STUDIES FOR REPLICATION IN CHILD DEVELOPMENT

STUDIES FOR REPLICATION IN CHILD DEVELOPMENT

Edited by
Morris E. Eson and H. Jean Wilkinson

State University of New York at Albany

HOLT, RINEHART AND WINSTON, INC.
New York   Chicago   San Francisco   Atlanta
Dallas   Montreal   Toronto   London   Sydney

Library of Congress Cataloging in Publication Data

Eson, Morris E.
   Studies for replication in child development.

   1. Child study—Addresses, essays, lectures.
I. Wilkinson, H. Jean, joint author.   II. Title.
[DNLM: 1.   Child development.   WS105 E76s]
BF721.E78   370.15   74-22203
ISBN: 0-03-085405-9

ACKNOWLEDGMENTS

For permission to reprint copyrighted materials, the editors are indebted to the following:

F. K. Graham, P. W. Berman, and C. B. Ernhart, Development in preschool children of the ability to copy forms. *Child Development*, 1960, *31*, 339–359. Copyright © 1960 by The Society for Research in Child Development.

L. Ghent, Form and its orientation: A child's-eye view. *American Journal of Psychology,* 1961, *74*, 177–190. Reprinted by permission of the author and the University of Illinois Press.

E. J. Gibson, J. J. Gibson, A. D. Pick, and H. Osser, A developmental study of the discrimination of letter-like forms. *Journal of Comparative and Physiological Psychology*, 1962, *55*, 897–906. Copyright 1962 by the American Psychological Association. Reprinted by permission.

R. Rudel and H. L. Teuber, Discrimination of direction of line in children. *Journal of Comparative and Physiological Psychology*, 1963, *56*, 892–898. Copyright 1963 by the American Psychological Association. Reprinted by permission.

C. U. Shantz and C. D. Smock, Development of distance conservation and the spatial coordinate system. *Child Development*, 1966, *37*, 943–948. Copyright © 1966 by The Society for Research in Child Development.

J. Smedslund, The effect of observation on children's representation of the spatial orientation of a water surface. *Journal of Genetic Psychology*, 1963, *102*, 195–201. Copyright 1963 by The Journal Press.

J. Kagan and J. Lemkin, Form, color, and size in children's conceptual behavior. *Child Development*, 1961, *32*, 25–28. Copyright © 1961 by The Society for Research in Child Development.

I. E. Sigel, Developmental trends in the abstraction ability of children. *Child Development*, 1953, *24*, 131–144. Copyright © 1953 by The Society for Research in Child Development.

D. Elkind, The development of the additive composition of classes in the child: Piaget replication study III. *Journal of Genetic Psychology*, 1961, *99*, 51–57. The development of quantitative thinking: A systematic replication of Piaget's studies. *Journal of Genetic Psychology*, 1961, *98*, 37–46. Both copyright 1961 by The Journal Press.

H. W. Stevenson and M. E. Bitterman, The distance-effect in the transposition of intermediate size by children. *American Journal of Psychology*, 1955, *68*, 274–279. Reprinted by permission of the author and the University of Illinois Press.

J. F. Wohlwill and R. C. Lowe, Experimental analysis of the development of the conservation of number. *Child Development*, 1962, *33*, 153–167. Copyright © 1962 by The Society for Research in Child Development.

G. Gratch, The development of the expectation of the nonindependence of random events in children. *Child Development*, 1959, *30*, 217–227. Copyright © 1959 by The Society for Research in Child Development.

J. Berko, The child's learning of English morphology. From *Word*, 1958, *14*, 150–177. Reprinted by permission.

C. Chomsky, Stages in language development and reading exposure. *Harvard Educational Review*, February 1972, *42*, 1–33. Copyright © 1972 by President and Fellows of Harvard College.

K. T. Alvy, Relation of age to children's egocentric and cooperative communication. *Journal of Genetic Psychology*, 1968, *112*, 275–286. Copyright 1968 by The Journal Press.

R. E. Hartley, Children's concepts of male and female roles. *Merrill-Palmer Quarterly*, 1960, *6*, 83–91. Reprinted by permission of the author and the Merrill-Palmer Quarterly—Behavior and Development.

L. Boehm, The development of conscience: A comparison of American children of different mental and socioeconomic levels. *Child Development*, 1962, *23*, 575–590. Copyright © 1962 by The Society for Research in Child Development.

PREFACE

Laboratory experiences in undergraduate psychology courses could play an important role in advancing the students' understanding, not only of the methodology employed in psychological research but, more importantly, of the concepts being studied. Over the years we have tried by various means to provide our students in the child development course with opportunities to learn about development through some kind of actual direct contact with children. At one point we introduced observation of children in various settings but found that this failed largely because the student-observer was unable to estimate the significance of what he saw or to interpret the observed behavior in terms of the concepts being taught in the course. We also tried to have the students set up their own investigations, but this procedure also failed because the students were unable to formulate a problem with sufficient clarity and within a reasonable time to be able to undertake such a project and carry it to completion.

About ten years ago we hit upon the idea of selecting a group of some twenty studies reported in the literature. The students selected one or two studies and proceeded to replicate them with appropriate modifications. As a result of our experience with some sixty or so different studies we are able to present in this collection those that have withstood the test of time, having held the students' interest, being within the range of ability of the typical undergraduate student, and having best met the criteria that we developed in choosing the studies. Our selection was based on the following considerations: (1) the student should be able to complete the study in the course of a single term; (2) no complex apparatus should be involved; (3) the topic should be of some significance in child development; (4) the number of subjects needed should be reasonable; (5) gathering the data should be based on face-to-face interaction with the subjects rather than obtained from groups; (6) the results should be of such a nature that they could be treated with few simple statistical procedures. Although many of the studies were originally reported more than a decade ago, their replication will remain a contemporary task for many years to come.

We estimate that a project reproducing one study can generally be carried out in less than 25 hours, including the preparation of the written report. One of the benefits of having the studies available in one place is that the student can conduct two or possibly three studies in the course of one semester with much smaller increments of time for the subsequent studies. In many cases the same subjects can serve as sources of data for more than one project without unduly extending the time that they serve as subjects. Having the reports available in one volume has allowed us to refer back and forth to various appropriate procedural adaptations and methods of data analysis. The volume can also serve as a readings collection to support the usual text. Students have frequently reported that one result of having carried out the replication has been a sharper appreciation of the text discussion, particularly when that discussion is based upon research literature. When a student replicates one or more studies, his appreciation for the others in the collection, even if not duplicated, is greatly enhanced.

We have encouraged students to work in groups of three or four, although most of the studies can be done by one investigator. We have found that requiring an individual report works out much better than group reports. When students work in groups we suggest that each look upon the other as a research assistant. We also suggest that they meet with each other before going out to seek subjects so that the procedures can be carefully reviewed and the assignment of particular categories of subjects (*e.g.*, age and sex) can be made. In this way students can avoid the aggravation of not being able to pool data because the members of the group had failed to make clear their agreement on specific testing procedures or kinds of subjects. One of the side benefits reported by many students who have worked in groups is the pleasure of knowing a fellow student with whom one is cooperating in a learning experience. We have found that the studies can be replicated by students with relatively little research experience. Students who have had a course in statistics and research methods can, of course, approach these projects with greater sophistication, but we find that those who are less well prepared develop an awareness that these research tools are worth learning; they subsequently enter these courses with a greater sense of purpose.

Locating subjects can be a difficult problem. In the early years of our experience with these projects we tried to locate nursery and elementary schools for our students. We found that we soon wore out our welcome in the limited number of local facilities. We then reluctantly turned over the task to the students themselves, a procedure that has worked out reasonably well and has even resulted in some unexpected benefits. Sometimes a letter from the instructor smoothes the way for the students as they make their own contacts with various agencies, Sunday schools, neighborhood centers, Boy Scout and Girl Scout groups, and public or private elementary schools. We have strongly urged our students to make contact with similar agencies in their own home communities. This not only serves to lighten the pressure on the pool of possible subjects in the university area, but also puts the student more at ease since he is placing his request with the director of a school or agency where he has some familiarity. Requiring the student to locate subjects has proven to be of some benefit in that the student learns to present himself, to make a case for himself, and to develop a sense of accountability both to the requirements of the course and to the children of the community. Often the student finds that he is more successful in obtaining cooperation if he volunteers some small measure of service to the agency providing the subjects, such as leading a group of children on a project or simply conducting a story hour. We have urged students to write letters of thanks and to take the time to send a summary report of the project and the findings. We have had occasional minor mishaps resulting from misunderstanding, but the overwhelming majority of contacts with the community has resulted in strengthening the ties between the university and the community which it serves.

The studies in this book are organized into four sections: perceptual–motor development, cognitive development, language development, and social development. After each study the editors offer suggestions for modifications. The best procedure for the student is to read the study and the editorial comments, and to prepare a written proposal on the precise procedures, sample selection, and expected treatment of data that he plans to use. If the student is going to work in a group, the various proposals of the group members can then be shared and modified in accordance with the group's decisions. The instructor may take an active role in offering suggestions at this point, or he may choose merely to note that the written proposal is completed and the study can be undertaken.

The several hundred students who have performed these replication studies have uniformly reported that they enjoyed them. The end-of-term course evaluations have consistently indicated that the project was the most worthwhile segment of the course. The students often assert that their understanding of the concepts of child development came alive, and for many this produced an enthusiastic determination to explore other concepts in psychology in the same way. We are pleased to offer other teachers of child development the opportunity to provide their students with similar pleasures in learning.

Albany, N. Y.   M. E. E.
September 1974   H. J. W.

CONTENTS

STUDIES FOR REPLICATION IN CHILD DEVELOPMENT

ONE

ETHICAL CONSIDERATIONS IN PSYCHOLOGICAL RESEARCH WITH CHILDREN

In selecting the studies presented in this volume we have been exceedingly conscious of the ethical problems associated with conducting research with human subjects, particularly children. With the increase of the number of investigations using clandestine procedures or some form of deception as part of the methodology, the issue of ethics has become a matter of great concern. Even those who conduct the type of research with human subjects where there can hardly be a question about the ethics of the procedures involved must be prepared to deal with some of the suspicion and hostility that have grown up around psychological investigations.

Webb *et al.* (1966) point out that "social scientists can go too far in intruding on privacy. . . .Manipulations aimed at the arousal of anxiety or extreme aggression could conceivably produce lasting damage to the psychological health of experimental subjects" (pages vi-vii). In presenting their novel methods of conducting social science research using "unobtrusive measures," Webb *et al.* indicate that they purposely avoided consideration of the ethical issues involved in such procedures. Brandt (1972), on the other hand, argues that the clandestine quality of various methods used in the study of behavior in natural settings "is not only right and proper but absolutely essential" (page 27). The issue has received so much attention that the American Psychological Association (1973) issued a statement on ethical principles discussing in some detail the ethical dilemmas involved in research with human participants.

While we do not wish to join the ranks of those who condemn the use of clandestine procedures and methods of research involving deception of subjects, we do not wish in any way to encourage the use of such techniques. There is much to be learned about child development without ever having to resort to such questionable

1

practices. As long as such is the case, and we predict that this will be so for the foreseeable future, we do not feel it essential to contribute further to the suspicion connected with social science investigation. We have, therefore, scrupulously avoided those studies where the subject is not informed of his participation or is misinformed about the intention of the study. In each study the student investigator can openly and honestly inform the subjects and their guardians as to the purpose of the study.

In those instances where the studies have reported such information as IQ and other personal data we have tried to point out how the study might be conducted without such information. We have avoided those investigations that seek to manipulate the arousal of anxiety, aggressive behavior, and the like. Some may feel that by not including studies of this sort we have eliminated some that would be of great interest to student investigators. Yet because of the hazards involved and because we have found that a high level of interest can be generated by investigating the more "neutral" psychological functions, we feel justified in having selected a more restricted range of studies for replication.

The studies presented in this collection have been selected so that some of the more cumbersome procedures regarding permissions can be avoided. In most cases the kinds of questions that the researcher would be asking would be similar to those that a teacher would ask in assessing the child's understanding. It is felt that if the teacher understands the nature of the investigation and grants permission for the interrogation of the children under her care, then the matter of permission has essentially been covered. We would, however, strongly recommend that any child who indicates a reluctance to participate as a subject should be graciously excused. Further, in the several years of using these studies we have not encountered any incident where there was any reason to suspect that one of the subjects has been in any way harmed by the investigation.

The American Psychological Association (1973) has published a statement on ethical standards of psychologists, which deals quite generally with the many kinds of ethical problems, including those dealing with the rights of subjects used in psychological investigations. The Division on Developmental Psychology of the American Psychological Association has an ongoing Committee on Ethics, which has given attention to the application of the generalized ethical standards to the particular problems in conducting research on children. One of their recent newsletters (1968), presented below, included a statement of ethical standards for those conducting investigations on children. These standards may appear overly stringent, but it should be noted that they were designed to cover many different kinds of investigations, including those that we have discussed above. The student investigator is urged to read these standards carefully and to be sure that his conduct is guided by them.

Children as research subjects present problems for the investigator different from those of adult subjects. Our culture is marked by a tenderness of concern for the young. The young are viewed as more vulnerable to distress (even though evidence may suggest that they are actually more resilient in recovery from stress). Because the young have less knowledge and less experience, they also may be less able to evaluate what participation in research means. And, consent of the parent for the study of his child is the prerequisite to obtaining consent from the child. These characteristics outline the major differences between research with children and research with adults.

1. No matter how young the subject, he has rights that supersede the rights of the investigator of his behavior. In the conduct of his research the investigator measures each operation he proposes against this principle and is prepared to justify his decision.

2. The investigator uses no research operation that may harm the child either physically or psychologically. Psychological harm, to be sure, is difficult to define; nevertheless, its definition remains a responsibility of the investigator.

3. The informed consent of parents or of those legally designated to act *in loco parentis* is obtained, preferably in writing. Informed consent requires that the parent be given accurate information on the profession and institutional affiliation of the investigator, and on the purpose and operations of the research, albeit in layman's terms. The consent of parents is not solicited by any claims of benefit to the child. Not only is the right of parents to refuse consent respected, but parents must be given the opportunity to refuse.

4. The investigator does not coerce a child into participating in a study. The child has the right to refuse and he, too, should be given the opportunity to refuse.

5. When the investigator is in doubt about possible harmful effects of his efforts or when he decides that the nature of his research requires deception, he submits his plan to an *ad hoc* group of his colleagues for review. It is the group's responsibility to suggest other feasible means of obtaining the information. Every psychologist has a responsibility to maintain not only his own ethical standards but also those of his colleagues.

6. The child's identity is concealed in written and verbal reports of the results, as well as in informal discussions with students and colleagues.

7. The investigator does not assume the role of diagnostician or counselor in reporting his observations to parents or those *in loco parentis*. He does not report test scores or information given by a child in confidence, although he recognizes a duty to report general findings to parents and others.

8. The investigator respects the ethical standards of those who act *in loco parentis* (e.g., teachers, superintendents of institutions).

9. The same ethical standards apply to children who are control subjects, and to their parents, as to those who are experimental subjects. When the experimental treatment is believed to benefit the child, the investigator considers an alternative treatment for the control group instead of no treatment.

10. Payment in money, gifts, or services for the child's participation does not annul any of the above principles.

11. Teachers of developmental psychology present the ethical standards of conducting research on human beings to both their undergraduate and graduate students. Like the university committees on the use of human subjects, professors share responsibility for the study of children on their campuses.

12. Editors of psychological journals reporting investigations of children have certain responsibilities to the authors of studies they review: they provide space for the investigator to justify his procedures where necessary and to report the precautions he has taken. When the procedures seem questionable, editors ask for such information.

13. The Division and its members have a continuing responsibility to question, amend, and revise the standards.

REFERENCES

American Psychological Association, *Ethical Principles in the Conduct of Research with Human Participants.* Washington, D.C.: American Psychological Association, 1973. Originally published in the *Newsletter*, Spring 1968. Minneapolis: Committee on Ethical Standards of Division 7, Institute of Child Development.

R. M. Brandt, *Studying Behavior in Natural Settings.* New York: Holt, Rinehart and Winston, 1972.

E. J. Webb, D. J. Campbell, R. D. Schwartz, and L. Sechrest, *Unobtrusive Measures: Nonreactive Research in the Social Sciences.* Chicago: Rand McNally, 1966.

STUDIES IN PERCEPTUAL–MOTOR DEVELOPMENT

DEVELOPMENT IN PRESCHOOL CHILDREN OF THE ABILITY TO COPY FORMS [1]

FRANCES K. GRAHAM,* PHYLLIS W. BERMAN,
University of Wisconsin

and CLAIRE B. ERNHART
Washington University

The present paper reports changes with age in the ability of preschool children to make a paper and pencil copy of simple forms presented visually. The study was undertaken to provide knowledge of normal development of an ability which is of special significance in studying the brain-injured.

A major purpose of the present paper is to contrast two methods of conceptualizing developmental changes in form reproduction—one emphasizing continuity in development, the other hierarchic organization and discontinuity in development. From the continuity point of view, quantitative changes on single dimensions are studied. From the discontinuity point of view, the interest is in studying qualitative characteristics typical of particular developmental periods. In order to encompass both approaches, two methods of analyzing reproductions were used in the present study.

The first method was to judge the accuracy or correctness of the reproductions in terms of eight characteristics. From the continuity point of view, accuracy in reproducing each characteristic should be a monotonic increasing function of age. From the discontinuity point of view, there should be stages of development which would be reflected in differential rates of change of the characteristics with age. The characteristics judged were whether or not the drawing had some form, whether it reproduced the open-closedness and curvature-linearity of figures, whether there were the correct number of parts, whether there was the correct relationship of parts, whether orientation on the background was correct, whether size relation-

---

* 219 Infirmary Building, University Hospitals, Madison, Wisconsin.

[1] This investigation was supported by a Research Grant B1550 from the National Institute of Neurological Disease and Blindness of the National Institutes of Health, Public Health Service.

Child Develpm., 1960, 31, 339-359.

ships of parts were correct, and whether the intersection of parts was correct. These particular categories do not, of course, exhaust the possibilities for analysis of differences between a drawing and an original. They were chosen either because of their historical interest or because it appeared likely that they would show a wide range of variation within the age group under investigation.

The second method of analysis was to judge whether reproductions were more "primitive" than the original designs. From the discontinuity point of view, "primitive organization" is characteristic of early stages of development, and three hypotheses stemming from this approach may be tested: Are primitive characteristics more frequent in younger children than in older? Are primitive characteristics more frequent than nonprimitive characteristics in young children? Do primitive and nonprimitive characteristics change differentially with age?

Primitive organization was judged by rating three characteristics— whether the reproduction was more closed than the original, simpler, or more symmetrical. The logical opposites of these, opening figures, complicating them, and making them less symmetrical, were also judged and were considered to be evidence of nonprimitive organization. The characteristics of primitive organization, as these are revealed in children's copies of geometric figures, have been most explicitly and clearly described by Werner (5, p. 122):

1. The strong emphasis on qualities-of-the-whole:
   a. Making a figure more uniform, indivisible: $\square \rightarrow \bigcirc$
   b. Closing an open figure: $\supset \rightarrow \odot$

2. In the homogeneization of directions and parts by:
   a. Making parts alike: $\lrcorner\!\!\lrcorner \rightarrow \urcorner\!\!\lrcorner$
   b. Simplifying directions: $* \rightarrow \not\!\!\not\!$
   c. Using symmetry: $\int \rightarrow C$

The description of these characteristics is in terms which should make it possible for an observer to identify the presence or absence of the characteristics. They overlap to some extent, however, and seem reducible to the three characteristics mentioned above. To these clearly defined characteristics, Werner adds another which he calls the "chain type" of reproduction. This is described as "the concatenation of pieces of the whole, an arrangement in which the distinguishing marks of higher geometric forms—the subordination of single parts, the presence of centers, and so on—are lacking. . . . The distinguishing sign of the chain type of drawing is the relative lack of definiteness in the relation of the parts" (5, p. 123-124).

We found it difficult to specify the distinguishing characteristics of this type of reproduction. A "relative lack of definiteness in the relation of parts" could be applied to any figure which did not accurately reproduce the original. It also might be interpreted as a figure in which the parts were more separated or spread out than the original rather than simplified and closed, or in which the figure was less uniform rather than more uniform than the original and so on. If either of these interpretations were employed, the theory of a primitive kind of organization would reduce to the statement that there are accurate reproductions and inaccurate reproductions and that inaccurate reproductions may be more or less uniform, more or less closed, or more or less symmetrical than the originals.

METHOD

Subjects

The subjects of the main experiment were 108 children, 18 in each of six age groups, proceeding by half-year steps from two and a half years to five years. In each half-year age group, there were nine boys and nine girls, of whom three of each sex were Negro and six were white. Half of the white children were under private medical care and half were under clinic care. Children were not included in the study if they were known to have behavior problems or if there was any history of neurological disease, convulsions, head injuries, or other evidence suggesting injury to the brain. All were products of single, full term births which had occurred without complications or operative intervention. Intelligence, as judged by a vocabulary scale, ranged from IQ 75 to IQ 173 with a mean of 119.4 and standard deviation of 23.3. Mean IQ estimated from this vocabulary scale was seven IQ points higher than the mean Binet IQ among a separate group of three-year-old children to whom both tests were administered. Mean and variance of the vocabulary scores did not differ significantly among the six age groups.

An additional 20 Ss were studied in a second experiment, differing from the main experiment only in the order of presentation of stimuli. The criteria for inclusion were the same as in the main experiment. No effort was made to specify age, sex, and race distribution, but all groups were represented. Subjects were obtained through the cooperation of medical facilities, individual physicians, and nursery schools.[2]

Stimuli

Stimuli consisted of the 18 forms reproduced in Figure 1. They were drawn in India ink on 5×8 inch white cards, with one design to a card. There were three curvilinear drawings. The remainder were line drawings

---

[2] The authors wish to acknowledge the cooperation of the Madison Department of Public Health, the Madison Neighborhood Centers, the Salvation Army Nursery School, and St. Louis Children's Hospital, the St. Louis Maternity Hospital, the University of Wisconsin Children's Hospital, and the University of Wisconsin Nursery School. We should like especially to express appreciation to the many individual physicians, teachers, and parents who contributed their help and time.

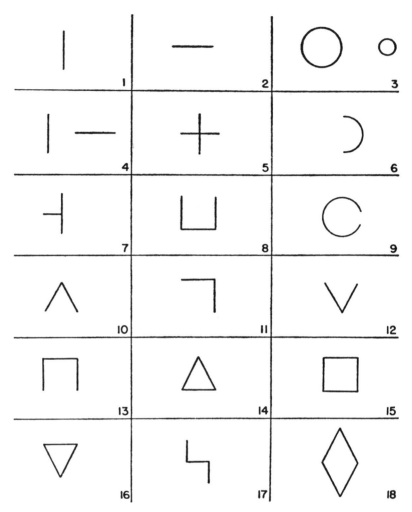

FIGURE 1—Stimuli.

varying primarily in the number of lines employed, the point at which the lines intersected, the size of the angle formed by their intersection, and their orientation on the background. The four "primary" figures—circle, triangle, square, and diamond—were included, and various combinations of parts of them were presented as separate figures. The number of each form indicates the order of presentation used in the main experiment. This order was roughly in terms of difficulty, estimated after preliminary work, except that identical designs, differing only in orientation on the card, were never presented in succession. Because of the age range of our sample, it was desirable to present material in an increasing order of difficulty so that the youngest would not lose interest in the task before they had an opportunity to demonstrate the limits of their ability.

A different order of presentation was used in the second experiment, which was designed to estimate the effect of order. In this experiment the order (18, 2, 17, 1, 16, 3, 15, 5, 14, 4, 13, 9, 12, 6, 11, 7, 10, 8) was such that designs occurring near the end of the main experiment occurred near the beginning in the second experiment, but were alternated with easier figures. The interspersion of easy designs was again necessary to maintain the interest of the youngest *S*s. The order of designs which were duplicates, except for their position, was reversed.

Procedure

Each subject was tested individually, the copying of forms procedure being inserted in a test session which lasted about an hour. The point at which the procedure was introduced was varied at the discretion of the examiner so as best to maintain the child's cooperation throughout. At the same time that the first stimulus card was exposed, the *S* was given a pad of five by eight paper and told, "See this? You make one just like it. Make yours right here." All 18 stimuli were presented except when three successive drawings had been made which were too poor to receive a form rating or when there had been three successive repetitions of the immediately preceding form. If a child embellished a drawing after having completed it or engaged in irrelevant drawing play, the examiner indicated this on the protocol. Such productions were not considered in analyzing the data. Spontaneous repetitions of a drawing were permitted, and in these cases the best reproduction was used in the analysis.

Measures of Primitive and Nonprimitive Organization

For each design a rating was made of whether the reproduction was more closed or more open than the original, more complicated or more simplified, more symmetrical or less symmetrical. Only instances in which the change was clearly evident and unequivocal were so rated. When there was any doubt as to the presence of a change, or if the change appeared to involve both of the opposed characteristics—as where one portion of the figure was more closed and another portion was more open—"no change" was recorded. Markings which did not represent an attempted reproduction, scribblings or perseverations without reference to the original design, were not included in this analysis (see "no-form" rating below). Allowance was made for lack of motor skill, especially in judging symmetry. If strict adherence to quantitative measurement were followed in comparing symmetry of an original and a copy, very few drawings would show increased symmetry. A drawing was judged to be more symmetrical when the reproduction resembled a form which would be more symmetrical than the original if it had been executed skillfully.

The reliability of the judgments was determined on a sample of 50 cases distributed among all subgroups of *Ss*. Correlations of two judges independently rating this sample ranged from .81 for more openness to .88 for more closure. These are satisfactorily high, especially since no period of training or practice was given prior to making the ratings. There was a significant difference, as well as a high intercorrelation, between the judges in rating decreased symmetry. The ratings used in the analysis were based on the judge who observed decreased symmetry less often.

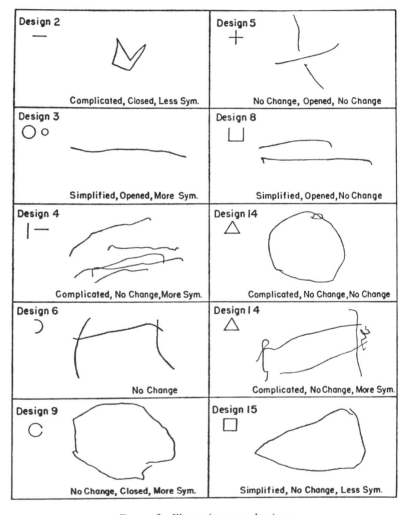

FIGURE 2—Illustrative reproductions.

Ten reproductions made by subjects in the three and three and one-half year groups are shown in Figure 2. The reproductions were selected to illustrate the ratings and to show as wide a variety as possible. Each drawing was made by a different child except for the reproductions of designs 6 and 9. These were included to indicate the difference in approach which can characterize the reproductions of a single subject.

Measures of Accuracy

Ratings of the presence or absence of the eight accuracy characteristics were made for each reproduction. If a reproduction did not possess any form, it automatically could not be correct in any of the other characteristics. The other characteristics were therefore rated, not as incorrect, but as unscorable. This policy was followed whenever a characteristic was incorrect because of failure to reproduce some other characteristic. It was not possible to judge the correctness of orientation, for example, unless enough of the general configuration had been reproduced to make the figure recognizable. Those features necessary to make a judgment depended upon the characteristics being judged and the particular figure, but for each figure and each characteristic these could be specified.

Detailed instructions, including illustrative samples, were prepared in order to make the judgment sufficiently objective. An abbreviated description of these is given below. The instructions were completed before the beginning of the experiment on the basis of a preliminary sample of drawings, and only minor clarifications of them were made subsequently. The general orientation underlying them was that all drawings called correct in a particular respect should appear equally similar or dissimilar to the sample from which the S had made the copy.

Correlations of two judges independently rating the sample of 50 cases ranged from .92 for intersections to .99 for orientation and for organization. The judges had had prior experience in rating a preliminary sample.

Abbreviated descriptions of the criteria used in rating follow.

Form. Form was scored for a reproduction which was more than a scribble, whether or not it resembled the sample. If S made four successive repetitions of the same form and there was no evidence, through eye movements or other behavior, that he was attempting to copy the sample, testing was terminated. The first of the repetitions was considered to have form, but the following three were considered perseverations and were rated as not having form.

Open-closed. The 18 stimuli can be divided into three groups: open, closed, or semiclosed figures. If the general configuration of the reproduced figure would be classified in the same group, credit was given for this characteristic. An open or semiclosed figure might be reproduced as more closed than the original and still be classified as an open figure. Similarly, a closed figure might be reproduced by drawing lines which did not actually join but whose general configuration would still be that of a closed figure.

The intent, in rating this characteristic, was to judge whether the gross gestalt of openness or closedness had been reproduced and not, as in the rating described earlier, to classify the direction of any perceptible change. A single closed figure, as a reproduction of the two circles, was given credit.

Curved-linear. A linear figure was judged as correctly reproduced when the reproduction was composed predominantly of lines even though there might be some curvature in parts of the figure or rounding of the angles. Similarly, portions of the circles and partial circles might be reproduced by straight lines, but as long as the reproduction was composed predominantly of curved lines it was considered correct.

Number of parts. Credit was given for a reproduction having the same number of parts as the original, without regard to the arrangement of the parts. A part was defined as either a change in direction or a discontinuity. Both designs 5 and 11 are two-part figures by this definition. It is not possible to specify the number of parts of a curved figure in any such rational manner. The arbitrary decision was made that design 3, the two circles, consisted of two single-part figures and that designs 6 and 9, the partial circles, consisted of from one to three parts. In counting the number of parts in a reproduction, the same criteria were followed. A circle was considered to be a single part and was therefore *not* credited as a reproduction of the number of parts of a triangle or a square. It was given credit as a reproduction of either of the single lines (designs 1 and 2) or of the partial circles (designs 6 and 9). Subjects sometimes drew curved lines or arcs in reproducing linear figures. These were arbitrarily rated in the same way as the original designs 6 and 9; that is, they were judged to consist of from one to three parts. In deciding whether such an arc was a correct reproduction of the number of parts of the original, the decision was always made in favor of crediting the subject, if this was possible. Thus, both) and 3 were accepted as reproductions of a figure with two parts.

Organization. Credit was given for a reproduction in which the parts preserved the same spatial relationship to one another as was true in the original although they might be incorrect with reference to their absolute placement on the background. For eight of the figures—the two lines, the two partial circles, and the four closed figures—this criterion was automatically satisfied when the four characteristics defining the general gestalt were correctly reproduced, that is, form, open-closed, curved-linear, and number of parts. In the remaining figures most of these characteristics had to be correct before organization could be judged, but they did not completely determine the rating. A definitely circular form was required on design 3. Concentric circles or embellishments were not credited, nor was markedly elliptical shape. It was not necessary to have two circular forms, however. For designs 4 and 7 to be correct, the two parts had to be roughly perpendicular. They might join, but not cross, at any point except their ends. On design 5 the two parts had to be crossed. On designs 8, 10, 11, 12, and 13 the parts had to be joined at their ends, if formed by lines. If formed by curves, these had to be broadened at the base for designs 8 and 13 and narrowed at the base for the other three figures. For design 17 the changes in direction of the three parts had to be in the same quadrant as the original.

Orientation. This rating was based on the relationship of the figure to the ground. The relationships of parts of the figure to one another did not have to be correct as long as the general configuration could be recognized. Reproductions were rated as correct, reversed (a rotation of 90 or 180 degrees), or tilted (a rotation of 30 to 45 degrees).

Size. Credit was given for reproducing the correct size relationship of parts, not the correct absolute size. For this characteristic to be judged, the organization of the parts had also to be correct. Different absolute standards of accuracy were required for the different figures in order to give perceptions of equality. With open figures, reproductions of equal lines appeared roughly correct if the difference between them was less than one-half the length of the shorter line. With closed figures, however, equal lines appeared equal only if the difference between them did not exceed one-third the length of the shortest side. In the case of designs 8 and 13 a difference in the sides of these figures which exceeded one-fifth the length of the shorter side destroyed the appearance of equality. Reproductions of bisections were called correct when a line was intersected at any point along the middle one-half of its length. Reproduction of the two circles was considered correct when one was clearly larger than the other. If there was uncertainty in making the judgment, credit was not given.

Intersections. This characteristic was rated as correct when angles of figures were roughly accurate in size. An error of 17 per cent was permitted, that is, $\pm 10°$ for 60° angles and $\pm 15°$ for 90° angles. They could be formed by the intersection of two lines if these did not overlap by more than two mm. or were not separated by a space of more than one mm. They could not be rounded or dog-eared. The number of angles did not need to be correct but the majority of them should meet the criteria for this rating. For design 4 the two lines should *not* be joined.

RESULTS

Primitive and Nonprimitive Organization

The total frequency of each of the primitive and nonprimitive characteristics and the percentage of attempted reproductions showing these characteristics are arranged in Table 1 by age groups. Frequencies have been included in the table only to show the size of the *N* on which the percentages are based. It is not possible to interpret meaningfully the change in frequencies with age since, unlike percentages, they are not independent of the increase with age in the number of attempted reproductions. In judging primitive and nonprimitive organization, an attempted reproduction was one which was more than a scribble or a perseveration. The results

TABLE I

NUMBER OF REPRODUCTIONS OF 18 DESIGNS SHOWING PRIMITIVE AND
NONPRIMITIVE CHARACTERISTICS AND PERCENTAGE OF ATTEMPTED
REPRODUCTIONS SHOWING THESE CHARACTERISTICS

Characteristics	A G E G R O U P S (N = 18 in each group)										
	2½	3		3½		4		4½		5	
	No.	No.	%	No.	%	No.	%	No.	%	No.	%
Nonprimitive (Complicated) .	6	49	29	51	27	44	15	44	14	30	9
Primitive (Simplified)	1	37	21	36	17	54	18	33	11	24	8
Nonprimitive (Opened)	1	46	28	33	15	33	11	39	12	20	6
Primitive (Closed)	3	31	18	29	14	49	16	22	7	7	2
Nonprimitive (Less Symmetry)	2	57	33	48	25	81	27	71	22	51	16
Primitive (More Symmetry) ..	0	23	14	44	21	30	10	16	5	13	4

of the two and one-half year group will be omitted in handing the data since the N on which they are based is too low to provide a reliable estimate. The main value of including the group is to show that the ability to reproduce forms is being measured near its zero point.

The group figures shown in Table I may be examined in the light of the three hypotheses to be tested. The first hypothesis, that primitive characteristics are more frequent in the drawings of younger children than in those of older children, would probably be confirmed. However, the second hypothesis, that primitive organizations are more frequent than the opposite or nonprimitive organizations, is disproved on the basis of these group percentages. Results indicate that they are, if anything, less frequent. The answer to the third hypothesis, that there is a differential change with age in primitive and nonprimitive characteristics, is not clear from inspection of the table.

Before testing these hypotheses statistically, it is necessary to consider whether, with the 18 designs used, there is equal opportunity for primitive and nonprimitive characteristics to occur. While any figure might be changed through primitivation of the original pattern, primitivation is expressed in various ways and not all of these ways would be possible with every figure. A square, for example, can not be made more closed, although it could be simplified by making it circular. A straight line, on the other hand, could not be made more open although it could be made more complicated. In comparing symmetry and simplification, therefore, the two straight lines (designs 1 and 2) should not be included since the possibility of obtaining a primitivation characteristic is not as good, a priori, as the possibility of obtaining nonprimitivation. For the same reason, only the 11 semiclosed designs should be included in comparing opening-closure tendencies.

The number of reproductions of these designs on which a subject showed a particular primitive (or nonprimitive) characteristic was expressed as a percentage of the total number of his attempted reproductions of these same designs. An angular transformation of the percentages was made, and the mean transformed percentages are shown in Figure 3 for each age

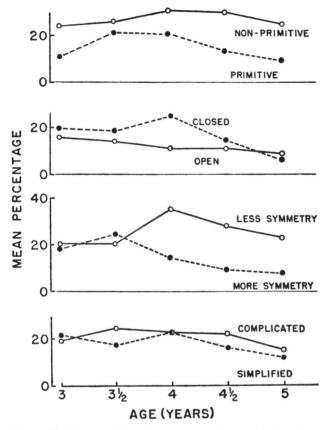

FIGURE 3—Mean transformed percentages of reproductions showing various primitive characteristics or the opposite characteristics.

group and for each pair of characteristics. Figure 3 also shows the mean transformed percentage of reproductions which showed *only* primitivation characteristics or *only* nonprimitivation characteristics. An example of a reproduction in which the change is one of primitivation is design 9, in Figure 2. Design 5, in the same figure, illustrates a change which is non-primitive. With one exception, the remaining reproductions in Figure 2 possessed both primitive and nonprimitive characteristics.

TABLE 2

ANALYSES OF VARIANCE OF AGE CHANGES IN THE TRANSFORMED
PERCENTAGE OF PRIMITIVE AND NONPRIMITIVE CHARACTERISTICS

		MEAN	SQUARE		
Source	df	Simplified vs. Complicated	Closed vs. Opened	More vs. Less Symmetry	Primitive vs. Nonprimitive
Ages (A)	4	432.29	764.17	455.04	491.62
linear	1	1109.93*	2402.81*	456.88	170.29
quadratic	1	539.73	488.84	1141.21*	1662.25**
cubic	1	59.71	38.34	68.79	124.14
fourth degree ...	1	19.81	126.71	153.25	9.80
Ss within ages	85	277.18	353.88	231.26	200.64
Characteristics (C) ..	1	129.64	1007.16	4710.00**	5419.07**
A × C	4	90.27	330.03	1167.64**	224.63
Pooled Ss × C	85	281.82	323.62	280.92	176.86

* $p < .05$.
** $p < .01$.

Table 2 shows the results of the four analyses of variance comparing
the pairs of primitive and nonprimitive characteristics. The main purpose
of statistical analysis was to determine whether there is an interaction between the kind of characteristic (primitive or nonprimitive) and age—
specifically, whether there is a differential change with age such that primitive characteristics are relatively more frequent at the youngest ages and
relatively less frequent at older. The only comparison showing such an interaction was the increase or decrease in symmetry of a reproduction. The
closed-opened and simplified-complicated characteristics show a significant
linear decrease with age but there is no differential change. Analysis also
reveals that the percentage of reproductions showing only nonprimitive
characteristics is significantly higher than the percentage showing only
primitive characteristics. This is presumably due to the frequency with
which a reproduction is produced as less symmetrical. Although the graph
of only primitive and only nonprimitive characteristics suggests that primitive organizations may rise to a peak at the youngest ages and then decline,
the interaction is not statistically significant.

Accuracy

Table 3 shows the total frequency of the eight accuracy characteristics
in each age group. The characteristics have been listed in the order of
decreasing frequency, and it will be observed that this order is the same
at each age. There are more correct reproductions of general characteristics

TABLE 3

MEAN NUMBER OF REPRODUCTIONS JUDGED CORRECT ON EIGHT
ACCURACY CHARACTERISTICS

(Each *S* reproduced 18 designs.)

Accuracy Characteristic	A G E G R O U P ($N = 18$ in each group)					
	2½	3	3½	4	4½	5
Form	0.7	9.7	11.9	16.8	17.9	17.7
Open-closed	0.6	7.4	9.7	14.9	16.2	17.0
Curved-linear	0.4	7.0	9.6	12.8	13.9	16.0
Number of parts	0.3	4.9	6.7	10.7	13.8	14.8
Organization	0.3	3.7	6.0	9.4	12.0	14.4
Orientation	0.2	2.6	4.8	7.6	9.2	12.3
Size	0	1.4	2.7	4.8	6.9	8.8
Intersection	0	0.6	1.7	2.7	5.5	7.1

determining the "whole-quality" (form, openness or closedness, curvilinearity or linearity, and number of parts) than of correct reproductions of details of design. This does not mean that general characteristics are easier to reproduce than details, however. Such a conclusion would overlook the fact that the characteristics are not independent of one another, as mentioned earlier. If a reproduction does not even possess form, it automatically could not be correct in any of the other characteristics. Similarly, it was found that on eight of the figures the organization or relationship of parts was automatically judged correct when the four characteristics defining the general gestalt were correctly reproduced and, conversely, that it was not possible to make a judgment of the relationship of parts unless most of these general characteristics were correct.

The frequencies of the individual accuracy characteristics were therefore expressed as a percentage of the number of designs which could be independently scored for that characteristic. The frequency of number of parts, curved-linear and open-closed characteristics were expressed as a percentage of the number of designs which had form, since these characteristics could be judged independently of one another. The frequency of correct organization and of correct orientation was expressed as the percentage of the number of designs which had form and two or three of the characteristics defining the general gestalt. The particular characteristics required for a particular design were not necessarily the same from design to design or for both organization and orientation but were specified in each case. The same procedure was followed in specifying the characteristics a reproduction must possess before the handling of its size relationships and intersections could be judged. In general, the organization (relationship of parts) needed to be reasonably accurate in order to make either of these judgments. The

TABLE 4

MEAN TRANSFORMED PERCENTAGES OF INDEPENDENTLY SCORABLE
REPRODUCTIONS JUDGED CORRECT ON EIGHT ACCURACY CHARACTERISTICS

Accuracy Characteristic	AGE GROUP ($N = 18$ in each group)				
	3	3½	4	4½	5
Form	51	61	83	88	88
Organization	53	69	76	78	86
Open-closed	50	62	75	77	84
Curved-linear	54	61	65	66	77
Number of parts	36	44	55	62	71
Orientation	41	41	57	60	67
Size	36	29	49	52	53
Intersection	8	16	25	35	39

mean transformed (arc sine) percentages of correct reproductions are shown
for each characteristic in Table 4. They provide an index of the change in
a characteristic freed from the effect of change in other characteristics on
which it is dependent. The two and one-half year group is not included
because of the small number of attempted reproductions. The percentage
of reproductions with form is, of course, a percentage of the 18 designs
presented. It should be noted that the transformed percentages in this table,
and in Figure 3, are the means of the transformed percentages obtained for
each S separately. They can not be calculated directly from the group percentages of Tables 1 and 3.

As in Table 3, the eight accuracy characteristics increase from age to
age, with one reversal. The relative order of difficulty, however, is quite
different and changes, to some extent, from age to age. Organization,
instead of appearing to be more difficult than reproduction of the general
characteristics, appears to be quite easy. That is, if reproductions have
enough of the general configuration present so that it is possible to judge
of the correctness or incorrectness of the relation of the parts to one another,
the majority are correctly related. In contrast, reproducing the correct number of parts or the correct orientation of the figure appears to be relatively
difficult at all ages. The difficulty of reproducing the correct number of
parts is especially interesting because this characteristic, to a considerable
extent, determines whether or not the general gestalt is preserved. The most
difficult characteristics to reproduce are the "details"—size relationships and
intersections.

An analysis of variance of these data is shown in Table 5. The change
with age is significant as is the difference among the characteristics. There
is, however, no interaction with age. Although some characteristics may
be easier than others to reproduce, there is no evidence to suggest a sudden

TABLE 5

ANALYSIS OF VARIANCE OF AGE CHANGES IN THE PERCENTAGES OF
INDEPENDENTLY SCORABLE REPRODUCTIONS JUDGED CORRECT
ON EIGHT ACCURACY CHARACTERISTICS

Source	df	Mean Square	F
Ages (A)	4	21,567.5	13.14*
Ss within ages	85	1,641.5	
Characteristics (C)	7	25,576.0	91.91**
A × C	28	315.9	1.14
Pooled Ss × C	595	278.3	

* $p < .05.$
** $p < .01.$

emergence, gaps, or uneven development within the age range examined and within the definition of the characteristics employed.

Table 6 shows the results of a similar analysis by designs rather than by characteristics. A subject's total "score" on each design was computed by assigning one point for a correct reproduction of each of the six accuracy characteristics which could be judged on all designs. The detail characteristics (size and intersection) were not included in computing this score since size relationships could not be judged on the two single-line figures and intersections did not occur on five of the figures. Once again the two main variables differ significantly but there is no interaction. The general trend of increasingly accurate reproductions with increasing age must be assumed to be the same, within the limits of normal variability, for each of the designs.

The significant difference among the designs is of some interest. Apparently, although they all show a similar pattern of increasingly correct reproductions with age, at any one age the designs differ among themselves in

TABLE 6

ANALYSIS OF VARIANCE OF AGE CHANGE IN TOTAL SCORES
ON EIGHTEEN DESIGNS

Source	df	Mean Square	F
Age (A)	4	567.09	18.02**
Ss within ages	85	31.47	
Designs (D)	17	75.83	55.35**
D × A	68	2.45	1.79
Pooled Ss × D	1445	1.37	

** $p < .01.$

the extent to which they are correctly reproduced. It might appear self-evident that this is because some designs are harder than others, but since there is no independent criterion of difficulty, such a statement would be redundant. We may, however, define difficulty in terms of the correctness of reproduction and then examine the difficulty or correctness order of the designs to determine what aspects of the designs are related to this order.

TABLE 7

RELATIVE DIFFICULTY OF 18 DESIGNS AS SHOWN BY MEAN SCORES ON
SIX ACCURACY CHARACTERISTICS UNDER TWO PRESENTATION ORDERS
AND BY SCALE VALUES BASED ON THE COMBINED WEIGHTED SCORES

Design	Original Order		Changed Order		Scale Value
	Presentation	Mean Score	Presentation	Mean Score	
│	1	4.68	4	4.75	1
—	2	4.19	2	4.65	3.7
O o	3	3.92	6	4.20	5.7
: —	4	3.81	10	3.85	6.6
+	5	3.69	8	4.50	6.6
⊣	7	3.54	14	4.05	7.9
C	9	3.30	18	4.05	9.2
⊃	6	3.41	16	3.35	9.3
⊓	11	3.15	12	3.65	10.4
⊔	8	3.14	17	3.30	10.8
⊓	13	2.85	13	3.40	12.3
∧	10	2.81	15	3.15	12.8
□	15	2.43	9	3.35	14.7
⌐	17	2.33	7	3.60	14.9
V	12	2.44	11	2.65	15.3
△	14	2.16	5	2.95	16.5
▽	16	1.98	3	2.70	17.7
◇	18	1.81	1	3.35	18.0

The mean "score" on the six characteristics is shown for each design in the left-hand column of Table 7, and the order of these means may be said to define the relative difficulty of the designs. These mean scores are based on the total sample, but the relative difficulty of the designs is highly similar in the individual age groups. The means for each design in each of the age subsamples were correlated with the means for each design in the total sample. The correlations ranged from .91 to .96 for the five older age groups. The correlation was only .62 in the two and one-half year olds due to the large number of zero scores at this age. This is essentially a test-subtest measure of reliability of the difficulty order. A similar indication of reliability of the difficulty order is shown by correlations ranging from .88 for form to .97 for organization when the number of correct reproductions of each design on all six accuracy characteristics was correlated with the number of correct reproductions of each design for each of the accuracy characteristics separately. These correlations were calculated for the total sample.

It will be noticed that the relative difficulty of the designs is very similar to the order in which they were presented. The correlation of presentation order and mean accuracy score was −.97. This is not surprising since the presentation order was intended to approximate roughly the anticipated difficulty order. However, before inferring any relationships between characteristics of the designs and their difficulty, it is necessary to estimate separately what effect presentation order has on difficulty. The second experiment, using a changed presentation order with 20 Ss, was carried out for this purpose. The mean scores on each design with the changed order of presentation are also shown in Table 7. The correlation of presentation order and mean accuracy score in this case is only −.16, which does not indicate any significant relationship between presentation order and difficulty order, while the correlation between the two sets of mean accuracy scores under the two orders of presentation is .85, a correlation nearly as high as the test-subtest measures of reliability. The present evidence suggests that order does not contribute a major portion of the variance. However, there are a considerably larger number of variations in presentation order possible, and it would be surprising if this factor could not be shown to have an effect on difficulty which was significant, if minor.

The designs in Table 7 are listed in the rank order determined by the combined scores of both presentation orders, weighted according to the *N* in each sample. For convenience, these combined accuracy scores were converted to a scale on which the easiest design is assigned a scale value of 1.0 and the most difficult design a scale value of 18.0, as shown in the table.

What are the features of the designs themselves which appear to be associated with greater difficulty in reproducing them? The most obvious is the number of parts, defined as either a discontinuity or a change in direction. But there are two exceptions to this: the two acute angles are more difficult than the three-part figures, and the two triangles are more difficult than the square. It seems probable that the sharpness of the turn or change in direction is itself a factor contributing to difficulty. It is possible to reproduce any of the angles by joining two lines, and this method is, in fact, used by a number of Ss, not only to reproduce the single angles but also to reproduce the three- and four-part figures. The most common method, however, is to attempt to reproduce them with a continuous line which changes direction, and this method often leads indirectly to considerable distortion of the figure. This may explain why the three two-part figures in which the two parts are discontinuous appear to be easier than the right angle. As far as can be judged, without a more systematic investigation than the present experiment provides, right-left or up-down orientation of the figure does not affect its difficulty. There are no consistent trends when figures differing only in orientation are compared. The differences that do obtain between them are probably due to unreliability in part and in part to the absolute and relative order of presentation.

DISCUSSION

Previous studies of form reproduction by children have been largely stimulated by interest in Gestalt principles of perceptual organization. Werner has made the clearest statement of developmental changes which would be predicted on the basis of these principles. In addition to formulating a general developmental "law," he has stated that these principles applied to motor as well as perceptual behavior (5, p. 121) and has described explicitly the characteristics to be expected in children's drawings (5, p. 118 ff.). The present study attempted to determine whether the characteristics were present in reproductions which children between the ages of two and one-half and five made of 18 designs. Most of the descriptions stemming from the principle were not confirmed. Simplification and closure were more common in the reproductions of younger children than of older, but they were no more frequent than the opposite characteristics of complicating and opening reproductions. Both pairs of characteristics declined with age, but the decline was not differential. Increasing the symmetry of a reproduction was more common than decreasing the symmetry only in the three and one-half year group. The interaction with age was, however, significant and is in line with Werner's theoretical expectation.

It seems necessary to conclude that the explicit descriptive principles expounded by Werner are not an adequate means of conceptualizing development of children's ability to reproduce figures. Efforts were made to apply the descriptive principles objectively and reliably and with considerable allowance being made in favor of the theory. The results were largely negative. We have included a number of specific illustrations of drawing which we have judged to contradict the Gestalt formulation (*see* Figure 2). Any broadening of the Gestalt principles so as to encompass these negative instances would seem logically to require either or both (a) considering the accuracy of the drawing or (b) stating that the drawings of young children are either one thing or the opposite. That is, if the description is made sufficiently broad, there would be no conceivable drawing which would not be covered and the only distinction possible between the drawings of younger and older children would be in terms of the accuracy with which the original is reproduced.

It is precisely this method that we would suggest as the most meaningful way to organize the developmental data. Children's reproductions show increasing accuracy or veridicality with age. Of this, Werner has said, "an analysis of types of operations rather than measurement merely in terms of accuracy of performance often reveal the truer developmental picture" (6, p. 132). We are suggesting the reverse, that rises and falls in "types of operations" represent indirect consequences of the gradual improvement in accuracy of performance. The interpretation that three-year-olds close a partial circle because they are at a stage of development where there is a closure tendency is belied by the fact that opening the partial circle occurs just as frequently in three-year-olds. An interpretation which does accord with the facts is that in the course of learning to reproduce distances they err in both directions—they both under- and over-estimate.

Stating that increasing accuracy is the most satisfactory general concept to describe the developmental course does not imply that accuracy improves in every respect with every design. We found, in fact, that changes in the method of reproducing one aspect, as an angle, often resulted indirectly in less accuracy in reproducing some other aspect of that figure, as its general gestalt. The principle does imply that, over time and with an adequate sample of the population of figures, reproductions will increasingly approach the original in all dimensions. There may be differences with age in which dimensions are learned earliest or reach some comparable level. Piaget suggested that "open-closed" is learned before number of sides and angles (4). Our data are in agreement with this. But our data indicate that the child does not go through discrete stages of learning to perceive size or to make intersections or to make straight lines or to learn the number of parts. Rather, there is gradual improvement in each of these as a function of age and as a function of the specific stimulus and its difficulty.

The stimulus is probably as significant a variable in determining the reproduction as is age. What aspects of the stimulus are associated with its difficulty requires further systematic investigation. As studies by Harlow (3), Attneave and Arnoult (2), and others have demonstrated, characteristics which have been considered in qualitative terms can be profitably quantified. In the present investigation the aim was to select from the designs which could be reproduced by this age group a sample varying along as many dimensions as possible. We found that the order of difficulty of the 18 designs used was highly consistent in each of our preschool age groups and for the various characteristics of the reproduction that were judged. From this consistent order inferences could be drawn as to aspects of the designs which were related to difficulty. However, such inferences need confirmation and more precise definitions of the relevant dimensions.

From our results we inferred that the number of parts is an important dimension determining difficulty. This variable is similar to Attneave's Number of Turns dimension which he found accounted for nearly four-fifths of the variance in judgments of the complexity of shape (1). Both discontinuities, included in defining parts, and the acuteness of the change from one direction to another also appear to determine difficulty. These are variables whose effect may be more important for motor than for perceptual behavior. The orientation of a design did not appear to be important in the present study but the right-left, up-down changes in orientation which were employed maintained a parallel relationship of figure to ground. A change from parallel to oblique presentation might well change the difficulty.

SUMMARY

Changes with age in the ability to copy forms were studied in preschool children between two and one-half and five years of age. The sample consisted of 108 children, with 18 in each of six half-year age groups, balanced for sex and for population group (white private, white clinic, and Negro). Two methods of conceptualizing developmental changes were contrasted—a discontinuity point of view emphasizing qualitative organizations typical of particular stages of development, and a continuity point of view emphasizing quantitative changes in the accuracy of reproduction.

To test whether specified qualitative organizations characterized the reproductions, each reproduction was judged as to whether it showed a change from the original in being more "primitive" or more "nonprimitive." Three characteristics of primitive organization—simplification, closure, and increased symmetry—and their logical opposites were judged. The major findings failed to confirm the predictions of this theoretical point of view. Simplification and closure were found to be more common in the reproductions of younger than of older children, but they were no more common than the opposite characteristics of complicating and opening. Both pairs of characteristics declined with age, and the decline was not differential. Increasing the symmetry of a reproduction was more common than decreasing the symmetry only in the three and one-half year group. The interaction with age was, however, significant and thus in line with the qualitative organization type of theory.

The reproductions were also judged as to whether they accurately reproduced eight characteristics—form, curvature-linearity, open-closedness, number of parts, relationship of parts, orientation on the background, size relationships, and intersections. The percentage of accurate reproductions increased with age for each of the characteristics judged and for each of the designs. There were no significant interactions of age and characteristics or of age and designs.

In view of these results, it was suggested that the most meaningful general statement to be made about developmental changes in the ability to reproduce forms is that the reproductions increasingly approach the original in all dimensions and that, in the course of so doing, errors both of under- and of over-estimation occur.

The order of difficulty of the 18 designs used was highly consistent in each of the preschool age groups and for the various accuracy characteristics. What aspects of the stimuli are associated with its difficulty remains a matter for further investigation, although the number of parts and the acuteness of a change in direction appeared to be important variables in the sample of designs employed while spatial orientation apparently was not.

REFERENCES

1. ATTNEAVE, F.   Physical determinants of the judged complexity of shapes. *J. exp. Psychol.,* 1957, 53, 221-227.
2. ATTNEAVE, F., & ARNOULT, M. D.   The quantitative study of shape and pattern perception. *Psychol. Bull.,* 1956, 53, 452-471.
3. HARLOW, H. F.   Learning theories.   In W. Dennis (Ed.), *Current trends in psychological theory.*   Pittsburgh: Univer. of Pittsburgh Press, 1951. Pp. 57-84.
4. PIAGET, J.   How children form mathematical concepts.   *Sci. Amer.,* 1953, 189(5), 74-79.
5. WERNER, H.   *Comparative psychology of mental development.* (Rev. Ed.)   New York: International Universities Press, 1957.
6. WERNER, H.   The concept of development from a comparative and organismic point of view.   In D. B. Harris (Ed.), *The concept of development.*   Minneapolis: Univer. of Minnesota Press, 1957. Pp. 125-148.

EDITORIAL COMMENTS

Graham *et al.* attempt to contrast two conceptualizations of the development of reproduction of forms by children: (1) a continuous increase in accuracy of reproduction with age, and (2) changes with age that are primarily qualitative in nature. They conclude that their findings provide support for the former notion, but do not provide support for the particular qualitative changes that were derived from Werner's theory of development.

Modifications of Sample and Procedure

This investigation has two aspects. The major part of the study concerns the reproduction of forms by preschool children; a second part is concerned with a smaller project carried out to confirm the order of difficulty of the forms. This latter part has generally not been of as great interest to students working on this project, and could be omitted from the replication study.

Graham *et al.* matched subject groups on the basis of the type of medical care that they were receiving (private vs. clinic care), and they also excluded subjects from the study who were considered to have behavior problems or any medical history suggestive of possible brain injury. While this information will generally not be available to students, it is not necessary for the testing of the hypotheses with which the original investigators were concerned.

The rating of the drawings for accuracy and for degree of primitive and nonprimitive organization should be done by two judges. In this way, one can obtain a measure of the reliability of the raters' assignment of the drawings for each of the dimensions on which they are being judged. The percentage of agreement between the judges should be reported. In a study such as this the percentage of agreement should be over 85 percent. It would be well for the two judges to spend a short period arriving at some agreed-upon definitions for each of the points on the accuracy dimension and that of the primitive-nonprimitive organization.

Analysis of Results

Students may wish to work with simpler statistical procedures than those in the original study. However, any procedure used should take into account the problem posed by the fact that not all the figures can be scored for all the characteristics. Percentages of figures scored in any given category should be based on the number of figures that can be scored for that category rather than on the total number of figures employed.

An additional way of looking at the data obtained in such a project would be to attempt to determine the extent to which individual children are consistent in the types of errors or distortions that they make in reproducing the forms. In doing this analysis, the student may be interested in looking at the stage analysis done by Chomsky in a later article in this collection (see Chapter Four).

The attempt of Graham *et al.* to assess sequential changes in reproduction of geometric forms is a cross-sectional study. Since different children pass through qualitatively different stages at slightly different times or ages, cross-sectional or group data may obscure the similarities in the sequences of these stages. A stage analysis, such as suggested above, will highlight the stage sequence more clearly.

FORM AND ITS ORIENTATION: A CHILD'S-EYE VIEW

By LILA GHENT, The George Washington University

The orientation of pictorial material usually is determined by the position of the figure with respect to a frame of reference provided by the environment or by the observer. The figure is considered right side up, or correctly oriented, when it is in the usual or familiar position with reference to the frame. Nonrealistic, or geometric, figures are not, however, usually considered to have a 'right side up' orientation (except in certain esthetic judgments).

Some chance observations indicated that young children show preferences for the orientation of geometric forms, *i.e.* they consider certain nonrepresentational forms to be right side up in one orientation and upside down in another. Such a finding would be surprising in any age-group, but it is particularly unexpected in preschool children in view of the customary belief that young children are unresponsive to the orientation of forms. This report describes a systematic investigation of these curious preferences for orientation and discusses the implicatons of the results for the more general problem of the influence of orientation on the child's perception of form.

EXPERIMENT I

Children of various ages were tested to determine the consistency of preference at different ages, and various types of form were used in an attempt to analyze the aspects of the stimulus that determined preference.

Subjects. The Ss were 78 children between the ages of 4-8 yr. There were 22 aged 4 yr., 26 aged 5 yr., 14 aged 6 yr., and 16 aged 7-8 yr., with approximately the same number of boys and girls in each group. The children were enrolled in a child care center situated in a low-income area in New York.[1]

Procedure. Twenty-six pairs of pictures were presented to each child, and he was asked to point to the one that was upside down or wrong. The members of each

* Received for publication December 4, 1959. This study was begun at the Psychophysiological Laboratory, New York University-Bellevue Medical Center, and was supported by a grant to the laboratory from the Commonwealth Fund of New York. The work was continued at the Pediatrics Department of the State University of New York, Downstate Medical Center, and was supported in part by grant M-2444 from the National Institute of Mental Health, Public Health Service.

[1] The writer is indebted to the Director and teachers of the Bronx River Child Care Center for their coöperation.

pair of pictures were identical except that one was rotated 180° with respect to the other. Five pairs of realistic forms were presented first (rooster, flowerpot, shoe, cat, chair), then the 16 pairs of the nonrealistic forms shown in Fig. 1, and finally another 5 pairs of realistic forms (tree, boat, cup, clown, horse). The series was always shown in the same order.

E sat beside *S* and held two pictures of every form with vertical axes reversed (one in each hand) in front of *S*, with a distance of 4–6 in. between the closer edges of the cards. *S* was allowed as much time as he wished to make a choice and was allowed to change his choice, if he desired. He was not told, however, whether his choices were right or wrong, although he was encouraged in a rather general way throughout the testing procedure. The only exceptions were the very few instances in which *S* made an error on the realistic forms. When this happened, *E* said, "Are you sure that is the upside down one? Go slowly now, and always pick the one that looks upside down or wrong." The *S*s of 6 yr. and older frequently balked at choosing between the nonrealistic forms, but *E* urged them to guess.

Results. Perhaps the most striking result was the ready acceptance by the preschool children of the problem of choosing the upside down member of a pair of nonrealistic forms. When the pairs of nonrealistic forms were introduced, the *S*s of 4 and 5 yr. made their choices with the same speed and ease that they had shown with the representational forms. They did not hesitate, nor did they comment on the pictures at this point; in general, they behaved as though the problem had not changed. The children over 6 yr. of age usually hesitated for a few seconds when the nonrealistic forms were first presented, and they often were reluctant to choose between the cards. These older children would say, "I can't tell," or "It doesn't matter," or the like.

A summary of the responses to each pair of nonrealistic forms is presented in Fig. 1, which shows the percentage of children in each age-sex grouping choosing the card as upside down in the orientation shown here. In the 4-yr.-old group, the frequency of choosing the card as upside down in the orientation shown in Fig. 1 was significantly greater than would be expected by chance (5% level) for all cards except Forms 4, 7, 13, 14, and 16. The consistency of the response to some items was extraordinary in the youngest group, with more than 95% of the 4-yr.-olds choosing as upside down Forms 1, 3, 5, 9, 10, and 15.

With increasing age, the choices remained essentially the same, and significantly different from chance in all age-groups (with a minor exception) for Forms 5, 9, 10, 11, and 12. (The exception is that the responses of the *S*s of 7–8 yrs. fell just short of the 5% level of significance for Forms 11 and 12.) Responses that were consistent in the 4-yr.-old group, but random in the oldest group, occurred for Forms 6, 2, 3, and 15, with significant differences ($p < 0.02$) appearing between the youngest and oldest groups for the latter three items. Other items showed a change from ran-

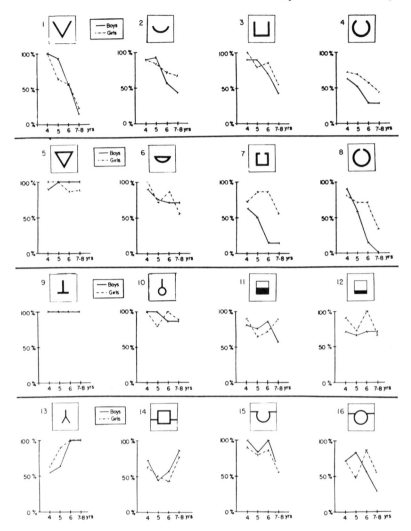

FIG. 1. PERCENTAGE OF BOYS AND GIRLS IN EACH AGE-GROUP CHOOSING
CARD AS UPSIDE DOWN IN THE ORIENTATION SHOWN.
Each card was 4 in. on a side and did not have the black border shown here.

domness to consistency (Forms 7, 13) or an actual reversal of preference
for orientation (Forms 1, 8).

When the incomplete circle (Form 8) was oriented with the gap on top,
the card was considered upside down by 86% of the 4-yr.-old Ss, whereas
it was considered right side up by 81% of the 7–8-yr.-old Ss ($p < 0.001$).

The responses to the incomplete square (Form 7) were random in the 4-yr.-old group, but the older boys consistently preferred the square with the gap on top. Comparison of the responses to the incomplete square of the 4- and 5-yr.-old boys with those of the 6–8-yr.-old boys showed a significant difference between the age-groups ($p < 0.02$).

Both for the incomplete circle and for the square, a sex-difference appeared in the older age-groups. Comparison of the responses of the boys and girls in the 6–8-yr.-old groups showed a significant difference between them for the incomplete square ($p < 0.01$) and the incomplete circle ($p < 0.05$).

It is clear that consistent responses to the orientation of form appear, not only for realistic figures, but also for geometric forms, in the 4- and 5-yr.-old child. Do these results reflect a true preference for orientation of nonrealistic forms, or is the preference due to the child's perception of the geometric forms as representations of real objects? The second interpretation is not supported by the children's spontaneous verbalizations, nor by their responses to questions. For example, the children did not consistently name, or say that they recognized, the card considered right side up. Sometimes, in fact, a child would give two names for each form, one for each orientation. (The crescent was called a bridge in one orientation and a bowl in the other by the same S, who nevertheless chose the 'bowl' as upside down.) When the young Ss were asked how they knew which picture was wrong, they usually replied, "I see it" or "I can tell" or the like. It is striking that not a single child suggested that the right side up picture was right because he could see what it was.

Granted that a genuine, although unexplained, preference for orientation exists, let us consider this phenomenon from the point of view of age. The frequency of preferences was highest in the Ss of 4 and 5 yr. of age, and essentially the same in both age-groups. There was a decline in preferences for orientation with age, but this change cannot be described as a simple decrease in strength of preference. A preference, when it appeared in the older S, tended to be as strong as in the younger S (Forms 5, 9, 10, 11, 12); fewer figures, however, evoked preferences in the older S. Perhaps the most puzzling change with age was the appearance of preferences that were not present in the young child. The changes in response to the 'V' (Form 1) and the 'Y' (Form 13) are not surprising, since the responses of the older Ss are consistent with the perception of these forms as letters. The changes in response to the incomplete circle (Form 8) and the incomplete square (Form 7) cannot be accounted for so simply.

An interesting aspect of the change with age in response to the figures with a gap is that the change occurred earlier in the boys than in the girls. An isolated finding of different responses to visual form by boys and girls would be of little significance in itself. It also has been found, however, that, in the same age-group, boys are better than girls in the recognition of tachistoscopically presented realistic forms.[2] The finding of two instances in which the response to form can be considered to be more developed in boys than girls is of significance for understanding sex-differences

---

[2] Lila Ghent, Recognition by children of realistic figures presented in various orientations, *Canad. J. Psychol.*, 14, 1960, 249-256.

in perception and raises the possibility that these changes (with age) in perception reflect related processes.

The most important problem raised by the finding of preferences for orientation is that of defining the characteristics of the cards selected as upside down. For this discussion, changes with age will be ignored, and the responses of the preschool *Ss* will form the basis for the analysis. Some of the forms were originally designed on the hypothesis that 'openness' in the top part of the figure characterized the upside down card. While most of the forms with an open top were considered upside down, the 'openness' did not appear to be essential, since the same forms with a partially or completely closed top also were considered wrongly oriented (compare, for example, Forms 1–4 and 5–8 of Fig. 1). Another possibility is that the upside down cards were unstable or top heavy, but the data do not support this view either (see Forms 9–12, 14, and 16).

The interpretation that appears to be most consistent with the data is that the card was upside down when the focal portion was in the lower half of the card. That is, let us assume that the figures eliciting significant preferences had one portion that caught the 'attention,' or drew the eye, more readily than did other portions. The angle of the *V*, the point of intersection of the *T*, the rounded portion of the crescent, and so on, each might be considered the focal portion of the particular form. When these portions of the figures were at the bottom, the cards were called upside down by the children.

EXPERIMENT II

The main difficulty with this interpretation is that the designation of 'focal' is made *post hoc*. For the experiment to be described now, a set of very simple cards was designed in which the focal part was designated beforehand, and, in most instances, there was little ambiguity as to whether or not the stated portion could be described as focal (Fig. 2). These simple cards were used to test the hypothesis that the cards were considered upside down when the focal portion was in the lower part. On the assumption that the hypothesis would be confirmed, an additional set of cards was included in the second experiment to explore some determinants of the focal portion of complex figures—brightness, size, and other variables.

Subjects. Forty children of preschool age were tested in the nursery school previously described, but none of these children had participated in the first experiment. The 4-yr.-old group consisted of 11 boys and 11 girls, and the 5-yr.-old group of 9 boys and 9 girls.

Procedure. Thirty-four pairs of cards were used, 10 realistic, and 24 nonrealistic forms. One member of each pair of the nonrealistic forms can be seen in Fig. 2 and Fig. 3. The realistic forms were the same as those previously used, but, for this experiment, one pair appeared at the beginning and at the end, and the remaining eight pairs were distributed throughout the series. The cards were presented in one

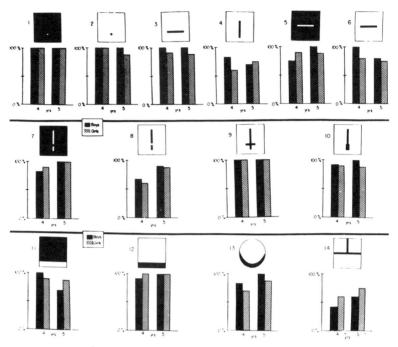

FIG. 2. PERCENTAGE OF BOYS AND GIRLS IN EACH AGE-GROUP CHOOSING
CARD AS UPSIDE DOWN IN THE ORIENTATION SHOWN.
With the exception of Card 13, each card was 4 in. on a side and did
not have the black border shown here.

sequence to half the children in each age-sex grouping, and in the reverse order to
the remaining children in each group.

Results. Fig. 2 shows the responses to the simple cards in which there
was little ambiguity, in most instances, as to which portion constituted the
focal part. The preferred position of a simple line or dot was investigated
with Cards 1–6. It is clear that the card was considered upside down when
the figure was in the lower part of the card. When the line was centered,
it was considered wrong when placed horizontally instead of vertically. The
next set of cards shows that, with a simple line interrupted in various ways,
the cards were considered upside down when the point of interruption
(the assumed focal portion) of the line was in the lower half of the card.
Finally, simply dividing the card itself, as in Cards 11–13, evoked the
response of upside down when the line of division was in the lower portion. Card 14 appears to be an exception to this generalization, and constitutes the only instance (in this group of cards) in which the predicted
choice was not made.

Fig. 3 shows the responses to the cards that were designed to explore the effects of differences in size and intensity in evoking preferences, or, in view of the results just described, in determining the focal portion. Black appeared to be more focal than white when the areas were equal (Card 5), even in the absence of a white background (cf. Fig. 1, Form 11). The preference for black on top was reversed, however, by the presence of dots in the white portion; that is, the dots were figural in contrast either to solid black (Card 6) or to solid white (Card 7). The effect of intensity was investigated further with the card consisting of three shades

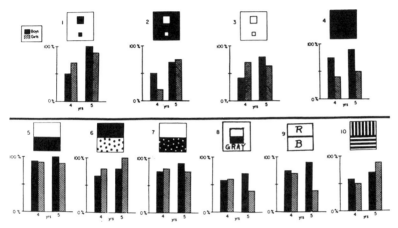

FIG. 3. PERCENTAGE OF BOYS AND GIRLS IN EACH AGE-GROUP CHOOSING
CARD AS UPSIDE DOWN IN ORIENTATION SHOWN
Each card was 4 in. on a side and did not have the black border shown here.
Card 8 consisted of three shades of gray, the background being
intermediate in brightness between the dark and light portions of the
figure. Card 9 consisted of a bright orange-red, and a dark royal blue.

of gray (Card 8); the responses were not different from chance. Preliminary investigation of responses to color (Card 9) indicated that 70% of the group considered the card upside down when the dark royal blue was at the bottom ($p < 0.02$); this preference could be due to difference either in color or in intensity.

The effect of the size of a figure in determining focal quality was investigated in relation to reversal of brightness between figure and ground, and in relation to the presentation of the figure in solid or outline form. The smaller figure consistently appeared to be the focal portion for the 5-yr.-old group, although the responses were significantly different from chance ($p < 0.02$) only in the case of the solid black square on the white ground. Consistent preferences did not appear in the 4-yr.-old group, and the choices of the 4- and 5-yr.-old groups were significantly different ($p <$ 0.05) for both cards with solid squares (Fig. 3, Cards 1 and 2). Reversal of the brightness-relations between figure and ground did not change the responses to the outline figures, but it did exert a significant effect with the solid figures. That is, 23 Ss made the same response to Cards 1 and 2 (Fig. 3). Thirteen Ss considered the card with the large square on top upside down when the background was white but right side up when the background was black, whereas only 4 Ss showed the converse change. Evaluation of the change in response to different cards by the same individuals yields a chi-square for correlated proportions of 4.76 ($p < 0.05$).

The only significant sex-difference found in this experiment was in response to the outline white squares on the black ground (Fig. 3, Card 4), with the boys, in contrast to the girls, showing a strong preference for the smaller square on the top. Since this type of response (to the cards with the squares) appeared more frequently in the children of 5 yr. than in those of 4 yr., the boys' response could be interpreted as more mature than that of the girls.

The results of Experiment II confirm and extend the observations reported previously. Again, young children showed marked preferences for a particular orientation of nonrealistic forms, and, furthermore, these preferences appeared to be related to the position of the focal part of the figure. The reader may inquire whether these preferences can be obtained with other methods. In work not reported here, the cards have been shown singly and S asked whether each card was upside down or right side up; in other instances, S has been given the pile of cards, in random order and orientation, and has been required to place each card in the right side up position. For most figures, the preferences remained the same and as strong, regardless of the method of presentation used. The data of Experiment II will be discussed with respect to three findings concerning the determinants of correct orientation of nonrealistic figures: (1) the position of the focal portion; (2) the role of the vertical; and (3) the effects of brightness and size in defining the focal part.

(1) It was clear that, when the focal portion could be defined in an unambiguous way, the card was considered upside down if this focal portion was in the bottom part of the card. When a single homogeneous figure, such as a dot or a line, was placed in the lower portion of the page, the card was considered to be upside down (Fig. 2, Cards 1–4). When a simple figure was interrupted by a gap or a line, producing a non-homogeneous figure, the card was considered upside down when the interrupted portion was in the bottom half of the card (Fig. 2, Cards 7–10). When the card itself was divided into unequal portions of black and white, the card was considered upside down when the line of demarcation was in the lower portion of the card (Fig. 2, Cards 11–13). An apparent exception to this general finding was the absence of consistent responses to Card 14 in Fig. 2. In this instance, it is possible that some of the children were responding to the position of the figure on the card, in which case it would be upside down when the bottom part of the card contained the figure, whereas other children were responding to the orientation

of the figure itself, in which case it would be upside down when the bottom part of the *figure* contained the focal portion (cf. Fig. 1, Form 9).

(2) The vertical axis appears to play a role in determining correct orientation that is separable, at least in part, from the position of the focal portion. The children showed a strong preference for a centered homogeneous line in the vertical as opposed to the horizontal orientation. Incidental observations suggest that the preference for verticalization may sometimes override the tendency to place a homogeneous figure in the upper space of the card. For example, with the pair of cards consisting of a horizontal line in the upper portion of one card and a horizontal line in the lower portion of the other card (Fig. 2, Card 3), one S spontaneously called them both wrong. (When asked which one was more wrong, he pointed to the one with the horizontal line at the bottom.) Further, the Ss who were presented with the cards one at a time and asked to put them right side up often turned these cards in such a way that the lines were in the vertical position. Some of the children also turned the cards that were divided into black and white portions in such a way that the line of juxtaposition of the black and white was vertical rather than horizontal (Fig. 2, Cards 11 and 12).[3]

(3) A subsidiary purpose of the second experiment was to explore the effects of relative brightness and size in determining the focal aspect of a figure. If the young child prefers the focal part in the upper portion of the figure (as indicated by the responses to the cards in Fig. 2), then the part preferred on top can be used as a measure of the portion of the figure perceived as focal. Other factors being equal, it appeared that black was more focal than white (Fig. 3, Card 5), and there was a tendency for darker portions in general to be more focal than lighter portions (Fig. 3, Cards 8 and 9). When a large and a small figure were opposed, the small figure was the more focal one in the 5-yr.-old group, but the 4-yr.-old children were equally divided in their choices (Fig. 2, Cards 1–4). Similar results have been reported for adults in the perception of reversible figures, where there is some dominance of black over white, and of small areas over large areas, in determining the figure seen.[4]

INTERPRETATION

It is clear that the young child is not insensitive to the spatial position of forms; on the contrary, he has preferences for the orientation of nonrealistic forms that have been hitherto unsuspected by his adult examiners. It will be proposed here that these preferences derive from some characteristics of form-perception in the young child, and that perhaps form-perception in the adult is not entirely free of similar influences.

Development of form-perception. There is general disagreement in the literature as to whether one can appropriately talk of the development of

---

[3] There were two kinds of response in the single-card situation to the cards that were simply divided into black and white portions—the line of demarcation was verticalized, or was placed in the upper part of the card. Since only a small number of children were tested in the single-card condition, it is difficult to account for the two types of response, but there was a tendency for the younger children to put the line of demarcation on top and for the older children to verticalize it.

[4] H. Goldhamer, The influence of area, position, and brightness in the visual perception of a reversible configuration, this JOURNAL, 46, 1934, 189-206.

form-perception. The Gestalt view is that the perception of simple forms does not show any genetic development, whereas the opposite position has been taken by such diverse writers as Hebb[5] and Piaget.[6] The present writer takes the latter position and leans in particular on the framework provided by Hebb for the development of the perception of form.

Let us first assume that the process underlying form-perception in the young child involves a sequential consideration of the figure, or scanning of its various parts. Let us further assume that certain portions of a figure catch the attention, or 'draw the eye,' more readily than do other portions. The scanning of a figure would, then, begin with such a focal portion.[7] The results of the experiments just reported indicate that the young child prefers this focal part to be at the top of the figure, and he prefers the main axis of the figure to be vertical. These two preferences both could be manifestations of a tendency to scan a figure in a downward direction. That is, it is suggested that scanning of a form does not proceed in a random order from one focal part to another, but tends to start at the top and continue downward.

If there is a preference for scanning in a top-to-bottom direction (in the developing stage of form-perception), then the position of the figure can conform to, or be in conflict with, this tendency. For example, the 'V,' with the angle at the bottom, would contrast with the preferred sequence of scanning, since attention would be drawn first to the angle in the bottom portion of the figure in contrast to the preferred tendency to start at the top and continue downward. When the 'V' is oriented with the angle on top, attention again would be drawn to the angle first, and the lines of the figure then would be consistent with the tendency to scan downward. From this point of view, a geometric form is considered right side up when the position of the form on the card conforms to, or reinforces, the preferred sequence of scanning,[8] and the form is upside down when it is placed in a position that opposes the preference.

---

[5] D. O. Hebb, *The Organization of Behavior,* 1949, 17-106.

[6] Jean Piaget, *The Psychology of Intelligence,* 1947, 56-66.

[7] The reader may object that the form must be 'perceived' as a whole before the focal point can be 'identified' and serve as the starting point of a scanning process. The sense in which the term 'focal' is used here does not require that the whole be 'perceived' first, but it does require that the whole figure fall on the retina regardless of which part of the figure is fixated first. This condition is fulfilled, as can be readily seen from the size of the card and its distance from the eye. That one portion of this retinal pattern may be more effective than another in producing an eye-movement, or 'drawing the attention,' is a reasonable assumption and hardly an original one (see discussion by Hebb, *op. cit.,* 82).

Although the objection that the focal aspect can be perceived only secondarily has been raised predominantly by Gestalt psychologists, the objection is more in the spirit of Helmholtz' 'unconscious inference' than of Gestalt field-effects. In the Gestalt view, the focal aspect of a configuration would be given as a primary quality resulting from the simultaneous interaction of the various parts of the field. The position taken here is entirely consistent with the assumption of field-effects, but departs from the Gestalt view in that form-perception is not assumed to be a single, unitary process.

[8] 'Scanning' could refer to overt eye-movements or to an internal motor process, *i.e.* the motor facilitation of a cell-assembly suggested by Hebb. It has been found that eye-movements are not necessary to elicit preferences for orientation (Lila Ghent, Lilly Bernstein, and A. M. Goldweber, Preferences for orientation of form under varying conditions, *Percept. mot. Skills,* 11, 1960, 46). 'Scanning' is used here to

This interpretation of the young child's preferences for orientation implies that the child makes a judgment of orientation radically different from the usual one. It generally is assumed that the judgment refers to a comparison of the relation between a given form and its framework with the relation between another instance of the form and its framework. In contrast, it is proposed here that the perception of orientation in the young child is a judgment of whether or not the form is oriented in such a way as to conform with factors that operate in the actual perception of the form.

The possibility that different types of judgment are made by the child and the adult may explain why earlier workers in this area have concluded that the spatial orientation of a form is irrelevant to the young child. The observations that have been made indicate that the young child does not compare, or does not match, the relations between forms and their environments.[9] It is appropriate to conclude from such data that the orientation of a form, in the adult sense, is not perceived by the young child, but it is inappropriate to conclude that the orientation of a form is without influence on the child's perception.[10] The child's lack of response to orientation in the adult sense appears to be due to an inability to make the complex comparison of the relations required for the judgment. An alternative type of judgment has been proposed to account for the child's sensitivity to orientation, as indicated by his preferences for orientation.

It has been stressed that the child's judgment of orientation does not relate the position of a form to its framework. Nevertheless, the 'top' of the figure and the 'downward' direction of scanning must be defined with respect to a framework. In principle, these terms could be defined either with respect to an environmental framework or to a retinal framework; the argument developed here, however, would seem to require that the framework be a retinal one. In a separate study, Ghent, Bernstein, and Goldweber investigated the determinants of the' phenomenal upright in preschool children by asking the children to judge the orientation of realistic and geometric figures while they were standing with their heads between their legs.[11] It was found that orientation was judged with respect to the retinal, and not the environmental, framework.

The interpretation offered for the preferences for orientation suggests that the judgment of the orientation of a figure is not separable, for the young child, from the perception of its shape. That is, a figure is called right side up if its position facilitates the tendency to scan in a top to bottom direction and hence facilitates the perception of the form. The burden

---

refer to an internal motor process facilitating perceptual activity in a particular sequence; this sequential organization conceivably could derive from overt eye-movements made in an early stage of development.

[9] Charlotte Rice, The orientation of plane figures as a factor in their perception by children, *Child Devel.,* 1, 1930, 111-43; Helen Davidson, A study of reversals in young children, *J. genet. Psychol.,* 45, 1934, 452-65; Davidson, A study of the confusing letters, B, D, P, and Q, *J. genet. Psychol.,* 47, 1935, 458-68.

[10] For example, it has often been claimed that young children recognize realistic figures equally well in any orientation. A direct test of this assumption has indicated that young children are particularly dependent on the right side up orientation of realistic figures for their recognition (Ghent, *op. cit.,* 249.)

[11] Ghent, Bernstein, and Goldweber, *op. cit.,* 46.

of proof of this argument rests on a demonstration that orientation does affect the recognition of form, and evidence in support of this position has been obtained. Ghent and Bernstein found that preschool children recognized geometric forms presented in the right side up position more frequently than forms presented in the upside down position.[12]

Changes with age. It has been suggested that the basis for the judgment of orientation is different in the preschool than in the older Ss, and the ready acceptance by the younger Ss of the problem of judging the orientation of non realistic forms did, indeed, contrast with the hesitant and questioning attitude of the older. The difficulty with this simple formulation is that the older Ss were, nevertheless, able to make consistent judgments of the orientation of the nonrealistic figures, as discussed in Experiment 1; furthermore, similar judgments of (or preferences for) orientation of nonrealistic figures have been found in adults.[13] The difference between younger and older Ss may be described by saying that the younger Ss have only one basis for the judgment of orientation, whereas the older Ss have two bases available; when the usual conceptual judgment cannot be made, the other basis for judgment comes into play. Although this formulation allows for the persistence of preferences in the older Ss, it does not account for the fact that the pattern of preference in the older Ss differs in at least two respects from that of the younger Ss. It will be recalled that the number of cards evoking preferences in the older Ss was less than in the younger Ss, and that the older Ss showed a few preferences that were significantly different from those of the younger Ss.

The finding that children of school age and adults showed fewer preference for orientation than preschool children is difficult to interpret. To some extent, the older S may look for meaning in the nonrealistic representations in an attempt to make the judgment of orientation on the usual basis; this tendency, acting on different figures for different Ss, would increase the probability of random responses appearing for the group. It is more likely, however, that the decrease in number of cards evoking preferences in the older Ss reflects some more general change in perceptual processes with age. The most obvious possibility is that sequential consideration of a form plays a diminishing role in form-perception in the older Ss; perhaps the definition of the focal part of a form does itself change with age.

The possibility that the focal aspect of a form may change is suggested, in part, by the responses to the figures with the gap (Fig. 1, Forms 7 and 8). The preschool children considered these figures upside down when the gap was on top, whereas

---

[12] Lila Ghent and Lilly Bernstein, Influence of the orientation of geometric forms on their recognition by children, *Percept. mot. Skills,* 12, 1961, 95-101.

[13] Significant preferences for the orientation of some nonrealistic figures have been found in two groups of college students, one group tested with the cards of Experiment I and the other group tested with those of Experiment II (Unpublished study).

the older children (and the group of adults referred to in Footnote 13) considered the figure upside down when the gap was on the bottom. This reversal of preference can most readily be interpreted by assuming that the line was focal for the younger *S*s and the gap for the older *S*s.[14] It will be recalled also that the response to the figures with the large and small squares (Fig. 3, Cards 1–4) showed some changes with age, suggesting that the small square might be considered focal for the 5-yr.-old *S*s and the large square for the 4-yr.-old *S*s. The possibility that the stimulus-characteristics defining 'focal' change with age in some instances raises difficulties for the definition of the focal part of a form, and there is risk of any definition becoming merely a tautology. To the extent, however, that further work can define the stimulus-characteristics preferred on top at different ages, the problems associated with the term 'focal' will be correspondingly diminished.

Although there is relatively little that can be said about developmental changes in the perception of form and its orientation after the preschool age, the existence of a type of judgment of orientation not heretofore considered has been suggested here. It seems reasonable to assume that the judgment of orientation of nonrealistic forms in the older *S*s is closely related to the judgment of the preschool *S*s. If the adult has a basis for judging the orientation of nonrealistic forms, and if this judgment indicates a tendency to scan form in a top-to-bottom direction, then one would expect these characteristics to manifest themselves in material other than that described here.

There are, in fact, a number of observations indicating asymmetry in the vertical axis in the perception of adults. Arnheim has reported that adults judge the orientation of abstract art with significant consistency—nonrealistic pictures appeared 'right' in one orientation and 'wrong' when rotated 90 or 180°.[15] Furthermore, all written languages of which the present writer is aware are read in a top-to-bottom direction rather than from the bottom to the top, although all other variations in direction seem to be present. Perhaps the asymmetry in the vertical axis most relevant to the results described here is that the perceptual center appears to be above the true center, as indicated by a constant error in the bisection of the vertical line,[16] and by the assumption by designers of advertising layouts that the 'optical center' is above (and to the left) of the midpoint of the page.[17] Presumably the same phenomenon accounts for the elementary rule in industrial design that a figure to be put in a frame, such as a picture on a mat or print on a page, must not be centered in the frame, since the figure would then appear to be below the center.[18] The apparent preference of adults for the placement of a figure above the true middle of the background might be described as an attenuated form of the preference shown by the young child for the placement of a figure in the upper portion of a card (Fig. 2, Cards 1–4).

---

[14] The Witte-König fusion-effect described by Helson and Wilkinson also indicates that a gap has a focal or dominant quality in the perception of adults (Harry Helson and A. E. Wilkinson, A study of the Witte-König paradoxical fusion-effect, this JOURNAL, 71, 1958, 316-20).

[15] Rudolph Arnheim, *Art and Visual Perception*, 1954, 18, 378.

[16] M. J. Delboeuf, Note sur certaines illusions d'optique, *Bull. de l'Académie Royale des Sciences, des Lettres, et des Beaux-Arts de Belgique*, 2me Série, 19, 1865, 195-216.

[17] Stephen Baker, *Advertising Layout and Art Direction*, 1959, 40.

[18] Harold Van Doren, *Industrial Design*, 2nd. ed., 1954, 151-52.

It has been proposed here that the sequential consideration of form in a downward direction plays a role in perception of young children and, to a lesser degree, in the perception of adults. It has already been suggested that sequential organization in a particular order could derive from movement of the eyes in scanning a form during the development of form-perception. The recent work of Ivo Kohler[19] and of Held and Hein,[20] in line with the theory of Von Holst,[21] indicates that organization of the perceptual world is strikingly affected by self-initiated movements of the organism; the role of such movements may be manifest primarily in the early stages of development (infancy) or of reorganization (*e.g.* after prismatic distortion).

SUMMARY

Investigation of the response of preschool children to pictures varying in orientation revealed that young children show remarkably consistent preferences for a particular orientation of nonrealistic figures as right side up. Such preferences are surprising, since they are clearly not learned from adults in the culture, and they seem to contradict the customary belief that young children are particularly unresponsive to the spatial orientation of visual forms.

Analysis of the stimulus-configurations eliciting preferences indicated that the young child prefers the focal part of the figure to be in the upper portion of the figure or the card; some data suggested, in addition, that the child prefers the main axis of the form to be in the vertical orientation. These preferences have been interpreted as indicating that, in the development of form-perception, scanning of form proceeds in a downward direction.

When the position of the focal part is such as to conflict with this sequential consideration of the form in a downward direction, the child considers the form to be upside down. Judgment of the orientation of a form is usually considered to be based on the relation of the position of a particular figure to the position of other figures in the environment, whereas it is suggested here that, for the young child, the judgment may be based on whether the position of the form facilitates, or conflicts with, movement-tendencies of the child.

---

[19] Ivo Kohler, Experiments with prolonged optical distortions, paper presented at the International Congress of Psychology, Montreal, Canada, 1954.

[20] Richard Held and A. V. Hein, Adaptation of disarranged hand-eye coördination contingent upon re-afferent stimulation. *Percept. mot. Skills,* 8, 1958, 87-90.

[21] E. von Holst, Relations between the central nervous system and the peripheral organs, *Brit. J. Animal Behav.,* 2, 1954, 89-94.

EDITORIAL COMMENTS

It has frequently been noted that young children are able to recognize pictures equally well in any orientation and that they confuse letters that are mirror images of each other, for example, *b* and *d*, *p* and *q*. Thus, until relatively recently, it was assumed that orientation was not a variable in the form perception of young children. However, contrary to this assumption, Ghent's study demonstrates that children as young as four years of age are able to discriminate between stimuli that differ only with respect to orientation, and also that they frequently show a preference for a particular orientation of nonrealistic or geometric figures as being right-side up. Thus it would appear that children are able to discriminate differences in orientation when this is an intrinsic part of the task that they are asked to perform.

Modifications of Sample and Procedure

Ghent's study consists of two experiments that are relatively independent. Students could replicate either one of the experiments, or both, depending on the time and subjects available. If a student elects to replicate only the second experiment, careful reading of the first study would be necessary in order to do this satisfactorily.

The sample that Ghent employed in her study was made up of children enrolled in a day-care center in a low-income area in New York City. If a different sample were chosen, this might provide an interesting comparison with the results of the original study. Ghent's subjects were grouped into four age groups—4, 5, 6, and 7–8 years. It might be more satisfactory for students to reduce this number to two groups (4–5 and 7–8), rather than attempting the replication with a very small number of children in each of four groups.

In the article, samples of the nonrealistic forms that Ghent utilized are presented, and these could be produced by students without much difficulty. However, while the content of the realistic forms is given, the actual forms are not shown and thus it will not be possible to reproduce these forms. Since the nonrealistic forms are line drawings, it might be best to use line drawings of the suggested items for the realistic pictures. (For students who are unable to obtain such pictures, children's coloring books provide a source from which pictures of objects could be traced.)

Ghent's discussion of her procedure does not indicate whether the presentation of the two forms of a pair was controlled for right or left position, a control that could be easily implemented by presenting alternate pairs in the opposite position for half of the subjects in each group.

Ghent reports that "children over 6 years of age usually hesitated for a few seconds when the nonrealistic forms were first presented, and they were often reluctant to choose between the cards." When children balked at choosing between the nonrealistic forms, they were urged to guess. When subjects cannot make a consistent choice between forms, this will result in selection of a form as upside down in a particular orientation at a chance level, that is, approximately 50 percent of the time. However, in replicating this study, some students have reported difficulty with this particular aspect of the procedure. One way of dealing with this problem is to encourage the subject to make a choice, and then if he persists in his uncertainty, to allow him to indicate no choice. Then, half of these responses would be arbitrarily regarded as right-side up, and the other half as upside down in the analysis of the results.

Treatment of Data

Ghent has presented her results in graphic form. It might also be helpful to the reader and to the student if the results were also presented in tabular arrangement. For each form, a table could indicate the proportion of boys and girls in each group choosing the orientation shown in Ghent's Figure 1 as upside down. The significance of differences between age and sex groups could also be indicated in such a table. Ghent's report of her investigation indicates that a statistical analysis of the results was carried out, and she reports that the frequency with which some figures were chosen as upside down in a specific orientation was significantly greater than would be expected by chance. However, she does not indicate which statistical test she employed. The data of this study are amenable to the use of the chi-square test with 50 percent selected as the level of chance expectancy (see appendix).

Experiment II

Having determined that children do discriminate between different orientations of geometric forms, an obvious question concerns the basis on which the choice of a figure as right-side up or upside down is made. On the basis of her findings in the first experiment, Ghent suggested that the young child's judgment of orientation is based on whether or not the form is oriented in such a way as to conform with the way in which visual scanning of the picture occurs, namely, in a top to bottom direction. She hypothesized that the figure is identified as upside down when the "focal portion" is in the lower half of the card. In order to examine this notion, she designed cards where she specified the part of the figure that was to be considered as "focal"—the portion of the figure that catches the viewer's attention—and thus she predicted which orientation of the figure should be chosen as upside down.

Ghent was also interested in considering the contribution that several variables, such as brightness and size, made to the determination of the focal point, and thus some of the figures were varied with respect to these characteristics.

For this experiment only preschool subjects (not used in Experiment I) were used, as these children had shown the most definite and consistent preferences in defining the "correct" orientation of the figures in the first study.

Ghent's discussion of the procedure for this experiment is brief and incomplete. However, it may be assumed that this second study utilized the same procedures as employed in the first. The suggestions made for replication of the first study would also apply to the second.

Journal of Comparative and Physiological Psychology
1962, Vol. 55, No. 6, 897–906

A DEVELOPMENTAL STUDY OF THE DISCRIMINATION OF LETTER-LIKE FORMS[1]

ELEANOR J. GIBSON, JAMES J. GIBSON, ANNE D. PICK, AND HARRY OSSER

Cornell University

It has generally been assumed in psychological analyses of the reading process that ability to discriminate letters is a prerequisite for reading and that children of 6 yr., when they begin to read, can in fact distinguish one letter from another with reasonable accuracy. The relevant literature is summarized by Vernon (1957, pp. 20 ff.). Some studies have used drawing as a criterion, some naming, and some matching. No one study has traced the development of letter differentiation as related to those dimensions or features of letters which are critical for the task and which may present more or less difficulty.

A method of studying this problem was suggested by an experiment of Gibson and Gibson (1955) in which children of two age groups and adults identified "scribbles" which were systematically varied on three separate dimensions (number of coils, compression, and orientation). The scribbles were somewhat comparable to strokes used in cursive writing. The results showed that the difficulty of the task was greater the younger the S, that errors varied in number with the dimension varied, and that systematic variation along at least three dimensions was possible. It also showed that confusion errors (primary generalization) provided an effective criterion for measuring ability to differentiate line drawings of this type.

The present experiment was designed to study the development of the ability to discriminate visually a set of letter-like forms in children 4 through 8 yr. of age. The aim was not merely quantitative comparison of different age levels, but primarily a qualitative developmental study of types of error as related to certain critical features of letters.

To secure information on qualitative changes, the plan was adopted of constructing

specified transformations for each of a group of *standard* letter-like forms. The transformations were chosen on an intuitive basis with regard to the distinctive features of letters as a set. Three types of transformation were included which were considered critical for discriminating printed letters, and one which was not.

Letter-like forms were selected, rather than actual letters, in order to keep specific experience with the forms as equal as possible. Matching, rather than identification, was the task, since simple discrimination (seeing a difference) was the criterion desired.

METHOD

Materials

Construction of standard forms. An analysis was made of actual letters (printed capitals, upper case, of the simple type customarily used in primary texts) in terms of number of strokes, straight vs. curved lines, angles, open vs. closed forms, symmetry, etc. This procedure provided a set of "rules" which describe generally the construction of letters. New forms were generated which follow the same constraints. A large number of forms resulted from which 12 were chosen as standards for the experiment. Of these half were symmetrical and half asymmetrical, half open and half closed, some combined straight and curved lines, some were composed only of straight lines, some only of curves, and the number of strokes varied from two to four. The standards are pictured in the first column of Figure 1.

Construction of transformations. The transformations chosen were as follows: three degrees of transformation of line to curve or curve to line (1, 2, or 3); five transformations of rotation or reversal, i.e., 45° rotation, 90° rotation, 180° rotation, right-left reversal, and up-down reversal; two perspective transformations, a 45° slant left and a 45° backward tilt; and two topological transformations, a break and a close.

The transformations are pictured in Figure 1 in the columns from left to right, each one in the same row as its standard. They were constructed by a draftsman, tracing from the standard whenever possible so that no change other than the intended one would be introduced. The perspective transformations were made by photographing each standard at the desired slant or tilt. The copies to be used for the experiment were reproduced by a photostatic process from the master copies. They were then mounted on 1¼-in.-sq. cards and covered with plastic.

It will be noted that half the forms (the symmetrical

[1] This research was supported in part by a grant from the United States Office of Education, Department of Health, Education, and Welfare.

The authors wish to express their gratitude to the principal and teachers of South Hill School, Ithaca, for their interest and generous cooperation.

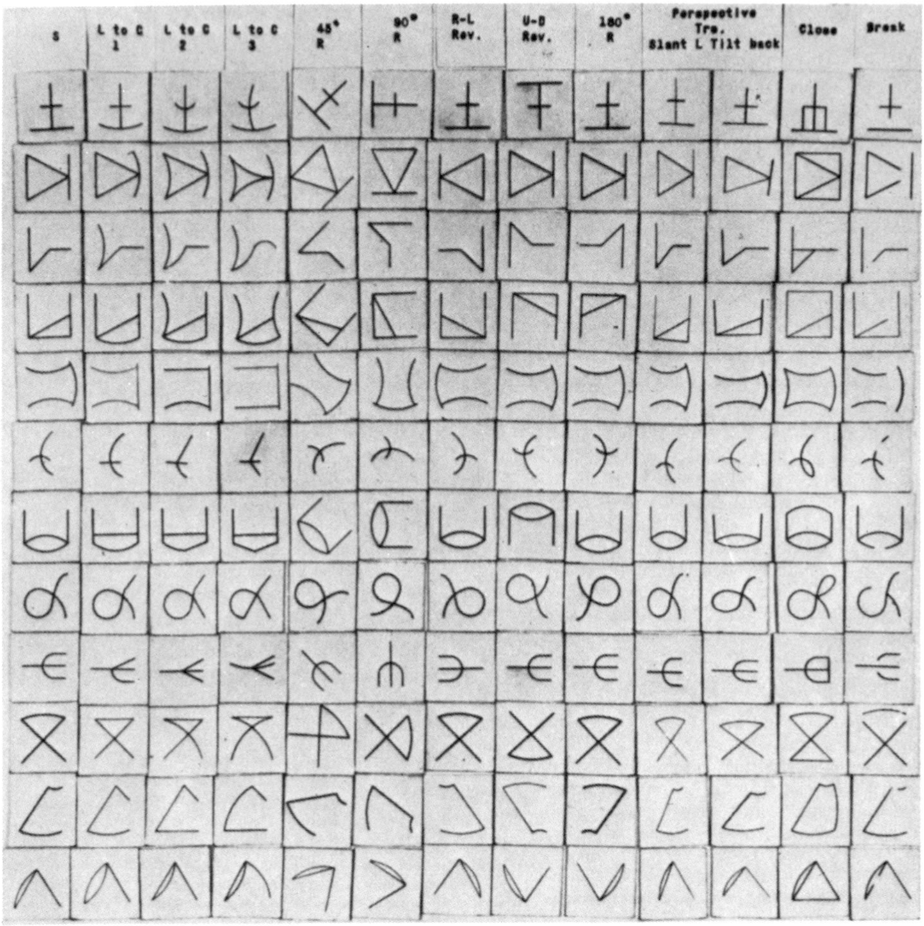

Fig. 1. The standard forms and their transformations.

ones) lacked two transformations, since either the right-left reversal or up-down reversal was identical with the standard and the 180° rotation was identical with the other. The cells in these cases were filled with the standard.

Procedure

The task. The discrimination task required S to match a standard with an identical form, in the following manner: A standard form was placed in the center of the top row of an apparatus which might be thought of as a matrix board (see Fig. 2). It was constructed of black-painted wood and contained four slotted rows below the top one, tilted so that S's angle of regard would be the same for each row. Each row held 13 cards. In any single row, a given standard and its own trans-

formations were placed in a random order. Three boards were available, so that 12 rows, one for each standard and its transformations could be set up before the experiment began. For the forms which lacked two transformations, three copies of the standard were mixed with the transformations. The others had one copy each of the standard in the row. This unequal number of exact matches per row had the advantage of preventing S from finding one and then stopping without scrutinizing the other cards.

After E had put the appropriate standard in the center of the top row, S went through a given row, searching for any form which was "exactly like the standard." When he found one, he removed it and handed it to E and continued until he had scanned the entire row. The display on the board at any given time had four filled rows, except for spaces left where S had

Fig. 2. Apparatus for displaying forms in the matching task.

removed a presumed match. All Ss matched for all 12 standards in counterbalanced orders.

The instructions were given very explicitly, so as to make absolutely clear that only an exact match was wanted. A demonstration was given first with very large sample forms (real letters) which included two reversals. The E asked if they were the same and corrected S if he responded incorrectly. Repetition and other terms such as "equal" or "exactly like" were used if necessary. Then S was given a practice row on the matrix board, again with real letters, but with a standard at top and filled board so that conditions simulated the final task. The S scanned across the row indicated by E, matching the standard, and E corrected his errors and explained the task again, if needed. If S lost his place or seemed not to be looking at every letter, his regard was directed across the board by E's indicating each one in turn. His attention was recalled to the standard if errors were made. No correction was given after the main task was begun, but the younger children had their attention directed back to the row and were guided across if their gazes wandered. There was no time limit.

Scoring. When S withdrew a form from the board and gave it to E, it was filed in a box and later classified as a correct match or an error. An error could be of two kinds: (a) failure to recognize a standard or (b) a confusion error, that is, selection of a transformation as identical with a standard. In the latter case, errors were classified according to type of transformation.

Subjects

The Ss were 167 children aged four through eight. The Ss from kindergarten through third grade were obtained at the same school, where the experiment was run during school hours. When grades were grouped according to progress, samples were taken from each group. The younger children were obtained at three nursery schools, the Cornell University Nursery School, a church nursery school, and a public nursery school at a settlement house. Numbers varied somewhat for age groups, but each age group contained at least 24 Ss, in order to rotate twice through the order.

Validation Experiment

It seemed desirable to have a check on the validity of the "letter-likeness" of the forms as well as a replication of the transformations with other standards. For this reason, a second experiment was run in which

the standards were 12 real letters (roman capitals, of the type used to formulate the rules in the first place). The 12 transformations were the same as those of the main experiment, and the material was constructed in the same way (see Fig. 3). The task and the apparatus duplicated the first experiment.

The Ss were the kindergarten chi¹lren tested in the main experiment, except for two who were no longer available. There was a 2-mo. interval between experiments.

RESULTS

Order Effects

A check was made to see whether order (position of the standard in the series of 12) was a source of variance. By Tukey's test of differences among a group of means (see Ryan, 1960), no difference was significant. Order was therefore disregarded thereafter and the data were combined.

Pooled Errors by Age Groups

There were very few errors of omission (failure to select the true match)—these errors did not vary in any orderly way, as Table 1 shows; therefore, all further discussion will be concerned with confusion errors, that is, identifying a variable as a standard. Pooled mean errors of this latter type declined with age, as would be expected (see Table 1). The standard deviations indicate rather large individual differences, which also decreased with age except for the 6-yr.-olds, who were apparently an unusually heterogeneous group. The drop in mean error from 5 to 6 yr., furthermore, was not as great as that between other age groups. The difference in mean error between boys and girls was small for all five groups, favoring the girls through 6 yr. and then the boys.

Analysis of Errors by Transformation

The mean errors for each type of transformation, presented in Table 2 for the five age groups, differ in frequency for different transformations as well as for age groups. There was a decrease in errors for all transformations as age increased, but some transformations were harder to discriminate from the standard than others, and rate of improvement varied with the type of transformation.

The errors for both the topological transformations—the changes of close and break—were few even for the 4-yr.-olds and declined

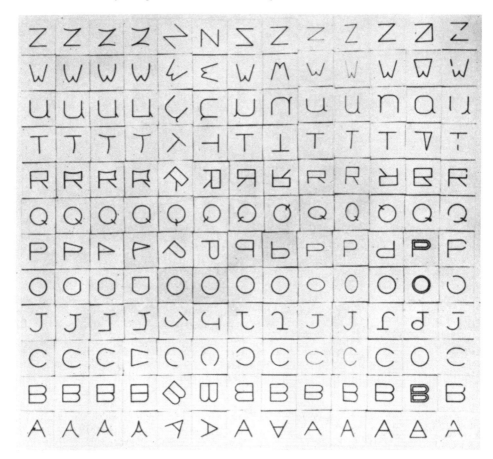

FIG. 3. Real letter standards and their transformations.

to almost zero for 8-yr.-olds. For both perspective transformations, on the other hand, the errors started very high ($M = 9.88$ and 9.23 at 4 yr., out of a possible 12), and were still high at 8 yr.

The errors for rotations and reversals started high, but by 8 yr. had declined almost to zero.

The errors for changes of line to curve were relatively great at 4 yr. for the first degree transformation and dropped low by 8 yr. For these transformations, mean error varied with the number of changes. Gradients of generalization for the three degrees of transformation can be compared by age groups. Generalization was greater, the younger the child, except for the overlapping of 5- and 6-yr.-olds,

and in every case decreased as the degree of change increased.

The differences in development of discrimination depending on type of transformation are most easily seen in Figure 4. Errors were combined for each of the four transformation groups. The curves not only look different from one another but the differences are statistically significant at most points of comparison. Ryan's (1960) method for making multiple comparisons was applied to proportions of errors to test the differences between the four types of transformation. At age four, all the differences were significant, and at five, six, and seven, five of the six differences were significant. At eight, where errors were few, the

TABLE 1

POOLED MEAN ERRORS BY AGE GROUP

Measure	Age				
	4	5	6	7	8
N	26	35	29	30	32
Omission errors	1.31	1.83	.41	.87	.94
Confusion errors					
Boys	61.69	40.42	37.76	24.53	16.63
Girls	54.54	38.31	36.25	27.85	22.88
M	58.12	39.46	37.14	25.97	19.75
SD_M	25.39	20.75	23.20	11.00	10.95

TABLE 2

MEAN ERRORS MADE FOR EACH TRANSFORMATION
BY AGE GROUPS

Transformation	Age Groups				
	4 ($N =$ 25)	5 ($N =$ 35)	6 ($N =$ 29)	7 ($N =$ 30)	8 ($N =$ 32)
Curve to line (1)	5.85	4.06	4.00	2.53	1.28
Curve to line (2)	4.42	2.60	2.69	1.33	0.53
Curve to line (3)	3.04	1.46	1.76	0.60	0.31
45° rotation	5.19	2.14	1.79	0.53	0.78
90° rotation	4.31	1.48	1.28	0.03	0.34
Right-left reversal[a]	6.56	3.96	2.07	0.97	0.59
Up-down reversal[a]	6.47	3.55	2.44	1.56	1.08
180° rotation[a]	5.24	2.74	1.10	0.14	0.38
Perspective, hor.	9.88	9.20	9.69	9.27	7.34
Perspective, vert.	9.23	8.97	9.31	8.20	6.81
Close	1.19	.69	0.83	0.43	0.31
Break	2.62	1.86	1.86	1.07	0.59

[a] These figures have been corrected to allow for the fact that opportunities for error were less than for the other transformations.

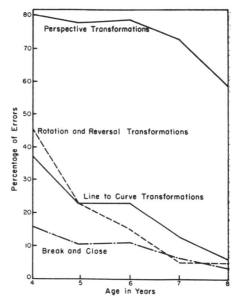

FIG. 4. Developmental error curves for four types of transformation.

differences were significant only between perspective transformations and the other three types.

The slopes of the four curves suggest that there is the greatest developmental change between 4 and 8 yr. in tendency to confuse rotation-reversals, with line-to-curve errors showing the next greatest drop, perspective errors next, and topological errors least. To test the differences in drop in error with age, the two youngest age groups were combined and the two oldest combined and the mean amount of drop computed for each type of transformation. Then t tests were made of differences between these mean drops for all six transformation comparisons (see Table 3). The difference in error decrease between perspective transformations and topological transformations is not significant, but all the other differences in slope are valid.

Correlations between Types of Error

With reference to the four curves of Figure 4, some justification should be given for pooling errors within transformation groups. There

TABLE 3

COMPARISON OF MEAN AMOUNTS OF DROP IN ERROR
FOR DIFFERENT TRANSFORMATIONS

Transformations Compared[a]	Difference in M Drop	
TT-PT	0.92	1.12
TT-CL	5.18	7.01*
TT-RR	10.94	7.03*
RR-PT	10.22	5.94*
RR-CL	5.81	4.57*
CL-PT	4.25	4.29*

[a] TT = topological transformations; CL = curve to line transformations; RR = rotation and reversal transformations; PT = perspective transformations.
* $p < .01$.

were several reasons for so doing: First, ad hoc or intuitive reasons, because the transformations combined were of the same geometrical types and because the curves, when drawn individually, resembled each other within transformation groups. Furthermore, the differences between curves of *different* transformation groups were overall significant. It was also possible to obtain a third kind of evidence, i.e., the intercorrelations between different kinds of transformation error.

Correlations were run between errors for each of the 12 transformations and every other, separately for each age level. This gave a 12 × 12 correlation matrix for each age level. Because space does not permit printing all the five matrices, the information yielded by the correlations is summarized in Table 4. The correlations *within* a transformation group, where there is more than one, have been averaged. So have the correlations between that transformation group and all others. For instance, the mean correlation between the three line-to-curve transformations is +.88 for the 4-yr.-olds, but the mean of the line-to-curve transformations with other types (rotations, reversals, perspective transformations and topological transformations) is lower, +.62. A similar comparison can be made at each age level for each transformation group. The *N* in Table 4 refers to the number of correlation coefficients which have been averaged for any mean in the column. (The *S N* is always the same for any age group.) Ranges are presented under the means in brackets to indicate the lowest and highest of the coefficients averaged in any mean.

It will be noted that in 18 of the 20 comparisons within and between transformation groups, the mean correlation is lower between different transformation types. In the two atypical cases (rotation-reversal and topological transformations at the 7-yr. level), correlations are low and insignificant. The reason for this is that errors of these types had dropped to zero for nearly all *S*s. The correlations for the 7- and 8-yr.-olds are less meaningful than those at four, five, and six because of the lowness of the error scores for everything except perspective transformations. The topological transformations showed less contrast than the others, probably because they are not as "clean" transformations. The break or the close had to be inserted somewhat arbitrarily, so that configurational changes in addition to the desired one probably resulted in some instances.

The high intercorrelations between transformations of the same type furnish strong supportive evidence for the inner consistency of the types of features chosen for qualitative analysis of errors.

Comparison with Real Letters

A check on validity, both of the material used and the functioning of the different transformations, was furnished by the repetition of the experiment with 12 real letters and the same 12 transformations. Only the kindergarten group took part. In Table 5 the mean

TABLE 4

MEAN CORRELATIONS WITHIN AND ACROSS TRANSFORMATION GROUPS

Age	L to C		R & R		P.T.		T.T.	
	Within $N = 3$	Across $N = 27$	Within $N = 10$	Across $N = 35$	Within $N = 1$	Across $N = 20$	Within $N = 1$	Across $N = 20$
4	.88	.62	.77	.54	.73	.43	.59	.52
	(.85 to .91)	(.32 to .81)	(.63 to .91)	(.28 to .81)		(.25 to .59)		(.25 to .75)
5	.76	.55	.74	.43	.68	.33	.65	.52
	(.71 to .83)	(.29 to .85)	(.61 to .87)	(.01 to .73)		(.01 to .53)		(.28 to .85)
6	.90	.54	.78	.42	.85	.40	.55	.48
	(.87 to .93)	(.37 to .88)	(.64 to .95)	(.18 to .66)		(.15 to .60)		(.15 to .88)
7	.70	.22	.07	.14	.81	.26	−.19	.17
	(.66 to .77)	(−.19 to .79)	(−.20 to .38)	(−.17 to .50)		(−.15 to .57)		(−.19 to .79)
8	.58	.46	.77	.34	.75	.35	.48	.18
	(.45 to .73)	(.04 to .73)	(.60 to .97)	(−.05 to .74)		(−.05 to .53)		(−.03 to .45)

TABLE 5

MEAN ERRORS BY TRANSFORMATION FOR LETTER-LIKE
FORMS AND LETTERS, AND THE CORRELATIONS
BETWEEN THEM

Transformation	M		Correlation between Forms and Letters
	Forms	Letters	
Curve to line (1)	4.33	4.25	.56
Curve to line (2)	2.78	1.98	.37
Curve to line (3)	1.60	1.15	.42
45° rotation	2.48	1.18	.84
90° rotation	1.90	1.18	.84
R-L reversal	3.33	2.25	.77
Up-Down reversal	2.93	1.03	.75
180° rotation	1.53	.65	.75
Perspective, hor.	9.38	7.85	.49
Perspective, vert.	8.95	7.13	.37
Close	.88	.68	.63
Break	1.85	1.23	.59

number of errors for each transformation can be compared for the letter-like forms and the letters. Errors were fewer for letters. This trend might be expected, since the children were familiar with letters (they could print their names) and they were 2 mo. older. But the correlations between transformations are are significant in every case.

One can also ask whether the order of difficulty of transformations corresponds in the two cases. The rank-order correlation between the forms and the letters, ordering the transformations according to mean number of errors, is +.87, showing that there was high correspondence.

Correlations within transformation types and across them were obtained for the letters, as they were for the forms. Mean r's within transformation groups were .83, .76, .73, .73; between groups, .56, .44, .38, .53. As was the case with the forms, the correlations within groups were considerably higher than across groups.

These results appear to confirm very satisfactorily the qualitative differences produced by different transformations in the first experiment. From this evidence, it is concluded that transformation type is a good predictor of confusion errors.

Comparison of Forms

Although characteristics of the individual standard forms were not a matter of primary interest for the experiment, it is possible to

classify and compare them in certain respects (e.g., symmetrical vs. asymmetrical) to see if these qualities are associated with greater or less discriminability. The "perceptibility" of forms in relation to such contour characteristics as symmetry, continuity, etc. has been studied by Fitts, Weinstein, Rapaport, Anderson, and Leonard (1956) and recently by Klemmer (1961). Undoubtedly, the role played (if any) by a dimension such as symmetry in "pattern difficulty" (to use Klemmer's term) would vary with the judgment required and with the set of other items also being judged. Under the conditions of the present experiment, symmetry did have a significant effect. Symmetrical standards were confused with their variants less often than asymmetrical ones were confused with theirs. The difference appeared in all five age groups ($p < .02$ in every case and $< .001$ in three cases), but the magnitude of the difference was very small. This finding agrees with the two studies mentioned.

Klemmer investigated, also, the effect of continuity and of a closed loop. All our standards were continuous, but since half the standards possessed a closed loop and half did not, they were compared for the latter characteristic. Here the results disagreed with Klemmer's; more errors were made when the standard possessed a closed loop. The difference was not significant at every age level, although it was in the same direction.

The straight-curved classification in our experiment was a three-way one, for four standards were all straight, four all curved, and four mixed. When these three types were compared, the all-curved standards were associated, at all age levels, with more errors than all straight. But the mixed figures occupied an ambiguous position with respect to them.

These "absolute" characteristics of a standard seem to us trivial as predictors of identifiability when compared with the transformations within the set to be judged. In other words, the influence of similarity within a set (here the transformations in relation to the standard) seems to us more important than any characteristic of the standard as such.

DISCUSSION

The most obvious and hardly unexpected outcome of the experiment was that the visual discrimination of letter-like forms, using a matching procedure which requires a judgment of same or different, improves from age four to eight. What are the reasons for improvement? Better ability to keep the task in mind and follow it through cannot be wholly ruled out, but preliminary practice, instruction, and assistance in scanning when required rendered this factor minimal. Maturation of retinal processes is still continuing during this period, but acuity as such should have been adequate even for the 4-yr.-olds. It seems, rather, that children between four and eight learn something about letter-like forms which makes possible better discrimination even between ones they have not seen before.

Our results suggest that what they learn are the features or dimensions of difference which are critical for differentiating letters. Some are critical, but some are not, and the latter variations in letters must in fact be tolerated. Here it is useful to consider Roman Jakobson's concept of "distinctive features" of phonemes (Jakobson & Halle, 1956). Phonemes, like graphemes, must be differentiated from one another, but many variations are permissable without destroying identifiability; the same phoneme pattern is recognizable when it is delivered by a high-pitched or low-pitched voice, whispered, shouted, sung, and so on. Brown (1958) has referred to this as "constancy of the phoneme." But certain features—the "distinctive" ones—are invariant and must be heard as such. It is our hypothesis that it is the distinctive features of grapheme patterns which are responded to in discrimination of letter-like forms. The improvement in such discrimination from four to eight is the result of learning to detect these invariants and of becoming more sensitive to them.

The 4-yr.-olds do, of course, discriminate the letter-like forms up to a point. They have had some experience with alphabet blocks and picture books. But, more important, some of their previous experience with solid objects could transfer to this new discrimination task. Solid objects also have invariant qualities and distinctive features, and a 4-yr.-old has learned what he needs to distinguish many of these, perhaps at the same time he began to distinguish the invariants which permit constancy of shape and size as he moves about in space.

The question is, Why should the four types of transformation differ in difficulty at the outset and why do errors decrease at different rates?

The perspective transformations produced the greatest number of confusions in the 4-yr.-olds. Was this because the amount of physical change was small? We have no absolute measure for comparing degrees of change. Nevertheless a 45° slant is very appreciable; acuity is good for it with judgments of moving perspective transformations (Gibson & Gibson, 1957) in adult Ss. But there was no motion in the present experiment—i.e., no indication of a depth difference. Furthermore, perspective transformations are not distinctive features for object identification. On the contrary, these variations must be tolerated for shape constancy to occur. Therefore, no transfer from discriminating solid objects of the world can be expected for this dimension, since the compression-like changes which result have never been critical for judging objects as same or different. Consequently, errors occurred at a very high rate when S was asked to match letter-like forms differing only by this type of transformation.

The decrease in these errors with age was also very slight because perspective transformations are no more distinctive features of letters than of objects. More or less compression must be tolerated in reading the same letter when the page is held at various angles to the line of sight.

At the other extreme are topological transformations—changes produced by breaking or closing a line. Differences of this type are not continuous, and they are critical for object discrimination. Piaget and Inhelder (1956) showed that children discriminate them with solid objects at a very early age. The difference is perceived as well in line drawings. The error curve for breaks and closes of lines began low initially and dropped, reaching zero at 8 yr., because this feature is critical for distinguishing letters as well as objects (i.e., the difference between C and O).

Initial errors for reversals and rotations would also be expected to be high because transformations of this type are not critical for identification of objects as same or different. Rotation gives information about the position of an object. If habits formed for object-discrimination are used when the child begins to make graphic discriminations, confusions due to rotation are to be expected, and in fact occurred. A right-left reversal (mirror reversal) is equivalent to turning over a flat object from front to back and again is not significant, usually, for distinguishing solid objects. Although this curve started high, it fell rapidly to near zero at 8 yr., for the child learns during this period that transformations of rotation and reversal *are* significant for distinguishing graphic forms (i.e., the difference between M and W, C and U, d and b, p and b).

The error curves for line-to-curve transformations need a more complex interpretation. For solid forms, the equivalent transformation would be a deformation of a rigid object, and in that case a critical one. But for living things or plastic objects, elastic transformations of line to curve do occur (i.e., changes of facial expression) and are not significant for identifying an object as same or different; they indicate, rather, a change of state. Transfer to graphic discriminations is therefore equivocal. The amount of the change (one to three changes) was important here. With three changes the error curve was initially low, but with one it was high. The prediction for eventual discrimination, however, is clear. These changes are critical ones for graphemes (i.e., the difference between U and V), and the error curve, at eight, has dropped almost to zero.

The developmental error curves for the four types of transformation that were studied can, then, be interpreted successfully and convincingly by the hypothesis that the child has to learn the distinctive features of letters and that he does not start "cold" because of transfer from his already good ability to differentiate critical features of objects. It may occur to the reader that we have not dealt with all the features by which one letter differs from another. This is of course the case; the set of distinctive features of letters is greater than the set of variables chosen here. Also, the set of noncritical variations of a letter was not fully explored (size, for instance). An attempt is at present being made to work out a fuller set of distinctive features for graphemes. When the set is available, predictions can be made and tested with a confusion matrix.

Another question of interest is how the distinctive features are detected by the child. Teachers apparently give a good deal of concentrated and highly verbal attention to reversal and rotation errors. But there is no evidence that teaching is required. It may be that the child learns which varying dimensions of letters are significant and which are not by simply looking repeatedly at many samples containing both varying and invariant features. The distinctive features of phonemes are not taught but they are nevertheless learned.

Helping the child to pay attention to the distinctive features can hardly hurt, however. If we knew the set of such features, they could be incorporated in some of the "reading readiness" tasks which involve visual discriminations. There is little or no evidence that these experiences transfer to reading. But if the typical matching tasks used variables which are significant for letter discrimination (instead of pictures of objects), there would certainly be greater potential transfer value.

SUMMARY AND CONCLUSIONS

This experiment studied qualitatively as well as quantitatively the development of visual discrimination of letter-like forms in children four through eight. The forms were constructed according to the same constraints which govern formation of printed capitals. Twelve were chosen as standards, and 12 specified transformations were constructed for each standard. The transformations were three degrees of change from line to curve or vice versa; five changes in orientation; two perspective transformations; and two topological transformations. The discrimination task required *S* to match a standard form with an identical form. All *S*s matched for all 12 standards. Errors were classified according to type of transformation erroneously identified with the standard. The experiment was repeated for the 5-yr.-old group using real letters.

Overall error scores decreased with age, but difficulty of discrimination was different for different transformations. Initial errors were greatest for perspective transformations and least for topological transformations, with changes of rotation and reversal in between.

Changes of line to curve varied in difficulty depending on the number of changes.

The slopes of the curves differed, as well as the initial error. The four classes of transformation showed similarity of slope within the class, but significant differences between them.

Errors made with real letters correlated significantly with errors made with letter-like forms. The correlation between mean errors for different transformations in the two sets of material was +.87, showing that the kind of transformation defining similarity or difference between two forms is a good predictor of confusion errors.

The differences between the developmental error curves for the four types of transformation were interpreted in terms of a hypothesis of distinctive features. Features which have been in the past critical for distinguishing objects are assumed to transfer to graphic discriminations. Discrimination learning continues from this point for distinctive features of letters, but proceeds slowly, if at all, for those varying features of graphemes which are not critical for distinguishing them.

REFERENCES

BROWN, R. *Words and things.* Glencoe, Ill.: Free Press, 1958.

FITTS, P. M., WEINSTEIN, M., RAPAPORT, M., ANDERSON, N., & LEONARD, J. A. Stimulus correlates of visual pattern recognition: A probability approach. *J. exp. Psychol.,* 1956, **51**, 1-11.

GIBSON, J. J., & GIBSON, E. J. Perceptual learning: Differentiation or enrichment? *Psychol. Rev.,* 1955, **62**, 32-41.

GIBSON, J. J., & GIBSON, E. J. Continuous perspective transformations and the perception of rigid motion. *J. exp. Psychol.,* 1957, **54**, 129–138.

JAKOBSON, R., & HALLE, M. *Fundamentals of language.* The Hague, Netherlands: Mouton, 1956.

KLEMMER, E. T. The perception of all patterns produced by a seven-line matrix. *J. exp. Psychol.,* 1961, **61**, 274–282

PIAGET, J., & INHELDER, B. *The child's conception of space.* London, England: Humanities Press, 1956.

RYAN, T. A. Significance tests for multiple comparison of proportions, variances, and other statistics. *Psychol. Bull.,* 1960, **57**, 318–328.

VERNON, M. D. *Backwardness in reading.* Cambridge, England; Cambridge Univer. Press, 1957.

(Received November 7, 1961)

EDITORIAL COMMENTS

Eleanor Gibson and her colleagues are interested in the development of perception and provide here another hypothesis for consideration. They suggest that the critical dimensions that the child learns to use as cues in differentiating figures, and which may also be important in his reproductions of geometrical figures, are those properties of objects, forms, symbols, and so on that are important for perceptual differentiation. The child's earliest experiences are with concrete objects that do not change even if their orientation in space is altered, if they have different colors or varying numbers of parts. For example, a chair is still a chair whether it is right-side up or upside down, whether it is green or red, or whether it has three rungs or four. The child must learn to respond to the "distinctive features" of stimuli, that is, to those features that are critical for discriminating objects from other different objects; he must also learn to ignore those variations that must be tolerated for shape constancy to occur, or which are not crucial to the object's basic identity.

In this study, Gibson *et al.* investigated the child's increasing skill in making perceptual differentiations between letterlike forms. They found that children improved with age in this skill, but they did so at different rates for different types of variants of standard stimuli. They interpreted the results as showing that those features critical in distinguishing among objects, for example, break–close, actually transfer to discrimination of letterlike forms, and thus these are the most readily discriminated transformations; such features are also shown to be those correctly identified by the youngest subjects. Variations such as perspective changes, on the other hand, are not distinctive features for object recognition, and thus are very difficult variations of letter-like forms to detect.

Modifications of Sample and Procedure

In general the materials and procedure utilized in this study are clearly described. In the original study the letterlike forms were drawn by a drafts-man, but students should be able to construct reasonably accurate copies of these forms from the examples provided in the article. The one instance where reproduction of the forms may cause a problem is the 45° backward tilt, which was produced by photographing the standard at the desired angle. By using the examples provided in the article, however, along with the con-ventions of perspective drawing, a reasonable copy can be produced.

Students may be able either to make an apparatus like Gibson's matrix board or to modify the procedure slightly by presenting only one form and its transformations at a time; this could be done by using either a single board with a groove to hold the cards or, as some students have done, by using holders from a Scrabble game. (Card order can be arranged in advance so that setting up each row does not increase the time necessary for each subject.)

In the original study, the standards (with their respective transformations) were presented to the subjects in counterbalanced order, that is, the first sub-ject was given Form 1 first, then Forms 2, 3, . . . , 12; the second subject was given Form 2, then Forms 3, 4, . . . , 12, 1, and so on. For each standard the order of presentation of transformations in the matrix board was random. Since it was found that order of presentation had no effect on the results (see Results: Order Effects), the procedure could be simplified by present-ing the standards, as well as their transformations, in random order. Each set of transformations could be shuffled and placed with the appropriate stand-ard in an envelope. The order of presentation of envelopes could then be determined by shuffling them in turn. This procedure would also eliminate the necessity for having any particular number of subjects in each group in order to counterbalance for order effects.

A number of modifications are possible in the selection of the sample. One example might be the use of a smaller number of subjects. Since the sex of the subjects in each of the age groups is not indicated in the original study, it might be interesting to select equal (or approximately equal) numbers of boys and girls in each group employed; the performance of the sexes on this task could then be compared, a procedure particularly relevant in view of the frequently reported sex differences in reading achievement.

Time per subject may be reduced, if necessary or desirable, by reducing the number of standards used. For example, the student might elect to utilize only 6 standards (with 12 transformations each). In this case, it would be desirable to select 3 symmetrical and 3 asymmetrical standards.

Another though less desirable modification is to reduce the number of transformations per standard, that is, to use all 12 standards but to reduce the number of transformations for each one, possibly using only one of each of the 4 types of transformations in each case.

In addition to the major experiment, the authors also carried out a validation study using transformations of real letters. In this study, using kindergarten children, they found results similar to the first study. Thus, this part of the project could be omitted in the interest of conserving time.

Treatment of Data

The statistical analysis of the results in the study may be too complex for some students to repeat. However, they could determine the mean and standard deviation for the distributions of the types of error for the age groups employed and present graphs of the percentages of types of errors as shown in Figure 4. This type of figure could also be utilized to present data concerning the four major types of transformations, showing the degree of similarity within each transformation group. Such graphs could illustrate the degree of similarity within transformation groups, as well as the differences between them.

Comparisons of sex groups and age groups could be done for each transformation, using the chi-square statistic. The student may also find it interesting to carry out a stage analysis (such as is done in the Chomsky article in this collection) considering the difficulty of the transformations at different ages. Thus, it could be determined if children who were able to discriminate those transformations that were developmentally more difficult were also able to deal with the earlier transformations successfully; that is, a developmental sequence might be demonstrated if the discrimination of transformations for individual children followed the order of developmental difficulty for the entire group of subjects.

Students who wish to exercise their own ingenuity might wish to design a study that would combine the procedures of the Graham *et al.* study on the development of the ability to copy forms with that of the Gibson *et al.* study. In such a case each subject would perform the copying of the figures of the Graham *et al.* study and the discrimination of forms of the Gibson *et al.* study. A correlation of the development of these two perceptual–motor skills should provide some interesting results.

Journal of Comparative and Physiological Psychology
1963, Vol. 56, No. 5, 892–898

DISCRIMINATION OF DIRECTION OF LINE IN CHILDREN[1]

RITA G. RUDEL AND HANS-LUKAS TEUBER

Massachusetts Institute of Technology

2 experiments were performed demonstrating similarity of pattern-discrimination learning in children to that of the octopus described by Sutherland. Young children (ages 3–4) confuse oblique lines oriented in opposite directions, just as the octopus does, although they can readily discriminate vertical from horizontal lines—again as seen in the cephalopod. Analogous results were obtained for U shapes in various orientations; transfer trials confirmed the lack of discrimination for obliques.

In searching for neural correlates of shape perception, comparisons between species may yield clues not readily obtained from studies limited to man. Such comparisons are often guided by the expectation that widely dissimilar nervous systems should mediate correspondingly dissimilar types of shape perception (Teuber, 1960). In fact, most studies of this kind have thus far shown the opposite: a surprising similarity of performance in different species. Shapes readily discriminated by man are also more readily discriminated by infrahuman forms. Conversely, animals often fail to distinguish shapes that are also confusing to man.

Such observations may be expected as long as comparisons are confined to higher species as closely related as man and anthropoid apes (Schiller, 1951), or man and monkeys (Klüver, 1933). It becomes more puzzling if we consider pattern perception in the rat (Lashley, 1938), since Lashley observed that levels of difficulty in visual discrimination learning were clearly analogous for rat and man. Evidence for such cross-species similarity has been extended further by Sutherland (1957, 1958, 1960). In his experiments on the octopus, Sutherland noted that this invertebrate could readily discriminate a vertical from a horizontal rectangle, yet could not respond differentially to an oblique rectangle paired with another inclined in the opposite direction. The present experiment was undertaken in the belief that these relative difficulties might exist in essentially similar fashion in the human child.

Two additional pairs of discriminanda were included, upright U vs. an inverted U, and a U rotated 90° to the left vs. one rotated 90° to the right, because here again the octopus managed to discriminate the former pair with much less difficulty than the latter. Similar findings had formerly been reported by Lashley (1938) for the rat.

EXPERIMENT 1: SIMULTANEOUS DISCRIMINATION

Method and Procedure

Subjects. The children were selected from a nursery in a low-income housing project and from a public elementary school in a mixed socioeconomic area (low and middle incomes). The elementary school had separated its children according to IQ and scholastic achievement; those for this study were selected from "average" classes only. There were 93 children in Experiment 1, 46 male and 47 female, comprising six age groups (3–6 to 8–5 yr. inclusive). (See Table 1.)

Equipment. Four pairs of plaques were used to display the discriminanda. The plaques were made of white opaque Plexiglas, cut into 5-in. squares. The figures on the plaques, i.e., vertical, or horizontal, or oblique lines, and U shapes were made of black plastic strips and pasted onto the Plexiglas. The strips were raised $1/16$ in. above the background; they were $1/4$ in. in width. The lines (horizontal, vertical, and oblique) were 3 in. long; the U figure consisted of three lines, each 2-$1/2$ in. long (see Figure 1). Other patterns for the transfer tests (black square and black diamond) were constructed in an analogous fashion (Figure 2).

Procedure. Each child was taken from his classroom to a small examining room where he was seated opposite E. Care was taken that the chair was the right size for the child and that

[1] The investigations of which this experiment forms a part are supported by Program Grant M-5673 from the National Institute of Mental Health, United States Public Health Service. The authors are indebted to N. S. Sutherland for a critical discussion of this paper.

his eyes were at reading height from the top of the table. Then, *E* read the following instructions:

> I am going to show you two cards; one of them is "right" and one is "wrong" that is, "correct" or "incorrect." At first you can only guess which is right, but after you've guessed, I will tell you whether you guessed correctly—that is, whether you were right or wrong. After that, you must always pick the card which is "right" and never the card which is "wrong."

If these instructions were not clear to the child, *E* added: "Let's try it and you'll see." The first pair of plaques was then presented together, side-by-side, approximately 2 in. apart, flat on the table in front of *S*.

The lateral position of the correct plaque in each pair was varied according to a Gellermann sequence (Gellermann, 1933). The order of presentation was designed so that each pair would appear first, second, third, and fourth in the series an equal number of times, yielding four sequences (see Figure 1). Each child went through four pairs (one sequence) of discriminanda. For half the children the vertical was designated as "correct," and for half, the horizontal was "correct." Similarly with the other pairs, for half the *Ss* one was "right," and for half, the other. If the child guessed correctly, he was told "right—now pick this one all the time," but if he chose in-

correctly, he was told "wrong—but you will have a chance to pick the right one from now on." When *S* had chosen the designated "correct" card on 9 out of 10 consecutive trials, *E* would say: "Now we will play the same game with this pair," and proceeded with the next three pairs. If, after 50 trials with any one pair, *S* showed no learning, *E* said, "Let's try it with another pair of cards" and went on to the next scheduled pair. (A pilot study demonstrated that only rarely would a child succeed with a particular pair of cards if he did not do so within the first 50 trials. To continue beyond this point often made *S* irritable and unfit to continue with the other pairs in the series.)

There were no rewards on any trials except for *E*'s "right" or "wrong." Although the three youngest groups were told that they could choose a candy bar from a display when they "finished the game," this reward was not related to individual success or failure. The older children received only verbal praise for their efforts.

A fifth discrimination was added for some *Ss* in the 6-, 7-, and 8-yr. groups. This consisted of either the vertical or horizontal figure paired with one of the obliques. It was always the last pair in the series and no further instructions were necessary. The *Ss* for this part were 11 6-yr.-olds (6 male, 5 female); 12 7-yr.-olds (5 male, 7 female); and 9 8-yr.-olds (4 male, 5 female).

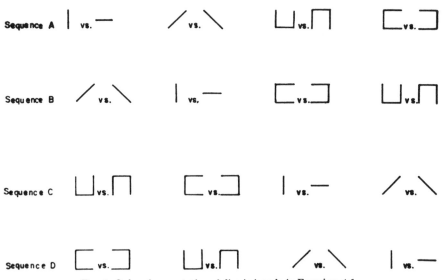

Fig. 1. Order of presentation of discriminanda in Experiment 1.

Results

In Table 1, the results for simultaneous presentations of discriminanda are given according to age group. Evidently, performance on the vertical-horizontal and right-side-up upside-down tasks are quite simple for the youngest children. On the other hand, almost all Ss in the 3-, 4-, and 5-yr. groups fail to learn the discrimination of the obliques or of the left-right oriented U figures.

The vertical or horizontal line paired with an oblique presented no difficulty for our 6-, 7-, and 8-yr. groups. There were no failures; the mean numbers of trials required to reach criterion (9 out of 10 correct) were, respectively, 10.1, 9.3, and 9.7. This suggests that simultaneous discrimination of vertical vs. oblique, or horizontal vs. oblique may be as simple as discrimination of vertical vs. horizontal. As one S expressed it, it would appear to be even simpler: "This is very easy because one of them is straight (the vertical) and one is crooked (the oblique); these two (vertical and horizontal) are both straight." It should be noted, however, that the discrimination tests for vertical or horizontal vs. oblique shapes came at the end of the trials schematized in Figure 1.

EXPERIMENT 2: SUCCESSIVE DISCRIMINATION AND TRANSFER TRIALS

Method and Procedure

Sixteen additional 5-yr.-old Ss (9 male, 7 female) were trained on a successive discrimination opposing either the vertical or the horizontal line to one of the obliques. The four pairs of discriminanda employed are shown in the left-hand columns of Figure 2. As can be seen, either the vertical or horizontal or one of the two obliques was positive.

For the successive discriminations, E presented one card at a time—say the one with the horizontal line—asked S whether it should be called "right" or "wrong," then removed the card and presented the other card of that pair (bearing an oblique line), asking again whether this second

TABLE 1
EASE OF LEARNING DISCRIMINATIONS BY AGE GROUPS
(Experiment 1)

Mean age (in yr. and mo.)	N		Discriminanda[a]							
	Boys	Girls		vs. —		/ vs. \		⊔ vs. ⊓		⊐ vs. ⊏	
			T	F	T	F	T	F	T	F
3–6	6	6	14.0	1	0.0	12	21.6	1	42.0	11
4–6	8	4	11.3	1	30.0	11	17.0	2	30.0	10
5–5	10	10	13.4	0	29.7	16	16.0	0	34.0	16
6–6	8	7	13.7	0	16.2	7	12.7	1	15.0	5
7–5	7	10	13.2	0	16.4	7	13.5	0	12.5	6
8–5	7	10	11.1	0	15.0	5	12.0	0	14.1	3
Totals	46	47								

[a] T—Trials to learn; F—Ss failing to learn in 50 trials.

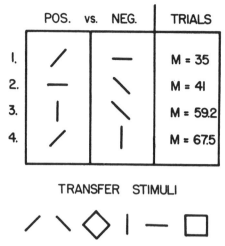

POS.	vs.	NEG.	TRIALS
1.	/	—	M = 35
2.	—	\	M = 41
3.	|	\	M = 59.2
4.	/	|	M = 67.5

TRANSFER   STIMULI

/ \ ◇ | — □

FIG. 2. Discriminanda used with 16 5-yr.-olds in transfer experiments. (The four pairs of discriminanda are shown, numbered 1 through 4. "Pos." and "Neg." designate the positive—rewarded—and the negative—unrewarded—number of each pair. The number next to each pair—right-hand column—refers to the mean number of trials needed to reach criterion on any given discrimination. The bottom row gives the six figures used in transfer trials.)

card should be called "right" or "wrong." The order of positive and negative cards was randomized. Trials with a given pair were continued until criterion had been reached, or until S had gone through 50 trials, whichever occurred sooner. The criterion of success was 9 correct responses to the positive card and an equal number of rejections of the negative in 20 successive presentations.

Following the training in successive discrimination, S was shown six figures (transfer stimuli in Figure 2, bottom line), one at a time, in a randomized sequence, so that each figure was presented three times in all. These transfer stimuli were the vertical and horizontal lines, the two obliques, and a diamond and a square. Thus, for any given child, two of these six transfer stimuli were the original training pair and the remaining four represented new figures not used during training. Regardless of whether a child called a given shape "right" or "wrong" during the transfer trials, E said "good," i.e., there was no differential reward. No child was trained on more than a single pair of discriminanda prior to these transfer tests.

Results

The third column of Figure 2 gives the mean number of trials needed to reach criterion by the 16 5-yr.-olds on successive discrimination learning for the pairs shown in the first two columns. As expected, suc-

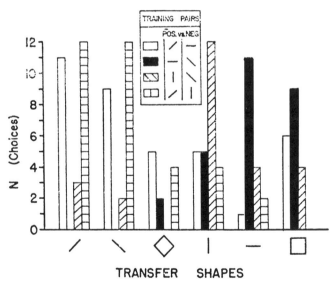

FIG. 3. Results of transfer tests for 16 5-yr.-old children in Experiment 2. (Ordinate shows numbers of choices—maximum 12—made on transfer trials for a particular shape—shown along abscissa.)

cessive discrimination learning under these conditions is more difficult than the corresponding tasks on simultaneous presentation of the discriminanda. However, successive discrimination of the horizontal line from the oblique (Pairs 1 and 2) is significantly easier than discrimination of the vertical from the oblique (Pairs 3 and 4) ($t = 2.12$, $p = .05$).

Each transfer figure could be called "correct" a maximum of 12 times after any given condition of training (4 Ss × 3 post-training trials). Figure 3 shows the number of responses to each of the discriminanda. It is apparent that when an oblique is positive (Conditions 1 and 4), the other oblique is called correct almost as readily on transfer trials. After training on Pair 1 (Figure 2), the originally positive oblique was chosen 11 times out of 12. No other transfer stimulus was chosen with a frequency exceeding chance, except for the square which was chosen 9 times out of a possible 12 when the horizontal line was positive (Pair 2) during the training trials. There was no transfer from either oblique, however, to the diamond.

DISCUSSION

The salient finding from this study is the similarity between child and octopus in several aspects of their discrimination of shapes. We shall describe these similarities and then turn to some possible differences.

Similarities

1. In the child, as in the octopus, identical figures are readily discriminated if one figure appears in a vertical and the other, in a horizontal orientation. The same figures are virtually indiscriminable if they are oriented obliquely, i.e., inclined at opposite 45° angles to the horizontal.

2. Analogously, both child and octopus discriminate right-side-up from upside-down U figures, while a right-left reversal in the U figure presents considerable difficulty.

3. Furthermore, after training on an oblique figure oriented in one direction (e.g., /), children as well as octopuses readily transfer their responses to an oblique figure oriented in the other direction (e.g., \).

4. Neither child nor octopus shows transfer from an oblique figure to a diamond. This failure of transfer is all the more remarkable in the child, since we used outline figures of the diamond shape which thus contained the same oblique lines employed in previous training. In his experiments with the octopus, Sutherland (1960) had used solid diamonds.

All in all, we have four important features of shape discrimination that turned out to be similar in the young child and the cephalopod, in spite of their totally different phylogenetic status. In view of such conspicuous similarities, one should search all the more thoroughly for possible discrepancies.

Differences

1. One possible difference might lie in the fact that for the octopus, discrimination of the right-side-up U vs. upside-down U was much more difficult than that of | vs. — . For the older children tested in our Experiment 1, both tasks were almost equally easy. For the youngest children, however, there was a distinct tendency to perform less well with the U figures than with ordinary verticals and horizontals. It is thus not clear whether one is dealing here with a true difference in performance of child and octopus, or with a similarity.

2. Another possible difference may be represented in our finding that for the child either vertical or horizontal lines opposed to an oblique (on simultaneous presentation) were at least as readily discriminated as vertical from horizontal; for the octopus, vertical (or horizontal) vs. oblique was a more difficult task than vertical vs. horizontal. However, it must again be noted that our tests opposing horizontals or verticals to obliques came at the end of training with other figures; the task of distinguishing verticals or horizontals from obliques might have been made easier for the children through a disproportionate amount of pre-training on other shapes.

3. The one salient difference between results for the two species was found in Experiment 2 involving successive rather than simultaneous discriminations. Here, 5-yr.-old children found it easier to discriminate horizontal lines from obliques than vertical

lines from obliques. For the octopus, the opposite seems to be true (Sutherland, 1958).

Except for these discrepancies, the results are remarkably similar for our widely dissimilar species. Instead of finding gross differences in shape perception (differences that would be somehow in correspondence with the differences in neural structures), we encounter, again, a rather similar organization in the perception of pattern.

Interpretations

What the neural basis for such an organization might be is difficult to guess. In dealing with his early findings in the octopus, Sutherland (1957) postulated a shape-analyzing mechanism for this species in which visual excitation was led into a two-dimensional array of cells. This arrangement was thought to permit a counting of excitation along rows (horizontal) and columns (vertical). As a result of such analysis along vertical and horizontal dimensions, vertical and horizontal extents should be maximally discriminable, while obliquely oriented figures should be difficult or impossible to distinguish. A further assumption involved in this model is that in the octopus, those parts of the visual system that are responsible for analyzing horizontal extents function more accurately than those for analyzing vertical extents of a figure (Sutherland, 1960). Such a provision could lead to the prediction that certain up-down mirror images are more readily discriminable than the corresponding right-left mirror images, a result obtained both for the octopus and for the child. The model would also predict that an oblique line would be more easily distinguished from a horizontal than from a vertical line; this result was in fact obtained in the present study with children but was not obtained for the octopus.

It is probably too early to expect full insight into the cerebral mechanisms that underlie the features of shape discrimination here discussed. Clarification may come from further work on shape discriminations in widely separated species, and from direct neurophysiologic studies of invertebrate and lower vertebrate visual systems with methods recently introduced by Hubel and Wiesel (1959) and by Lettvin, Maturana, McCulloch, and Pitts (1959). This is not to say that we expect necessarily identical

neural mechanisms in octopus and child: Similar features in perception may have arisen at different times in phylogeny, provided there are similar environmental pressures.

Whatever the actual mechanism might be, the biologic utility of some of the features here described is obvious. In child and octopus, vertically-oriented contours in the visual environment may play a special role, reflecting their importance for the maintenance of upright posture. Octopuses as well as children—in spite of other obvious anatomical differences—are similar in being bilaterally symmetrical organisms which attempt to maintain a preferred orientation of their receptors relative to gravity.[2] If analysis of patterned stimuli is performed in correspondingly preferred directions (a basic feature of Sutherland's theory), then it would be expected that up-down reversals (which are correlated with loss of posture would be of greater significance than right-left reversals. Similarly, as Sutherland has noted (1960), the equivalence of right-left mirror images may be related to the fact that one is converted into the other whenever the organism moves around and behind a given shape. The prevalence of right-left confusions may thus be not as puzzling as we have initially suggested. Yet, whether learned or built-in, the equivalence of certain right-left mirror images remains a remarkable feature of pattern perception in children and cephalopods.

SUMMARY

In a series of experiments on pattern perception in the octopus, Sutherland (1957, 1958, 1960) showed that this animal can

---

[2] The statocysts of the octopus continuously readjust the orientation of the animal's eyes during changes in head posture in such a way that the midvertical meridian of the retina remains vertical, or nearly so, at all times (Young, 1961). Following destruction of the statocysts (Boycott, 1960; Wells, 1960), this oculomotor mechanism is lost. The animal holds its head inclined to one side or the other, and its preoperatively acquired visual discriminations between horizontals and verticals become perverted (Wells, 1960). For the same reason, octopuses deprived of their statocysts seem incapable of acquiring a consistent discrimination of horizontals vs. verticals (Wells, 1960). Evidently, response to visual orientation depends in this species on the proper orientation of their retina, rather than on some central interaction of visual and proprioceptive inputs.

readily discrimnate vertical from horizontal rectangles but confuses rectangles oriented obliquely in opposite directions (/ vs. \ ). Essentially the same results were obtained in the present study for normal children.

In Experiment 1, 93 children (comprising six age groups from 3½ to 8½ yr.) had to learn simultaneous discriminations between vertical and horizontal lines (| vs. —); obliques (/ vs. \ ); right-side-up and upside-down ∪ shapes (∪ vs. ⊓); and ∪ shapes rotated 90° in opposite directions (⊏ vs. ⊐).

The majority of the younger children (3–4 yr.) and all of the older children mastered the vertical vs. horizontal, and ∪ vs. ⊓ discrimination. By contrast, none of the 3-yr.-olds (12 *S*s) and only 1 of the 4-yr.-olds (12 *S*s) learned to distinguish the oblique lines (/ vs. \ ); only 1 of the 3-yr.-olds and only 2 of the 4-yr.-olds learned to discriminate ⊏ from ⊐ . The older children (5½ to 8½ yr.) did increasingly better on these difficult discriminations, but even for the oldest group tested (8½ yr.), a marked difference in favor of the easily mastered discriminations (| vs. — , and ∪ vs. ⊓) remained.

In Experiment 2, 16 5-yr.-olds were trained on successive discriminations opposing a horizontal or a vertical line to an oblique, and then tested for transfer to other forms. The results of this second experiment agreed with those of the first by showing confusion between / and \ ; the experiment also disclosed that discrimination of the horizontal line from the oblique was significantly easier than discrimination of the vertical from the oblique, and that there was no transfer from obliques to diamond.

REFERENCES

BOYCOTT, B. B. The functioning of the statocysts of *Octopus vulgaris. Proc. Roy. Soc. Lon., Ser. B*, 1960, **152**, 78–87.

GELLERMANN, L. W. Chance orders of alternating stimuli in visual discrimination experiments. *J. genet. Psychol.*, 1933, **42**, 206–208.

HUBEL, D. H., & WIESEL, T. N. Receptive fields of single neurons in the cat's striate cortex. *J. Physiol.*, 1959, **148**, 574–591.

KLÜVER, H. *Behavior mechanisms in monkeys.* (Reprinted, 1957) Chicago: Univer. Chicago Press, 1933.

LASHLEY, K. S. The mechanism of vision: XV. Preliminary studies of the rat's capacity for detail vision. *J. gen. Psychol.*, 1938, **18**, 123–193.

LETTVIN, J. Y., MATURANA, H. R., McCULLOCH, W. V., & PITTS, W. H. What the frog's eye tells the frog's brain. *Proc. Inst. Radio Engng.*, 1959, **47**, 1940–1951.

SCHILLER, P. v. Figural preferences in the drawings of a chimpanzee. *J. comp. physiol. Psychol.*, 1951, **44**, 101–111.

SUTHERLAND, N. S. Visual discrimination of orientation by *Octopus. Brit. J. Psychol.*, 1957, **48**, 55–71.

SUTHERLAND, N. S. Visual discrimination of the orientation of rectangles by *Octopus vulgaris* Lamarck. *J. comp. physiol. Psychol.*, 1958, **51**, 452–458.

SUTHERLAND, N. S. Visual discrimination of orientation by *Octopus*: Mirror images. *Brit. J. Psychol.*, 1960, **51**, 9–18.

TEUBER, H.-L. Perception. In J. Field, H. W. Magoun, & V. E. Hall (Eds.), *Handbook of physiology.* Vol. 3. Washington, D. C.: American Physiological Society, 1960. Pp. 1595–1668.

WELLS, M. J. Proprioception and visual discrimination of orientation in *Octopus. J. exp. Biol.*, 1960, **37**, 489–499.

YOUNG, J. Z. Learning and discrimination in the *Octopus. Biol. Rev.*, 1961, **36**, 32–96.

(Received April 2, 1962)

EDITORIAL COMMENTS

Rudel and Teuber have carried out a study that demonstrates that relative difficulty in visual pattern discrimination is the same for children as has previously been demonstrated for both the rat and the octopus. The authors have also compared the responses of children in several different age groups, illustrating a developmental progression in visual discrimination.

In replicating this study, the sample of subjects does not need to be selected from schools of the same socioeconomic level as was done in the original study. The sample size for the first experiment could also be reduced by selecting children in three age groups (e.g., 4, 6, and 8 years), rather than using six age groups as in the original study. If possible, equal numbers of boys and girls in each group would control for sex differences between groups, and also facilitate comparison of the performance of boys and girls.

The Plexiglass plaques used in the study are carefully described by the authors. White bristol board or cardboard could be substituted for the Plexiglass, and the figures drawn on these materials, using the size specifications given in the original study.

This paper reports two experiments. The first of these involves learning to make simultaneous discriminations between horizontal or vertical lines, pairs of *Us* that differe in up–down or left–right orientation, and a pair of oblique lines, one of which slants to the right, the other to the left. A fifth task, discrimination of a horizontal or vertical line from an oblique one, was added for some subjects.

The results of this first experiment are presented in a table (Table 1), which indicates the mean number of trials required to learn each discrimination by the subjects of the different age groups, and the number of subjects in each group who failed to learn the discrimination in fifty trials. While no statistical analysis of the results was carried out by the authors, a chi-square test of independence could be utilized here (see appendix).

The second experiment in this paper involves sixteen additional five-year-old subjects who were trained in successive discrimination between a horizontal or a vertical line and an oblique line. Following the training procedure, subjects were shown the transfer stimuli presented at the bottom of Figure 2, one at a time in random order until each figure had been presented three times to each subject. If students elect to replicate the second experiment alone, it could be expanded by comparing the performance of subjects in two different age groups.

The authors of these studies discuss their results in terms of comparative development and brain mechanisms. It may be of interest to the student experimenter to consider the possible implications of such a study for the discriminations that have to be made by children in learning to read, such as between *d* and *b*, *p* and *q*. It would also be interesting to compare the findings of this study with those of Gibson *et al.* on the discrimination of letterlike forms. As noted at the conclusion of the editorial comments on the Gibson *et al.* study, some students may wish to administer the two tasks, one derived from Rudel and Teuber and the other derived from Gibson *et al.*, to the same subjects and to correlate the results.

Students who wish to pursue this topic further are referred to Olson (1970) and Piaget and Inhelder (1956).

REFERENCES

D. R. Olson, *Cognitive Development: The Child's Acquisition of Diagonality.* New York: Academic Press, 1970.

J. Piaget and B. Inhelder, *The Child's Conception of Space.* London: Routledge and Kegan Paul, 1956.

DEVELOPMENT OF DISTANCE CONSERVATION AND THE SPATIAL COORDINATE SYSTEM

CAROLYN UHLINGER SHANTZ

Merrill-Palmer Institute

CHARLES D. SMOCK

Purdue University

2 spatial concepts, conservation of distance and the Euclidean coordinate system, were studied to test Piaget's hypothesis that distance conservation is a prerequisite attainment for the achievement of the coordinate concept Second, drawings and objects as test stimuli were compared for possible differential effects on performance. 20 first-grade children were tested individually, being randomly assigned to order of concepts and type of stimuli. Data were generally supportive of the developmental priority of conservation of distance to a Euclidean coordinate system. Presentation of tasks using objects before drawings, in contrast to the reverse order, tended to facilitate correct responses.

Piaget and Inhelder (1956) and Piaget, Inhelder, and Szeminska (1960) postulated a sequential development of the child's representation of space, culminating in the acquisition of a Euclidean structuring of space. The coordinates of Euclidean space may be described as a grid of lines crossing each other perpendicularly in three dimensions. The presence of such a conceptual coordinate system is attested to when horizontality and verticality become independent of the perceptual properties of objects and immediate surround. Thus, the presence of the horizontal concept is demonstrated when the child is able to refer the water level in a tilted bottle to the table level, rather than to any particular property of the bottle. Likewise, if the child has acquired the concept of verticality, figures on a mountain, for example, are related to ground level rather than to the mountainside.

The authors wish to express their appreciation to Dr. Walter Emmerich for his assistance in the formulation of this study. Author Shantz' address: Merrill-Palmer Institute, 71 East Ferry Avenue, Detroit, Michigan 48202.

It is Piaget and Inhelder's contention (1956) that the conservation of distance is a prerequisite for the development of the coordinate system. There are two cognitive operations involved in distance conservation: (*a*) distance must remain constant whether the space between two points is filled or empty, and (*b*) distance must remain identical between two points regardless of the direction of travel (*AB* = *BA*). The developmental priority of distance conservation to the coordinate system has received empirical support, according to Piaget, in terms of the general age of emergence of distance conservation at approximately 7 years of age compared to emergence of the coordinate system at 9 years of age. However, Piaget notes that the use of a coordinate system appeared in his subjects from 6½ to 12 years of age. and equally large age ranges have been found by independent studies (Dodwell, 1963; Smedslund, 1963). The overlap in ages of emergence of distance conservation and the coordinate system does not provide a clear test for determining whether these two concepts emerge simultaneously or sequentially, particularly in the sequence hypothesized by Piaget. A more direct test of the hypothesis would be provided by testing both concepts in the same children. The purpose of the present study is to test Piaget's hypothesis that every child using the coordinate system also conserves distance, and every child who is unable to conserve distance is unable to demonstrate the coordinate system concept.

Studies by Dodwell (1963) and Rivoire (1961) suggest that the variability in age of emergence of the coordinate system may be due in part to the way in which the task is presented. Specifically, there appeared to be a differential performance associated with the use of objects or pictures as stimuli. Since the number of spatial dimensions of stimuli appears to be particularly germane to the study of space concepts, and there are indications of its effects, the second purpose of this study is to determine the comparability of data relevant to two spatial concepts derived from two-dimensional (drawings) and three-dimensional stimuli (objects).

METHOD

Subjects

Ten boys and ten girls from one first-grade class in a rural elementary school were subjects (*Ss*). Their ages ranged from 6 years, 4 months to 7 years, 10 months with a mean of 6 years, 9 months.

Experimental Measures

Distance conservation.—Five items were designed to determine whether *S* conserved distance (*a*) if the distance were filled or empty (FE), and, with five additional items, (*b*) if the direction of movement were changed (*DM*). To assess *FE* distance conservation with objects, for example, two 2½-inch trees were placed before *S* 8 inches apart, and *S* was asked whether the trees were "far apart" or "near together." A board higher than the trees was placed halfway between them and *S* was asked, "And now, are they far apart (or near together)?" A child who conserves distance will assert that distance remains the same whether the space is filled or empty; nonconservers make a variety of responses, the most common being that the distance is less because the board "uses up" some of the space between the trees. Four additional *FE* tests varied the type of figures (pigs or trees) and height of the interposed object (higher or lower than figures). Table 2 presents the exact combinations used in this and all other tests. The variations were designed to provide a more stringent test of conservation. For example, Piaget et al. (1960) found that some children conserve only if the barrier is lower than the figures.

The same basic *FE* task was presented in five drawings, but with a matching-to-standard method. A standard picture showed two trees 6 inches apart with no object between them. The *S* designated his preference for calling that distance "far apart" or "near together." The *E* presented three comparison pictures of the same figures at varying distances and said, "Now here are some trees—some have fences between them and some don't. Now find two trees that are just as far apart (or near together) as these [referring to the standard]." In the remaining four items, the same variations in figures and screen height were used as with objects; in some cases, the standard had a fence between the figures and the correct match did not, or vice versa.

Distance conservation with *DM* was determined with objects by asking *S* to indicate whether or not it is "just as far from here to here [left tree to right tree] as from here to here [right tree to left tree]." As this was said, *E* moved her finger at equal rates in each direction. A child who has the concept of conservation will assert the symmetrical character of distance regardless of travel direction; the child who does not will assert it is "further" in one direction. The four remaining tests varied the figures, height of figures, or one figure was raised 3 inches off the table.

The five *DM* tests with drawings were the same as with objects except for slight variations in the size of the drawn figures, and the method of inquiry was the same.

Coordinate system.—Five tests were constructed to assess each of the concepts of horizontality (*H*) and verticality (*V*). The former concept task with objects consisted of presenting an upright bottle one-quarter filled with dark liquid. The *S* indicated with his finger on an identical, but empty bottle, what would happen to the water level when the empty bottle was upside down. (At no time did *S* have an opportunity to observe the filled bottle change in orientation.) If *S* has acquired the horizontal concept, the water level is related to an external level, such as the table; if not, *S* may respond in many ways, such as relating the water level to a particular side of the bottle. Four additional items varied the orientation and shape of container.

With drawings, E presented a drawing of a quarter-filled bottle the same size as the actual bottle; S drew on "empty" drawings the water level he expected at orientations similar to those used with objects.

Verticality was tested by presenting a clay-covered styrofoam pyramid ("mountain") with a 60° slope on which figures with pins in their base were to be placed "nice and straight" by S at five sites verbally designated by E. If S has acquired the vertical concept, objects are placed on the mountain in reference to external axes, such as vertical to the table or parallel to the walls; if not, he relates objects to the most proximal perceptual configuration, that is, perpendicular to the slope of the mountain.

A drawing of the mountain with a 60° slope was presented for each S to draw freehand figures at similar sites under the same directions as with objects. The H and V responses with drawings and objects which deviated 10° or less from the correct axis were considered correct.

Procedure

Half the Ss were administered the tasks with objects and then drawings, and half had the reverse order. Within either sequence, half of those Ss had distance conservation tests first and coordinate tests second, or the reverse order. The Ss were randomly assigned to each of the four orders of testing. In all cases, the five tests of each concept (*FE, DM, H, V*) were administered sequentially in the order listed in Table 2. At no time was the adequacy of S's response indicated by E.

RESULTS AND DISCUSSION

The first hypothesis concerned the developmental priority of distance conservation, that is, every child using the coordinate system would also achieve conservation of distance, but failure to conserve would preclude success on the coordinate tasks. The criterion of successful performance was passing four or five of the five items of each concept. Contingency table distributions of Ss are presented in Table 1. Since such a distribution provides a direct test of the hypothesis, χ^2 analyses were not done.

The task using drawings yielded five Ss who used both concepts and seven who used neither. No child used the coordinate concept who did not show distance conservation. The eight Ss who evidenced conservation but not the coordinate concept constitute the most relevant supporting evidence for the hypothesis of priority of distance conservation. The same trends were found using objects with the exception of one S whose performance may be interpreted as a refutation of the hypothesis or a case of measure-

TABLE 1

DISTRIBUTION OF SUBJECTS ON TWO SPATIAL CONCEPTS
ASSESSED WITH DRAWINGS AND OBJECTS

DISTANCE CONSERVATION CONCEPT	DRAWINGS (COORDINATE CONCEPT)		OBJECTS (COORDINATE CONCEPT)	
	Pass	Fail	Pass	Fail
Pass............	5	8	4	7
Fail............	0	7	1	8

ment error. The assessment of both concepts in a larger number of Ss would be required to clarify which of the interpretations is more tenable.[1]

An item analysis of the percentage of correct responses is given in Table 2. There is evidence that Ss found distance conservation easier with drawings than objects. The major difficulty in applying the coordinate concept appears when the child is confronted with the *tilted* line both in drawings and objects.

The second aspect of the study concerned a comparison of drawings and objects as stimuli. The difference between stimuli in an analysis of variance of correct responses was not highly significant ($p < .12$). This trend toward a greater number of correct responses with drawings than objects was sufficiently strong, however, to warrant further analysis. Of 20 Ss, 19 passed the *FE* conservation task with drawings, while only 14 passed with the same items administered with objects. There are three factors which may have facilitated *FE* conservation with drawings. The drawings may have provided more cues for correct response, for example, the additional structure provided by the borders of the card. Several children were observed comparing the distance of trees from the edge of the card rather than distance between the trees. Second, the potential "movability" of tree-objects versus tree-drawings may have hindered identity of distance with or without barriers. And third, the matching-to-standard method with drawings may have assisted in recognition of identity. There is no theoretical or empirical reason (Piaget et al., 1960) to suspect that filled versus empty space conservation is an easier concept to acquire than conservation with change in direction of movement. Indeed, with objects, *FE* and *DM* conservation were passed by exactly the same number of Ss. A significant stimuli x concept interaction ($p < .05$) appeared to be primarily a function of the frequency of success with *FE* tasks with drawings.

The impact of the type of stimuli was further evident as an order effect: Ss who had objects first and drawings second performed better than

---

[1] An analysis of variance indicated significantly more correct answers on conservation items than on coordinate items ($p < .01$), which is also consistent with the hypothesis. There was no significant difference between sexes on the total number of correct responses.

TABLE 2
Percentage of Subjects Passing Each Item

Concepts and Items	Drawings	Objects
Distance conservation		
Filled vs. empty space:		
Trees with high screen..........	95	75
Trees with two low cubes.......	100	75
Trees with low screen..........	95	80
Pigs with high screen..........	100	70
Pigs with one low cube.........	95	80
Direction of movement change:		
Equal height trees.............	90	85
Unequal height trees...........	80	80
One raised tree................	65	65
Pigs on level..................	80	90
One raised pig.................	85	75
Coordinate system		
Horizontal:		
Bottle upside down............	100	95
Bottle tilted 45° left...........	35	60
Bottle on side.................	75	80
Box tilted 45° right............	30	35
Box on side...................	80	85
Vertical:		
Tree on right side.............	45	40
Doll on left side..............	35	25
Flag at summit................	100	95
Doll on level ground..........	100	100
Tree on left side..............	45	50

those under the reverse order of stimuli ($p < .10$). This finding not only indicates the importance of evaluating such order effects in repeated measurement designs but suggests that training of spatial concepts may be most effective with manipulation of objects preceding two-dimensional presentation of tasks.

In summary, the data are consistent in general with the hypothesis of the developmental priority of distance conservation to the coordinate system. A longitudinal analysis of the development of these concepts is a necessary next step in the investigation of the ontogeny of spatial representation.

REFERENCES

Dodwell, P. C. Children's understanding of spatial concepts. *Canad. J. Psychol.*, 1963, **17**, 141–161.

Piaget, J., & Inhelder, B. *The child's conception of space.* London: Routledge & Kegan Paul, 1956.

Piaget, J., Inhelder, B., & Szeminska, A. *The child's conception of geometry.* New York: Basic Books, 1960.

Rivoire, J. L. The development of reference systems in children. Unpublished doctoral dissertation, Univer. of Arizona, 1961.

Smedslund, J. The effect of observation on children's representation of the spatial orientation of a water surface. *J. genet. Psychol.*, 1963, **102**, 195–201.

EDITORIAL COMMENTS

Shantz and Smock tested the hypothesis proposed by Piaget that "conservation of distance is prerequisite for the development of the coordinate system." They contended that previous attempts to investigate this hypothesis have been cross-sectional in nature (i.e., compared groups of children of different ages) and that this does not provide as direct a test of the hypothesis as would be demonstrated by a study of the development of these concepts in the same children. If the age range when a particular development occurs is wide, so that there is overlap between two successive age groups, cross-sectional data do not provide a satisfactory basis for understanding individual change.

Shantz and Smock proposed that one way to investigate their hypothesis is to demonstrate that every child who is able to use the coordinate system to represent space is able to conserve distance, and that children unable to demonstrate distance conservation are unable to utilize the coordinate system. An additional interest in their study was to compare the development of these concepts with two-dimensional and three-dimensional stimuli.

Modifications of Sample and Procedure

The subjects in this study, 10 boys and 10 girls, were all in first grade in a rural elementary school. In replicating the study, students may wish to enlarge the sample, either by adding more subjects of the same grade level, or by selecting additional subjects from kindergarten or second grade.

The materials and drawings in the study are not described in great detail in the article, but enough information is given so that reasonable facsimiles could be produced with relatively little effort or expense.

Shantz and Smock describe their procedure in sufficient detail for the student to replicate the order of presentation of tasks to the children. However, the exact instructions that were given to the subjects for each task are not presented for all of the tasks involved. It would be desirable to give each task in the same way, as far as possible, to each subject. Thus it would be advisable for the investigator to use the same instructions for each child, and to include these instructions in reporting the study. If several students work together, agreement as to specific instructions to be used would reduce the possibility of variability in results as a consequence of varying instructions.

Analysis of Results

In analyzing their results, the authors compared the number of subjects who passed or failed the distance conservation tests with the number passing or failing the tests of the coordinate concept. The results of this comparison, for both drawing and objects used as stimuli, are presented in Table 1. The distribution of the subjects in this table was such that it provided a direct test of the hypothesis—children who could not conserve distance *without exception* were not successful on the coordinate tasks—and thus a statistical test was not necessary to demonstrate the significance of this finding. Should the results of the replication be more equivocal, then a statistical test of significance could be applied.

A second analysis by the authors compared the use of drawings with objects as stimuli. A comparison of correct responses using each of these was made, with an analysis of variance procedure, for the five tests of each of two aspects of distance conservation (filled vs. empty space) and for the five tests of two aspects of the coordinate concept (horizontal vs. vertical). This procedure could be simplified by utilizing a chi-square test of independence, with 50 percent selected as the level of chance expectancy for each group of five tests. A separate chi-square test can be done to provide an analysis of order effects, that is, whether being tested with drawings before objects gave different results than being tested with objects as stimuli first.

The Journal of Genetic Psychology, 1963, **102**, 195-201.

THE EFFECT OF OBSERVATION ON CHILDREN'S REPRESENTATION OF THE SPATIAL ORIENTATION OF A WATER SURFACE[*][1]

Institute for Social Research, Oslo, Norway

Jan Smedslund

A. Introduction

In their book "The Child's Conception of Space," Piaget and Inhelder (5) describe certain phenomena relating to children's representation of horizontality. A number of children, between four and 11 years old, were shown some pictures of variously tilted bottles, and were asked to draw the water surface in these bottles. They were also asked to point out the correct one among sets of differently drawn model pictures. It turned out that children up to seven-eight generally did not have a conception of the invariant horizontality of the water surface. This very slow development is in apparent contrast to the fact that tilted water and milk bottles are among the frequent daily experiences of children. Even more striking was the observation that children who did not have any concept of horizontality, apparently did not seem to profit at all from a period of close observation of the water surface in an actual bottle that was tilted in all directions. Only children

[*] Received in the Editorial Office on April 14, 1961.

[1] A relevant unpublished study by Mlle. P. Dadsetan is referred to in *Les Mécanismes Perceptifs*. J. Piaget, pp. 222-226 (Paris: Presses Universitaires de France, 1961). The results appear to confirm the present one with respect to representation, and, in addition, indicate that even simple perceptual estimates of horizontality are difficult at five-six years.

who already showed some beginnings of a conception of horizontality, did profit somewhat from direct observation.

Piaget and Inhelder interpret these findings in terms of their theory that there is never any direct feedback from the external world, and that the feedback always is determined by the way the subject assimilates the situation. The subject can only observe horizontality and deviations from it if he already has a schema of horizontality, and in the absence of this schema, no amount of observation will influence him. He is enclosed in an evil circle from which he can only emerge when the progressive development of spatial concepts gives rise to the beginnings of a schema of horizontality, which then may be empirically confirmed.

This original study by Piaget and Inhelder was conducted by means of Piaget's flexible "méthode clinique" and the results were not reported in extenso. We have repeated the study in a more systematic and objective manner.

B. Procedure

Twenty-seven five- to seven-year-old children in a nursery in Oslo participated as subjects. The design involved a pretest, a period of observation and a posttest. Each subject was first shown a picture of a bottle half-filled with water, and was asked to notice the position of the water in the bottle. Then six pictures of bottles tilted in various directions were presented, one at a time, and the subject was asked to draw the water surface in each case. See Figure 1.

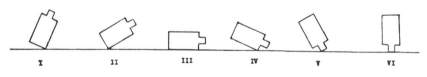

FIGURE 1
The Six Drawing-Test Pictures

Then a flat bottle half-filled with ink-water was presented. The subject was asked to pay close attention and the experimenter slowly tilted the bottle in steps of about 30° each time, with a brief period of rest in each position. The movement was continued 360°. After this, the initial six pictures of tilted bottles were presented again, and the subject was again asked to draw the water surfaces.

Finally, three sets of respectively eight, seven and eight model pictures of ink-water in a bottle were shown, and the subject was asked to point out the correct picture in each set. See Figure 2.

The scoring was open to a certain ambiguity, since it was sometimes difficult to decide whether a drawn line was approximately horizontal or not, and whether a drawing was improved from pre- to posttest or not. In order to make the procedure as reliable as possible, two judges scored the material independently. In the case of changes from pre- to posttest the categories of "better," "unchanged" and "worse" were employed. With six pictures and 27 subjects there were a total of 162 judgments to be made. The two judges agreed on 84 per cent of the cases. After some discussion and closer inspection of the drawings, agreement was reached on the remaining 16 per cent.

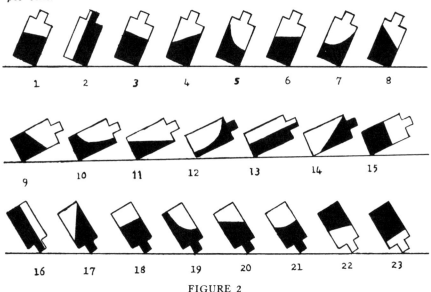

FIGURE 2
THE MODEL-CHOICE PICTURES

In the comparison between drawing on posttest and choice of model picture, the same ambiguity occurred. With the three categories "drawing better", "equal" and "choice better," the two judges agreed on 83 per cent of the 81 comparisons, and agreement was reached on the remaining cases after discussion and closer inspection.

C. RESULTS

The number of subjects with frequencies of correct drawing in the pre- and posttests as presented in Table 1.

The data in Table 1 show that one third of the subjects had no drawings correct in the pretest and only two subjects had all six correct. In the posttest there was a certain shift toward higher values in the middle categories, but the total number of subjects with no correct drawings and with all drawings correct remained unchanged.

TABLE 1

THE NUMBER OF SUBJECTS WITH VARIOUS FREQUENCIES OF CORRECT DRAWINGS IN THE PRE- AND POSTTESTS ($N = 27$)

Number of correct drawings	0	1	2	3	4	5	6
Frequency on pretest	9	8	5	2	1	0	2
Frequency on posttest	9	3	8	2	3	0	2

The changes of the individual subjects may be represented in terms of changes in number of correct drawings and in terms of the more sensitive measure of number of improvements vs. deteriorations. Table 2 presents the outcome of a comparison based on the former measure. The 25 subjects who had less than a perfect score in the pretest are divided into those who had no correct drawings in the pretest and those who had at least one correct drawing.

Table 2 shows a clear difference in the relative frequency of increment in number of correct drawings in the two groups. As to the size of the

TABLE 2

THE NUMBER OF SUBJECTS WITH ZERO AND WITH ONE OR MORE CORRECT DRAWINGS IN THE PRETEST WHO INCREASE VS. DO NOT INCREASE THEIR NUMBER OF CORRECT DRAWINGS FROM PRE- TO POSTTEST ($N = 25$)

	Number of correct drawings in pretest	
	0	$\geqq 1$
Improvement	1	9
No improvement	8	7

individual changes it should be mentioned that nine subjects had one more correct drawing and one subject had two more correct drawings. In terms of general improvement in drawings the difference between the two groups is even more pronounced. The results are shown in Table 3.

TABLE 3

THE PRESENCE VS. ABSENCE OF IMPROVEMENT IN AT LEAST ONE DRAWING FROM PRE- TO POSTTEST IN THE GROUPS WITH NO CORRECT DRAWINGS AND WITH AT LEAST ONE CORRECT DRAWING IN THE PRETEST ($N = 27$)

	Number of correct drawings in pretest	
	0	$\geqq 1$
At least one improvement	1	15
No improvement	8	1

The data in Table 3 show that nearly all the subjects who have no correct drawings in the pretest, do not profit at all from the observations of an actual tilted bottle, whereas nearly all the subjects who showed some initial traces of horizontality, do improve their drawings somewhat.

The data on the relative difficulty of the six drawing-test pictures and on the improvement on these pictures from pre- to posttest are shown in Table 4.

Table 4 shows that pictures no. III and VI are clearly easier than the others and even have a tendency to improve their relative superiority from pre- to posttest.

TABLE 4
THE NUMBER OF CORRECT DRAWINGS OF THE SIX TEST PICTURES IN PRE- AND POSTTEST

	Picture					
	I	II	III	IV	V	VI
Number correct in pretest	4	5	11	4	2	14
Number correct in posttest	6	4	16	3	4	16

Finally, we will report the findings concerning the choice among model-figures in the posttest. Table 5 shows the results of a comparison between drawing and model choice.

It may be gathered that the two tests are about equally difficult on the average. On the other hand, pictures I and V are clearly favorable to the choice-test and picture II to the drawing-test. Inspection shows that performance on the two tests is not very highly correlated; however, it is difficult

TABLE 5
THE FREQUENCY OF "DRAWING BETTER THAN CHOICE," "DRAWING AND CHOICE EQUALLY GOOD," AND "CHOICE BETTER THAN DRAWING" ($N = 81$)

	Picture			
	I	II	V	Sum
Drawing better	7	14	7	28
Equal	8	7	9	24
Choice better	12	6	11	29

to find any exact measure of this interrelationship. The number of correct drawings and choices is too small to allow one to calculate a meaningful correlation in terms of correct vs. incorrect performance. The irregular and sometimes curvilinear drawings and model-figures makes it impossible to give any simple quantitative estimate of amount of covariation.

The relative frequency with which the alternative model-pictures are chosen, is presented in Table 6. The results show that the correct figures

TABLE 6
FREQUENCY OF CHOICE OF ALTERNATIVE MODEL-PICTURES
(Nos. 6, 11 and 20 are correct)

Pictures							
Model pictures	1	2	3	4	5	**6**	7	8
f	3	5	4	7	2	**3**	1	2
Model pictures	9	10	**11**	12	13	14	15	
f	5	0	**4**	3	7	2	6	
Model pictures	16	17	18	19	**20**	21	22	23
f	4	3	3	6	**4**	1	3	3

are not chosen with any outstanding frequency. Even figures which depart radically from what is felt as reasonable by adult standards, are chosen fairly frequently.

D. DISCUSSION

The results generally support the conclusions of Piaget and Inhelder. The general absence of a representation of horizontality in the given age group was verified. Likewise we have observed the intermediate stage of development where the child understands horizontality only when the bottle is lying on its side or standing on its head (5, p. 384). Finally, the absence of learning in children who have no initial conception of horizontality was clearly confirmed, as was also the limited improvements of those who have initial traces of a concept of horizontality.

The comparison between drawing and model-choice shows that, although the average difficulty is equal, the individual pictures seem to be of unequal difficulty in the two tests.

The apparent variations in the relative difficulty of drawing and choice from one picture to another, and the small number of pictures (three), prevents us from drawing any conclusions as to the relative difficulty of drawing and choice in other situations. Furthermore, the absence of a high intercorrelation between the two tests indicates that they cannot be very pure measures of the same underlying factor ("representation of horizontality"). Further research is needed to reveal what processes are involved in the responses to the tests.

The absence of effects of the period of observation on those subjects who showed no initial traces of a conception of horizontality, seems to be of some theoretical significance. The results support the general point of view that learning cannot be conceptualized in terms of a simple empiricism, where the organism acquires habits or expectancies as a function of direct contact with the external world. Instead, every contact with external reality is patterned according to the existing schemata of the subject. Thus, to the subject, his representation of the water surface is not contradicted by his perception of the water surface in the actually tilted bottle, because neither his representation nor his perception involves a placing into relationship of the water surface and the surface of the supporting table. This placing into relationship (mise-en-relation) probably occurs as a part of a gradual process of organization of the subject's representation of space. The real water surface (distal stimulus) may be horizontal and the projection of the lines of the water surface and the table surface on the retina (proximal stimulus) may be parallel; nevertheless, the subject who has no schema of horizontality will remain uninfluenced by any confrontation with these stimuli. Some recent studies in other areas have shown an analogous absence of effects of empirical control in the absence of relevant supporting schemata. Cf. Greco's (1) study of the learning of complex empirical rules, Morf's (2) study of logical inclusion and Smedslund's (6, 7) studies of transitivity of weight, and of multiple probabilistic cues. Piaget's models of assimilation/accommodation and equilibration represent the most advanced existing attempts to conceptualize these phenomena (3, 4). It seems likely that data of this type eventually will lead to a radical change in current models of reinforcement.

E. Summary

Some five- to seven-year-old children were shown a series of six pictures of bottles tilted in various ways, and were asked to draw the water surface in each bottle (pretest). Then a flat bottle half-filled with ink-water was presented and was slowly tilted in various ways. After this, the pretest was repeated and in addition the children were asked to choose the correct picture in each one of some sets of drawn model-pictures. The pretest results show a general absence of an adequate conception of the spatial orientation of the water surface, and an absence of effects of the period of observation in those subjects who had no traces of an adequate conception in the pretest. The average difficulty of drawing and model choice was the same, but with great variations in the individual subjects and pictures.

References

1. Greco, P. Induction, déduction et apprentissage. *Études d'Épistémol. Génét.*, 1959, **10**, 3-59.

2. Morf, A. Apprentissage d'une structure logique concrète (inclusion): Effets et limites. *Études d'Épistémol. Génét.*, 1959, **9**, 15-83.

3. Piaget, J. Logique et équilibre dans les comportements du sujet. *Études d'Épistémol. Génét.*, 1957, **2**, 25-117.

4. ———. Assimilation et connaissance. *Études d'Épistémol. Génét.*, 1958, **5**, 49-108.

5. Piaget, J., & Inhelder, B. The Child's Conception of Space. London: Routledge & Kegan Paul, 1956.

6. SMEDSLUND, J. Apprentissage des notions de la conservation et de la transitivité du poids. *Études d'Épistémol. Génét.*, 1959, **9**, 85-124.

7. ———. The utilization of probabilistic cues after 1100 and 4800 stimulus-presentations. *Acta Psychol.*, 1961, **18**, 383-386.

Institute for Social Research
Muthes Gate 31
Oslo, Norway

EDITORIAL COMMENTS

In this paper, Smedslund reports a systematic study of Piaget's hypothesis that until a child has developed a concept of horizontality, that is, until he demonstrates a concept of horizontality that is independent of the perceptual properties of objects and immediate surroundings, he cannot draw water levels or a plumb line. Even direct observation of an invariant horizontal surface will not enable him to do this correctly.

Modifications of Sample and Procedure

In this study, Smedslund's subjects were 27 children, age 5 to 7 years, in a nursery in Oslo. In replicating the study, students may wish to select children in terms of school grade or age (in the same general age range as in the original study) and to specify the number of children of each sex at each grade level.

Smedslund's scoring procedure requires two judges. If two students work together, this problem is easily solved; students replicating different studies that both require the assistance of a second judge can provide this service for each other. The editorial comments for the Graham *et al.* study outline the procedure for the use of two judges to obtain a measure of the reliability of the ratings.

Treatment of Data

Smedslund presents his results in several tables, but he has made no statistical analysis of the findings. In interpreting the tables, it should be remembered that three scores are available for each subject:

1. number of drawings correct on pretest;
2. number of drawings correct on posttest;
3. number of drawings improved on posttest.

Table 2 presents the results for the first two of these scores. Two of the subjects in the original study had perfect scores on the pretest, so they could show no improvement in terms of number of drawings correct on posttest, or number of drawings improved on posttest. Thus, in the table a comparison is shown between those who had no drawings correct on the pretest (i.e., those who demonstrated no evidence for a concept of invariant horizontality) and those subjects who had at least one drawing correct.

Table 3 includes data for the same 25 subjects included in Table 2. (The indication of 27 subjects at the top of this table appears to be an error.) Again, the subjects who had no correct pretest drawings are compared with those who had at least one correct pretest drawing in terms of whether or not there was improvement in any of their drawings from pre- to posttest. A subject's drawing could improve, that is, the water level could be depicted as "more horizontal" than on pretest, but still not be sufficiently horizontal to be considered correct.

Table 4 indicates the number of correct drawings by all subjects for the six test pictures, thus showing the relative difficulty of the pictures. While no statistical comparison is made, it is quite clear that drawings III and VI are easier than the other pictures.

Finally, Tables 5 and 6 deal with the subjects' choices of correct bottle when shown a series of drawings of tilted bottles and requested to pick the bottle with the correctly depicted water level.

Smedslund found that some subjects performed better on the drawing test, while others performed better on the "choice" tests. There was likewise variability as to choice of the correct model. It might have been interesting to have analyzed these differences in relation to subjects' pretest performances demonstrating the presence or absence of the concept of horizontality. The student investigator may be interested in doing such an analysis. This could be done by analyzing separately the performances on the drawing test and on the "choice" test for those subjects who demonstrated the initial concept of horizontality on the pretest and those who did not.

The conceptual skills investigated in the Smedslund study are related to those studied in the Shantz and Smock investigation on the development of distance conservation and the spatial coordinate system. By combining the tasks used in the Shantz and Smock study and those used in the Smedslund study one could determine the relationship between distance conservation, the spatial coordinate system, and the concept of horizontality. A study by Ford (1970) does go into some of these matters.

REFERENCE
L. H. Ford, Jr., Predictive versus perceptual responses to Piaget's water line task and their relationship to distance conservation. *Child Development*, 1970, *41*, 193–204.

FORM, COLOR, AND SIZE IN CHILDREN'S CONCEPTUAL BEHAVIOR [1]

JEROME KAGAN* *and* JUDITH LEMKIN
Fels Research Institute

Although conceptual behavior of adult humans has always been a frequent problem for investigation, studies of conceptual processes in the child have attracted considerably less attention. The work of Piaget (4) has recently catalyzed a vigor in this area and has made psychologists aware of the lack of reliable empirical information available on children's conceptual behavior. This very brief note is the first in a series of studies which seeks to understand the way in which the child conceptualizes his environment. This particular research focuses on the tendency to use form, color, or size in classifying stimuli into conceptually similar groups.

Over 30 years ago, Brian and Goodenough (1) found that the child under 3 years of age preferred form to color in organizing his world into groupings of "similar" stimuli. From 3 to 6 years of age, the child shifted to color over form as the preferred basis for categorization. After 6, form once again became dominant over color. The recent interest in conceptual behavior is flavored with a concern for individual differences rather than statements about children in general. We are now more suspicious of statements which purport to hold for all children and expect that there will be important sex, age, and even personality differences in conceptual behavior. Although Brian and Goodenough reported no significant sex differences, a recent investigation (3) with children ages 7 to 11 found that more girls than boys used form rather than color as a basis for classifying stimuli into conceptual classes. The present study is, in part, a replication of this experiment with a younger group of children.

METHOD

The subjects (*S*s) were 35 girls and 34 boys ranging in age from 3-9 to 8-6 with a median age of 5-8. All *S*s were enrolled in either a nursery or the first grade of an elementary school. The junior author was the experimenter (*E*), and she initially spent several hours in the classes of the *S*s

* Fels Research Institute, Yellow Springs, Ohio.

[1] This research was supported, in part, by research grant (M-1260) from the National Institute of Mental Health, United States Public Health Service.

in order to promote familiarity and facilitate rapport for the individual testing situation which was to follow. Each *S* was tested individually in a room provided by the school. The *E* spent a few minutes gaining the child's confidence and then initiated the concept formation task.

Each of the nine stimuli in the series consisted of pieces of white paper upon which were pasted paper cutouts of geometrical forms differing in color, shape, and size.[2] The first three stimuli had two comparison forms on the top of the paper and a standard stimulus at the bottom. Stimuli 4 through 9 had three comparison forms on the top of the paper and the one standard stimulus at the bottom. The method used here was essentially similar to the procedure of Brian and Goodenough. For stimuli 1 through 3 the instructions were: "Here are some cutouts. Do you see this cutout down here? Which one up here (*E* points to the top of the page) is the same as the one down here?" For items 4 through 9 the instructions were: "Now we have one cutout down here and three up here. Which one up here is the same as the one down here?"

Each of the nine stimuli contained forms which could be classified with the standard stimuli on the basis of form, color, or size. For each stimulus only two of these three alternatives were possible as correct solutions. For stimulus 1, color was opposed to form; for stimulus 2, color vs. size; stimulus 3, size vs. form; stimulus 4, color vs. form; stimulus 5, form vs. size; stimulus 6, color vs. form; stimulus 7, form vs. size; stimulus 8, color vs. size; stimulus 9, color vs. size. The *E* recorded the child's answer and asked why the child had chosen that stimulus. All the children understood the task and performed appropriately, but usually were unable to answer why they had made the response they did.

RESULTS

Table 1 presents the percentage of boys and girls who chose form, color, or size for each of the nine stimuli. All children strongly preferred form to either color or size, and size was rarely used as a basis for conceptual similarity. For any one stimulus, there were no statistically significant sex or age differences in choice of color, form, or size. However, when the total number of form, color, and size responses were summed for all nine stimuli, two interesting results emerged.

Table 2 presents the average number of form, color, and size choices for boys and girls who were divided at the median into young and old groups. There was no difference between the responses of young vs. old boys. However, older girls were much less likely than younger girls to choose color ($p < .02$; two tails). Secondly, older boys were much more likely than older girls to use color as the basis for conceptualization ($p < .05$; two tails).

---

[2] The standard stimuli sampled one of three forms (triangle, square, or circle), one of four colors (orange, green, red or blue) and one of two sizes (large or small). The area of the large forms was approximately six times the area of the smaller forms.

TABLE I

PERCENTAGE OF BOYS AND GIRLS CHOOSING FORM, COLOR, OR SIZE
AS BASIS OF CLASSIFICATION

Stimulus	Alternative	Preferred Choices	Boys·	Girls
1	F vs. C	F	64.7	85.7
2	C vs. S	C	73.6	60.0
3	F vs. S	F	73.6	91.4
4	F vs. C	F	64.7	80.0
5	F vs. S	F	67.7	80.0
6	F vs. C	F	58.8	77.3
7	F vs. S	F	73.6	88.6
8	C vs. S	C	53.0	51.3
9	C vs. S	C	64.7	68.5

This finding agrees with the results of Honkavaara who found that more
girls than boys (aged 7 to 11) preferred form to color as a basis for conceptualization. The fact that color is not a preferred hypothesis for children
this age is supported by the unexpected finding that, when color and size
were present as the only bases for similarity, over 20 per cent of the Ss said
they did not know what the answer was and could not offer an answer to
E. That is, when the stimuli did not allow for the use of form but did
allow for the use of color, one fifth of the children did not know how to
respond. This indicates that a color hypothesis is not merely weaker than
form but, for some Ss, is unavailable when the child is asked the question,
"How are these stimuli the same?"

TABLE 2

MEAN NUMBER OF FORM, COLOR, AND SIZE CHOICES FOR ALL NINE
STIMULI BY SEX AND AGE

	Boys		Girls	
	Young	Old	Young	Old
Form	4.2	4.3	4.3	5.7
Color	3.4	3.6	3.4	1.6
Size	0.4	0.9	0.6	1.2

DISCUSSION

The results indicate that the preschool child's understanding of the phrase
"same as," in the present context, is influenced primarily by the shape or
form of the stimulus rather than its color or size.

The sex differences between older boys and girls is difficult to explain. One post hoc argument is presented. Since the verbal skills of young girls proceed precociously in relation to boys, it is possible that the girls implicitly apply the language labels, square, triangle, circle, to the stimuli more often than boys. Thus, for the girls, the stimuli are more likely to derive their meaning from the label attached to them rather than through the more direct physical quality of color. This explanation agrees with Sigel's (5) finding that, when school age children were asked to sort diverse stimuli into conceptually similar groups, the semantic meaning attached to the stimuli crowded out other bases for conceptualization (color, type of material, texture). Sigel concluded that the label attached to the stimulus is the primary basis for conceptualization in school age children. Brian and Goodenough reported that the brighter children were more likely to prefer form to color, and this incidental datum supports the present post hoc argument.

SUMMARY

This paper describes an experiment on the conceptual preferences of children when they were asked to group geometric stimuli differing in form, color, or size into similar pairs. Subjects, 35 girls and 34 boys (ages 3-9 to 8-6), were presented with nine stimuli in which a standard stimulus was presented simultaneously with other stimuli differing in form, color, and size. The child was asked to select the comparison stimulus which was the "same as" the standard. The result indicated that for both boys and girls form was distinctively preferred to color as a basis for similarity and that color was preferred over size. For boys, there was no age difference in this response pattern. However, older girls were less likely than younger girls to use color as a basis for conceptualization. Older boys, moreover, were more likely to use color than were the older girls. These results agreed with a recent investigation in this area, and it was suggested that the sex difference was a function of the girls' implicit labeling of the forms as square, triangle, or circle, which presumably facilitated the use of form as a basis for similarity.

REFERENCES

1. BRIAN, C. R., & GOODENOUGH, F. L. The relative potency of color and form perception at various ages. *J. exp. Psychol.*, 1929, 12, 197-213.
2. BRUNER, J. S., GOODNOW, J. J., & AUSTIN, G. A. *A study of thinking.* Wiley, 1956.
3. HONKAVAARA, S. A critical reevaluation of the color and form reaction, and disproving of the hypotheses connected with it. *J. Psychol.*, 1958, 45, 25-36.
4. PIAGET, J. *The construction of reality in the child.* Basic Books, 1954.
5. SIGEL, I. E. The dominance of meaning. *J. genet. Psychol.*, 1954, 5, 201-207.

EDITORIAL COMMENTS

The basis of children's classification of stimuli has been the subject of a number of investigations in the past several decades. In this study Kagan and Lemkin investigate the variables of form, color, and size.

The authors of this study specify the age range and grade range of their subjects. However, in carrying out a replication of this experiment, it might be more satisfactory to select an equal number of boys and girls in particular age and/or school classes.

Some student investigators may not be able to spend several hours in the children's classes in order to "promote familiarity and facilitate rapport." If this is not feasible, the assistance of the teacher in selecting subjects will generally prevent any possible problems.

The instructions given to the children and the basic characteristics of the stimulus materials employed in the study are described in the authors' report. For the first three stimuli, each of which has two comparison forms on the top and a standard form on the bottom, construc .. of the stimuli should present no problems. However, the remaining six stimuli each have three comparison forms on the top that are to be judged against the standard. In each instance, only two of the alternatives are to be possible solutions; that is, for Stimulus 4, one of the forms must be of the same shape (but not the same color) as the standard, one must be of the same color (but not the same shape), and none of the comparison figures should be of the same size as the standard (so that size would not be a possible basis of choice). One possible set of comparison and standard stimuli is presented below.

Alternative	Standard	Comparison
F vs. C	small orange triangle	large green triangle
		large orange square
C vs. S	small green square	large green circle
		small blue triangle
F vs. S	large blue circle	small red circle
		large orange square
F vs. C	large blue triangle	small orange triangle
		small blue square
		small red square
F vs. S	small orange square	small green circle
		large red triangle
		large blue square
F vs. C	small red circle	large blue triangle
		large red square
		large green circle
F vs. S	large green triangle	large red square
		small orange triangle
		small blue circle
C vs. S	small orange square	small blue circle
		large orange triangle
		large red circle

Alternative	Standard	Comparison
C vs. S	large red circle	large green triangle
		small red triangle
		small blue square

Analysis of Results

The results of the study can be evaluated by means of the chi-square test for independence, for differences between age or sex groups as to their preference for form, color, or size as a basis of classification.

THREE

STUDIES IN COGNITIVE DEVELOPMENT

DEVELOPMENTAL TRENDS IN THE ABSTRACTION ABILITY OF CHILDREN[1]

IRVING E. SIGEL *Merrill-Palmer School, Detroit, Michigan*

Abstraction is "a mental process in which some attribute or characteristic is observed independently of other characteristics of an experience as a whole." Werner (26) emphasizes that the ability to abstract does not appear suddenly in the course of the individual's development; rather it is present from the very beginnings of life but changes qualitatively with progress in maturation.

Different organizational patterns of response to environmental stimuli are observed in children of varying age levels (26). The abstraction behavior of very young children seems to be primarily on a sensori-motor level and can be designated as *perceptual*. In such a response the individual yields to demands of the situation, and the organization of the material is determined by the nature of the stimuli as well as by the limited maturity of the subject. A more mature individual would be expected to consciously impose organization on the material (1, 7, 14, 17, 19, 26) and classify the material into deliberately conceived categories. This is the *conceptual* level of abstraction.

The hypothesis that the younger the child, the more perceptual are his organizations has been stated (1, 7, 14, 26) but a search for specific details of the development encounters a paucity of data. The present study was undertaken to obtain information regarding changes in abstraction ability during the elementary school period.

PROCEDURE

Candidates for study were boys of lower-middle-class background who were in the correct grades for their ages and whose percentile ranks on the Raven Test of Progressive Matrices were between 25 and 75. From candidates 7, 9, and 11 years old, 20 were chosen at random to represent each age group.

[1] The data for this paper were contained in a dissertation presented in partial fulfillment of the requirements for the degree of Doctor of Philosophy in the Committee on Human Development, University of Chicago. The author wishes to express his gratitude to Drs. Helen L. Koch, Benjamin Bloom, and Robert T. Havighurst for their consistent encouragement in this research.

CHILD DEVELOPMENT, Vol. 24, No. 2 (June, 1953)

Toy objects were selected as the basic item for the grouping tests, and pilot exploration resulted in assembly of 24 items which were familiar to all of the children. Except for the snake, which was about 12 inches long, the maximum dimension of any object was 5 inches. The following objects were used:

1. Blue and red plastic lounge chair
2. Red plastic office chair
3. Brown and white plastic arm chair
4. Red plastic stool
5. White plastic dining table
6. Red plastic end table
7. Plastic man in black suit and white shirt
8. Plastic woman in blue dress
9. Flesh pink rubber baby doll
10. Flesh pink celluloid child doll
11. Brown metal soldier
12. Metal boy in blue suit
13. Green plastic truck
14. Blue plastic baby carriage
15. Purple plastic airplane
16. Red and yellow plastic tractor
17. Blue metal train engine
18. Red and blue plastic boat
19. Brown metal chicken
20. Red celluloid fish
21. Pink celluloid duck
22. Red plastic horse
23. Green wood snake
24. Black and white plastic dog

Five variants of the test situation were used:

Form I—Tactual-motor. The subject was permitted to handle the objects while making his groupings.

Form II—Visual-non-motor. The subject was not allowed to touch the objects but was asked to point to or name the objects and instruct the tester on grouping.

Form III—Pictures. Black and white photographs mounted on cards approximately 3.5 × 4.5 inches were substituted for the objects, and the subject was allowed to group the cards manually.

Form IV—Names. The name of each object was printed in large, black block letters on a card approximately 3 inches square, and the subject was asked to group the cards.

Form V—Names listed. The names of all objects were typewritten on the upper one-half of a sheet 11 × 13 inches, and the subject was asked to write the names in groups on the lower one-half of the sheet.

Within each age group the order in which the five forms were given was rotated so that four subjects of the twenty did Form I first, four did Form II first, etc. In the presentation of each form the materials were arranged in a circle on a table so that two objects obviously of the same class were not adjacent. The same arrangement of materials was employed with all subjects.

Before testing, each child was asked to identify the objects as they were placed on the table or to read the names on cards as listed. Before each test a subject was told to "put those things together in a pile (or list) that belong together or go together or are alike in any way, and those other things that go together or belong together or are alike in another way in another pile (or list). You may have as many or as few piles as you wish. Do you understand?" Some seven-year-olds found the concept of "belong-ingness" or "likeness" difficult to grasp. Examples were not given because they might set a pattern and deter spontaneous grouping. When a child seemed not to understand or asked whether there was a right way to group, the directions were repeated. Judged by the performances of the children, the task was comprehended.

Minimum control was exerted by the experimenter in the first test situation, the child being left to determine what made things similar or belong together. Trials were completed in not more than ten minutes. After completion of the first trial, a subject was asked to explain the reason for each group. The names of objects in each classification and the reasons for groups were recorded *verbatim*. To determine the upper limits of grouping and the effects of pressure, additional trials were used.[2] Each child was instructed to "group the things that are alike or belong together into fewer groupings than you made the first time," until the children could not reduce the number of groupings. After the objects were grouped, the reasons for grouping again were recorded *verbatim*. Identical procedure was followed with each of the five test forms. Each child was given one test daily for five consecutive days to reduce fatigue and perseveration.

Upon completion of the five test forms, each subject was given a class recognition test to determine his ability to recognize bases of groupings possibly more inclusive than any he had devised. Successively, a child was introduced to the groups of objects which could be classified as animal, human, vehicle, and furniture and was asked, "Do these things go together or belong together or are they alike in any way?" If these were identified, the experimenter presented to the child the 24 objects in two groups, those "living" and "non-living," and asked the same question. If these were identified, the 24 objects were placed in a single group, and the child asked the basis of it. Finally, the subject was exposed to the classifications "red" (office chair, stool, horse, fish, end-table) and "metal" (train engine, soldier, boy, chicken).

For scoring on the basis of the number of objects placed in each category, designations of groupings were classified as perceptual, conceptual, and miscellaneous; sub-categories were required for the first and last of the three classifications. The designations are similar to those used by Bolles (1), Goldstein and Scheerer (7), and Werner (26).

---

[2] The first and second trials were only used for analysis since too few children in the sample were able to reduce the groupings in Trial 3.

A. *Perceptual*

1. *Affective*—grouping based on feeling.
2. *Identity*—grouping based on identity of structure or function.
3. *Partial Identity*—grouping based on identity of certain aspects of structure or function.
4. *Centroid*—grouping based on belongingness in a geographical area.
5. *Functional*—grouping based on use.

B. *Conceptual*—grouping in which the objects were treated as members of a class even though gross structural differences were apparent. Designation by a class name was required for a grouping to be scored conceptual.

C. *Miscellaneous*

1. *Mixed-1*—grouping in which conceptual and perceptual classifications are combined and treated as perceptual.
2. *Mixed-2*—grouping in which two or more perceptual groupings are combined into a third perceptual category.
3. *Thematic*—grouping based on a story.
4. *Pseudo*—grouping which appeared incorrect in interpretation or information of reality.
5. *Non-Groupings*—objects which were not found to belong to any grouping and which were isolated intentionally.

The miscellaneous categories were derived from a pilot study and are recognized as a heterogeneous combination of sub-categories necessary to demonstrate adaptations in sorting behavior when "pure" conceptual or "pure" perceptual organization was not exhibited.

Results

The frequency with which the children of three age groups made use of the perceptual and conceptual classifications in Trials 1 and 2 is shown in Figure 1. By an analysis of variance technique (4) the age differences indicated in the chart for conceptual classifications in Trial 1 were significant at the .01 level of confidence. Differences in the use of conceptual categories also were significant for every age comparison in Trial 2. The age differences in perceptual classification in Trial 1 were significant between the group of children 7 years old and both of the older groups but were not significant between groups 9 and 11 years old. In no instance were dependable differences found between tests (18).

Comparisons between Trials 1 and 2 for groups of children 7, 9, and 11 years old did not show significant changes in the use of perceptual

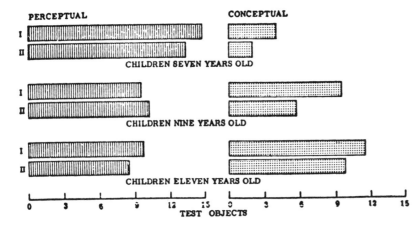

FIGURE 1—Comparisons of mean numbers of objects placed in perceptual and conceptual categories by children of three age groups.

type classifications although the direction of change was toward an increased use in Trial 2 by the nine-year-olds and decreased use by the other two groups. With respect to conceptual classifications all groups showed changes significant between the two trials at least at the .05 level of confidence. However, in both trials the trends with increasing age were similar downward for use of the perceptual categories and upward for the conceptual classifications.

The percentages of objects grouped according to the subcategories of the perceptual and miscellaneous[3] classifications are shown in Figure 2. The children never used the "affective" category and the "identity" category was omitted because with the test objects employed, identity might have been a conceptual approach in some instances and a perceptual approach in others.[4]

In both trials the children 7 and 11 years old employed the partial identity category as a basis of grouping significantly more than did the nine-year-old children. Similarity is apparent between the results for seven- and eleven-year-old groups, yet one would expect to find differences, since maturity is a factor in differentiating the types of classificatory approaches used. If the reasons offered for the groupings are considered, the seven-year-olds classified significantly more frequently on the basis of partial identity of action than did the nine- and eleven-year-olds. The two older groups

---

[3] It was felt that in view of the heterogeneity of the miscellaneous category, it would not be valid at this time to treat them as a single unit. Analysis of these results, however, will be presented later.

[4] Nevertheless, the use of what might be considered "identity" was rare. This might have been a function of the materials, since no two objects were identical.

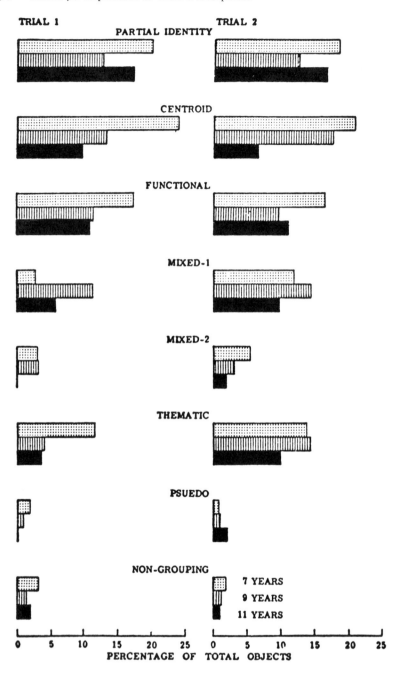

FIGURE 2—Comparisons of percentages of total number of objects placed in perceptual and miscellaneous categories in Trials 1 and 2 by children of three age groups.

tended to use partial identity of structure, although the differences between the nine- and eleven-year-olds is not significant. Partial identity of structure was used significantly more by the eleven-year-olds than by the seven-year-olds.

The centroid grouping was employed by the youngest children more significantly and use of that category was less for each older age group. Typical reasons given for the groupings were: "all belong in air," and "all belong in the house." Objects were organized in ways familiar to the child from his own experience or from stories and explanations. The trend described occurred in Trial 2 also, although the nine-year-old children increased their use of this type of classification.

The seven-year-old children also employed functional grouping significantly more than did the older children. Nine- and eleven-year-old children used the category almost equally. Under pressure to reduce the groupings, the eleven-year-olds increased the frequency of their use of this classification but the other two groups did not.

Examination of the uses of the miscellaneous groupings shows that in the first trial the combining of the perceptual and conceptual approaches (mixed-1) occurred most frequently among nine-year-old children. The combination of two or more perceptual categories (mixed-2) was used almost equally by the seven- and nine-year-olds, but rarely by the older children. In Trial 2, however, all groups increased their use of the mixed categories, the greatest increase being for the oldest children.

Use of the thematic category decreased with age, the seven-year-old group using it most frequently. In Trial 2, however, the nine-year-old children increased their use of this approach to an extent that results for the seven- and nine-year-old groups do not differ significantly. The eleven-year-old children also increased their use of thematic groupings in Trial 2.

Subsumed under the category "pseudo" are the groupings meaningless to us. This and "non-grouping" appeared rarely and most frequently in the seven-year-old group. The children had the most difficulty with the category "vehicle," which some did not use at all. More frequently, the failure involved only the baby buggy. Even eleven-year-old children often did not think of this classification. The difficulty may have stemmed from the fact that baby buggies have no motors as do the other vehicles represented. Another possibility is that the children may have considered it part of the family's furniture. The boat, the snake, and the fish also presented difficulties and frequently were left ungrouped, especially by the seven-year-old children.

The question arises, can the child who does not in spontaneous groupings use such categories as animal, vehicle, furniture, human, redness, and metal, identify such classifications when the groupings are made by the experimenter? The results of the recognition test are summarized in Table 1 and demonstrate that the ability to identify groupings increases with age.

TABLE 1

PERCENTAGES OF GROUPS OF CHILDREN WHO IDENTIFIED
GROUPINGS IN RECOGNITION TEST

Groupings	Age Groups (years)		
	7	9	11
Animal	50	75	90
Human	60	85	95
Vehicle	0	40	50
Furniture	40	90	90
Living	0	40	35
Non-living	0	15	15
Single Group	0	0	25
Red	5	20	10
Metal	0	0	10

The similarity between scores of the nine- and eleven-year-old children is greater than between those of either group and the seven-year-old children. Only the nine- and eleven-year-old youngsters were able to identify the category "living things" and only eleven-year-old children were able to give some adequate reason for grouping all the objects into one category. More of the nine-year-old group were able to identify the "red" category than either of the other two age groups. Only two eleven-year-old subjects were able to identify "metal" as a basis of classification, perhaps because the metal objects were painted. All children gave some basis for their designations of the groupings, but their reasons were not always correct in terms of conceptual response. Usually, the explanations were not different from those offered for their own classifications.

DISCUSSION

The classificatory behavior represented in the first trial indicates the child's ability in a situation which is minimally structured. The children were free to use the approaches they "felt most comfortable" with in determining similarity or belongingness. The trends are clear cut that regardless of the nature of the material, perceptual classifications declined and conceptual ones increased with age. This finding substantiates the hypothesis that with increases in age significant changes in classificatory behavior occur. The specific determinants effecting this change are difficult to isolate. Although the group trends reported are clear cut, individual variations within the groups in the use of "more mature" classificatory approaches were found. Some seven-year-olds were able to utilize conceptual as well as perceptual approaches. What accounts for the individual variations becomes a highly relevant and pertinent question. Since chronological age and social class are controlled, and since the mental ability range within the groups did not include extremes, the questions point to areas of experiential, personality and organic forces as possible determinants of the difference. Factors such as quality of experience with similar problems, early learnings of concepts, reality "boundness," and rate of constitutional maturation offer themselves as possible determinants of the variations observed. Further experimentation with variables such as these is necessary.

Whatever the reason, the results of this study tend to confirm those reported in the literature (1, 7, 15, 19, 21, 26). The various uses made of the sub-categories is an important consideration. The total perceptual score is a composite of all the perceptual sub-categories. Hence, to state that perceptual classifications decrease with age is merely a half truth. Examination of the perceptual sub-classifications reveals significant differences in the frequencies with which they were used. Partial identity was used by the two youngest age groups with about the same frequency. The results, however, differ qualitatively in a way that tends to confirm the view of Werner (26) and Koffka (12) that action and movement are abstracted earlier than structural aspects. Thus, this quality is a significant indicator of maturity differences. The seven-year-old child, perhaps since his early experiences with objects are in terms of movement, has not yet replaced this more primitive learning with that which is more sophisticated. The question also arises as to the relationship between partial identity of structure and conceptual classificatory ability. It is the oldest group, the one in our population most able to handle the material conceptually, that tends to use this approach. Is the structural approach intrinsic to or correlated with conceptual thought? It may be that the two are interdependent.

Similarly, in the centroid grouping the specification of location as a determinant of belongingness or similarity emphasizes the more concrete nature of the younger children and indicates inability to perceive the materials in the "abstract," that is, not tied to specific places or persons. That this approach declines so sytematically with age would support this premise. The same thinking holds with respect to the functional approach. The inability to see objects as representing classes of material; rather, the perception of them as similar by virtue of utility is further evidence of concreteness.

It is not surprising that seven-year-old children have difficulty in using the mixed-1 category frequently, for use of this approach is correlated with the ability to use the conceptual category. By definition, children could not be expected to use mixed-1 with any greater frequency than they were able to use the conceptual category. Of interest, however, is the frequency with which the nine-year-old children used this approach. Figure 2 indicates their preference for a combined approach in at least one conceptual category.

This suggests that not being quite ready to see the objects only as member components of a class of objects, they prefer to associate the objects with something concrete, thereby adding the perceptual concept to the classification. It is clear that mixed-2 is used infrequently by this group and the eleven-year-olds have no need to use the approach at all.

The rationale of using additional trials to indicate the extent of approach and, to some degree, the stability as well as the solution to a more complex request for grouping was substantiated by examining the shifts that did take place.

The changes that occurred in the second trial reflect the children's ability to reorganize their groupings in new ways. Some of the children included more objects within the groupings which they had already established. For example, a seven-year-old child who in Trial 1 made three centroid groupings, in Trial 2 merely brought them together into one centroid group. The idea used to explain the grouping was enlarged in scope and inclusiveness, but the type of grouping remained the same. This did not actually involve a shifting of the basis of the groupings, for the child did not select a new classificatory scheme by which more objects could be included. The child could shift within narrow limits, for he had to reorient the classificatory scheme applied to the objects, but he was not able to find an essentially different basis for groupings.

Some children were able to shift from perceptual to conceptual classifications, which involved utilization of classifications essentially different from those used in the previous organization. For instance, one change was from a grouping in which animals were placed together "because they live on a farm" to a grouping of the animals "because they are animals." The type of shifting involved in this situation requires a greater degree of flexibility than is required in the example cited previously, a reorientation of "attitude" toward the objects to perceive them in a basically different way. This ability to shift from perception to conception is evidence that a child is well established in the use of the categorical approach.

In Trial 1, one seven-year child made four groupings: (1) the fish, the snake, the duck, and the boat, "because they all belong in water" (scored centroid); (2) the boy, the man, the woman, the soldier, the doll, and the baby, "because they are all people" (scored conceptual); (3) the tractor, the truck, the plane, the train, "because they all run and run on the ground" (scored mixed-2); and (4) the horse, the dog, the chicken, "because they all walk" (scored partial identity). In Trial 2 he made three groupings: (1) the vehicles, except the baby carriage, "because they are all things you travel with" (scored functional); (2) all the animals "because they are animals" (scored conceptual); and (3) the furniture and the people "because people sit and use the furniture" (scored mixed-1). This record clearly shows shifting from the original approach and the inclusion of a new conceptual category not used in Trial 1. It is true that the child used a conceptual classification in the first trial, which might be related to his ability to make another conceptual grouping in Trial 2 and bring all the animals into one group regardless of differences in structure. He did not alter his original conceptual grouping, but to make fewer groupings, as directed, he had to group humans and furniture together in a mixed category.

Such findings indicate that individual differences in ability to handle some types of material conceptually and to shift are found as early as the seventh year. Whether vocabulary, unique experience favoring concept formation, certain types of innate ability, maturational factors, or personality determinants affect the abilities of the youngsters is still an open question.

Principally, shifting by the nine- and eleven-year-old children was toward combining classificatory types. The general trend was toward fewer items grouped conceptually and more items grouped in miscellaneous categories. However, nine-year-old children were able to expand their conceptual groupings in Trial 2 by changing to animals or to humans from centroid categories. The Raven scores of children able to effect these changes ranged from the 50th to the 75th percentile.

Only one eleven-year-old child, whose Raven score was around the seventy-fifth percentile, grouped all of the objects into one category "because God created all these." Although performance of this level is rare, it is significant that eleven-year-olds shifted from perceptual to conceptual approaches with greater frequency than did seven-year-olds. The fact that many of the children were unable to make fewer groupings in Trial 2 than in Trial 1 indicates a type of rigidity, a kind of "boundness" to the already achieved tasks. Our justification for qualifying rigidity is simply that we are using a limited measure of rigidity or flexibility, i.e., rigidity with respect to number of groupings. If we had asked that the children merely alter the groupings, without requesting change in number of groups, more intensive rigidity might have been detected. The two types of shifting described indicate that a reorientation in approach toward objects occurs as early as age seven. Developmentally the trend from shifting within a single approach to shifting from one classificatory scheme to another may well be a key to the maturity index of conceptual thinking. The seven-year-old who can do this, therefore, is more mature in his abstraction ability than the seven-year-old who cannot, if maturity be considered in terms of the degree of similarity of performance from the young to the older. It would be interesting and fruitful to explore this question further by finding out if such differences relate to language ability or problem solving ability.

The findings of the "Recognition Test" show interesting agreement with those of Welch (23), who tested the ability of children to learn certain abstract concepts rather than the frequency in the use of the concepts.

The recognition test showed that the use of hierarchic levels in grouping material increases steadily with age. The designation *conceptual* in this study actually was applied to groupings which Welch would have called second level—the "animal," "human," "vehicle," and "furniture" categories. The categories "living" and "non-living" are third level and "substance" is fourth level in Welch's system.

We have pointed out the difficulties seven-year-old subjects had in identifying even second level concepts, as well as their inability to identify third and fourth level ones. Although results of the study showed definite changes with age in the ability of children to identify groupings, the problem remains of explaining why certain groupings are more readily identified than others. The effects of qualitative differences in experience upon the formation of concepts needs further analysis.

Summary

Sixty white lower-middle-class children, 20 from age group 7, 9, and 11 years, who were in the correct grades for their age and whose percentile rank scores on the Raven Test of Progressive Matrices ranged from the 25th to 75th percentile, were selected as subjects. To each child five test situations, each containing 24 familiar toy objects, pictures of these toys, and word names of the toys were presented. They were instructed to group materials on the basis of similarity.

The data presented reveal a decrease with age in perceptual classification of items. This decrease between the ages of 7 and 9 years was significant, but not between 9 and 11, when children were asked to reduce groupings. The use of conceptual classifications increased steadily with age. Placement of items in miscellaneous categories was negatively correlated with age when the children were allowed free choice in grouping, but when urged to reduce the number of groupings, an age trend was not found.

Seven-year-old children principally used groupings of the thematic type in their first trials and repeated that approach when requested to reduce the number of groupings.

Nine-year-old children tended to use conceptual and perceptual classifications equally and made some use of the miscellaneous categories as well. When requested to reduce the number of groupings, they increased perceptual and miscellaneous classifications and reduced conceptual groupings.

Eleven-year-old children employed conceptual groupings predominantly but used the perceptual approach about as frequently as did nine-year-old youngsters. Miscellaneous classifications were infrequent when grouping was spontaneous. With pressure to reduce the number of groupings, conceptual and perceptual classifications still were used, but recourse to the miscellaneous category increased.

When groupings of the objects were made by the experimenter, the chidren's effort to identify the bases he had in mind did not reveal essentially different patterns of thought than did the groupings made by the children themselves.

BOLLES, MARY MARJORIE. The basis of pertinence: A study of the test performance of aments, dements, and normal children of the same mental age. *Arch. Psychol., N.Y.,* 1937, No. 212.

BRIAN, CLARA H., and GOODENOUGH, FLORENCE L. The relative potency of color and form perception at various ages. *J. exp. Psychol.,* 1929, 12, 197-213.

COLBY, MARTHA G., and ROBERTSON, JEAN B. Genetic studies in abstraction. *J. comp. Psychol.,* 1942, 33, 385-401.

EDWARDS, A. L. *Experimental design in psychological research.* New York: Rinehart, 1950.

FEIFEL, H., and LORGE, I. Qualitative differences in the vocabulary responses of children. *J. educ. Psychol.,* 1950, 41, 1-18.

GOLDSTEIN, K. *The organism.* New York: American Book Co., 1939.

GOLDSTEIN, K., and SCHEERER, M. Abstract and concrete behavior: An experimental study with special tests. *Psychol. Monogr.,* 1941, 53, No. 2.

HEBB, O. *The organization of behavior.* New York: Wiley & Sons, 1949.

HEIDBREDER, EDNA. The attainment of concepts: A psychological interpretation. *Trans. N.Y. Acad. Sci.,* 1945, 7, 178-188.

HUMPHREY, G. The problem of generalization. *Bull. Canad. Psychol. Assn.,* 1944, 4, 37-51.

JOHNSON, B. The development of thought. *Child Develpm.,* 1938, 9, 1-7.

KOFFKA, K. *The growth of the mind: An introduction to child psychology.* Trans. Ogden. 2nd ed. rev. New York: Harcourt, Brace, 1928.

LING, BING-CHUNG. Form discrimination as a learning cue in infants. *Comp. Psychol. Monogr.,* 1947, 27, No. 2.

McNEMAR, Q. *Psychological statistics.* New York: Wiley & Sons, 1949.

PROTHERO, E. T. Egocentricity and abstraction in children and aments. *Amer. J. Psychol.,* 1943, 56, 66-77.

RIMOLDI, H. A study in some factors related to intelligence. *Psychometrika,* 1948, 13, 27-46.

SIGEL, I. E. Developmental trends in abstraction ability in children. Unpublished Ph.D. dissertation, Univ. Chicago, 1951.

SIGEL, I. E. Dominance of meaning. *J. genet. Psychol.* In press.

THOMPSON, JANE. Ability of children on different grade levels to generalize on sorting tests. *J. Psychol.*, 1941, 11, 119-126.

WARREN, H. C. *Dictionary of psychology.* Boston: Houghton Mifflin, 1934.

WEIGLE, E. On the so-called processes of abstraction. *J. abnorm. soc. Psychol.*, 1941, 36, 3-33.

WELCH, L., and DAVIES, H. I. The theory of abstraction and its applications. *Psyche*, 1935, 15, 138-145.

WELCH, L. A preliminary investigation of some aspects of the hierarchical development of concepts. *J. genet. Psychol.*, 1940, 22, 359-378.

WELCH, L. The genetic development of the associational structures of abstract thinking. *J. genet. Psychol.*, 1940, 56, 172-206.

WERNER, H. The concept of rigidity: A critical evaluation. *Psychol. Rev.*, 1946, 53, 43-52.

WERNER, H. *Comparative psychology of mental development* (rev. ed.). Chicago: Follet Publishing Co., 1948.

Manuscript received July, 1953.

EDITORIAL COMMENTS

A similar study is reported by Olver and Hornsby (1966). In that study six groups of ten subjects each, ranging from age six to eighteen, were used. The materials differed somewhat and the categories for classifying responses also differed in some respects. The student investigator may find it useful to read the Olver and Hornsby report in setting the categories for the analysis of the responses and for a better understanding of the procedures.

Modifications of Sample and Procedure

In selecting a sample it would *not* be necessary to obtain scores on the Raven Test. It can be assumed that if the sample is taken from a normal school population the intelligence test scores would fall within the normal range.

The size of the sample used can be reduced by selecting subjects from two, instead of three, age levels: ages seven and eleven. Further reduction could be achieved by reducing the sample size in each age group from 20 to 15. Sigel does not report the sex distribution of his subjects. If the investigator wishes to compare performance according to sex, then the size of the population at each age level should be retained at 20—10 boys and 10 girls at each age level.

The objects used in the sorting task can be obtained in the toy department of most department stores. If this presents a problem then pictures of these objects can be obtained (see pictures used in Olver and Hornsby 1966).

The variants of the test situation can be reduced to two: either the tactual-motor (Form I) and the names (Form IV), or the pictures (Form III) and the names (Form IV). The order can be varied so that half the subjects receive the names first, and the other half either the tactual-motor or the pictures first.

Because Sigel used five variants of the test situation it was necessary to test the subjects on five separate days in order to avoid fatigue. If only two variants are used, as suggested here, the subjects could be tested in one sitting.

In order to be sure that the categorization of responses is being done with some degree of reliability, two judges should be used. The judges should confer and reach agreement on a small sample of responses, about ten. They then should categorize the remaining responses independently and the percentage of agreement should be indicated in the report. This percentage should be above 85 percent. If agreement is less, then another conference should be held on an additional small sample of responses and a second independent categorization should be done. Those responses on which there remains disagreement can be classified alternately according to each of the judges. (See editorial comments for the Graham *et al.* study.)

Analysis of Results

Sigel employed an analysis of variance technique for testing the various age differences. It would be possible to employ the chi-square technique.

REFERENCES
R. R. Olver and J. R. Hornsby. On equivalence. Chapter 3 in J. S. Bruner, R. R. Olver, and P. M. Greenfield, *Studies in Cognitive Growth*. New York: Wiley, 1966.

The Journal of Genetic Psychology, 1961, **99**, 51-57.

THE DEVELOPMENT OF THE ADDITIVE COMPOSITION OF CLASSES IN THE CHILD: PIAGET REPLICATION STUDY III*

UCLA School of Medicine

DAVID ELKIND[1]

This is the third[2] study in a series devoted to the systematic replication of experiments originally performed by the Swiss psychologist, Jean Piaget. For its starting point the present study takes one of Piaget's (1942) investigations dealing with the child's ability to additively compose classes (include partial classes within a total class.) In his work Piaget assumed that the ability to include classes indicated the attainment of logical (abstract) class conceptions. By studying the ability of children of various ages to include classes Piaget sought to trace the developmental steps in the formation of abstract conceptions of classes.

To test for the child's ability to additively compose classes Piaget made use of the "wooden beads" experiments.[3] The purpose of these experiments was to determine whether the child could tell that the number of elements in a total class was greater than the number of elements in one of its sub-classes. For example the child was shown a box of brown wooden beads and a box of less numerous white wooden beads. After the child agreed that all the beads were wooden, he was asked whether there were more wooden or more brown beads in the two boxes.

Experimenting with children of various ages Piaget found three age related stages in the development of the ability to include classes. At the

---

* Received in the Editorial Office on September 16, 1959.

[1] This study was carried out while the author was staff psychologist at the Beth Israel Hospital in Boston. The author is grateful to Dr. Grete L. Bibring, head of the psychiatric department, and the members of the research committee for granting him the time to make the study.

[2] For the first two studies cf. Elkind (1961a; 1961b).

[3] For an identification, questionnaire, and learning approach to the study of class inclusion cf. Welch (1940).

first stage (usually ages five-six) children had a general, gestalt-like, impression of a total class and demonstrated[4] they knew the wooden beads were also brown and white. But when forced to break down this impression and compare part against whole (the brown with the wooden beads) the children behaved as if the whole class was destroyed and compared one partial class (the brown beads) with the other partial class (the white beads).

Children at the second stage (usually ages five-six) had a more differentiated conception of a general class and its sub-classes. When these children were asked to compare part with whole, the whole was not destroyed but identified with the part. The children at this stage said that the brown beads were "the same" as the wooden beads. Sometimes by trial and error children at the second stage were able to discover that the brown beads were less than the wooden beads.

Third stage children (usually ages seven-eight) had an abstract conception of classes and said immediately that the wooden beads were more than the brown beads because there were white (wooden) beads as well.

Because the class "wooden beads" was artificial in the sense that it had no specific name, Piaget used several control tests with total classes having proper names. One of the control tests involved asking the child whether there were more boys (girls) or more children in the classroom. This control test was only briefly reported by Piaget and the present study attempted to replicate it using a large number of subjects. One purpose of the replication study was to determine whether Piaget's stages were significantly related to age.

B. Method

1. *Subjects*

One hundred children attending the Claflin School[5] in Newton, Mass., were tested. Twenty-five children were selected at random from each class from kindergarten to third grade. The mean age and standard deviation for each class was: Kindergarten, M = 5-8, SD = 3.0; Grade 1, M = 6-9, SD = 3.9; Grade 2, M = 7-8, SD = 3.6; Grade 3, M = 8-7, SD = 3.8 months. The majority of the children came from middle to upper middle class homes. The mean IQ for all the children in the school was 109 (on the Kuhlmann-Anderson Intelligence Test).

2. *Procedure*

Each child was seen individually and asked the following questions: (a) How many children are there in your class? (b) How many boys in the

---

[4] Piaget's first and second stage subjects grasped without difficulty that if all the wooden beads were taken out and put in an empty box there would be none left whereas if only the brown ones were taken out the white ones would remain.

[5] The author is grateful to Dr. Harry Anderson, principal of the Claflin School, and to the teachers for their very friendly cooperation.

class? (*c*) How many girls in the class? (*d*) Are there more boys (or girls depending upon the sex of the child being questioned) or more children in your class? Those children who answered incorrectly were asked (*e*) What are children? and then question (*d*) was asked again. The questions were repeated as often as necessary to insure the child's attention and understanding.

3. *Categorization of Responses*

Questions (*a, b, c*) were asked only to orient the children to the problem and to help them differentiate the classes. Ninety-two of the children had no idea of how many children, boys, or girls were in the room and simply said they didn't know. Three of the children made up fantastic figures. Of the older children only five actually knew the correct number of boys, girls, and children in the classroom.

The responses to question (*d*) were categorized according to Piaget's stages. All responses indicating the partial class was greater than the total class (e.g., more boys than children, more boys than girls = children) were categorized as Stage I responses. Responses indicating that the partial class was identical with the total class (e.g., they are the same, boys are children) were categorized as Stage II responses. Those answers which stated that the children were more than the boys or the girls were categorized as Stage III responses.

C. RESULTS

Table 1 shows the per cent of children giving Stage I, II, or III responses for the four age groups. The χ^2 for all the cells in the table was 12.59 and was significant beyond the .05 level. The stages were related to age in agreement with Piaget's findings. The small per cent of subjects at the second stage was unexpected. However, since it is a transitional stage it may be shorter in duration than the other two stages and perhaps does not occur at all in some children.

TABLE 1
PER CENT OF CHILDREN AT EACH STAGE OF ADDITIVE COMPOSITION
OF CLASSES FOR FOUR AGE LEVELS

N	Age group	Stage I	Stage II	Stage III
25	5	50	12	48
25	6	32	12	56
25	7	12	12	76
25	8	8	—	92

To make concrete the children's performance at each of the stages, records from the present study are presented below.

Joan, age 6, No. 10

How many children are there in your room? "Twenty." How many girls? "I don't know." How many boys? "I don't know." Are there more girls or more children in your room? "There are more boys than girls." Are there more boys than children? (Joan counts to herself) "More boys." And what are children? "They are boys and girls." Then are there more boys or more children in your room? "More boys."

Joan knows at the verbal level that boys and girls are children but as soon as part and whole must be compared, dealt with logically, the total class is apparently destroyed and only the parts are retained in the child's mind for comparison. This example is much like those presented by Piaget in reporting his bead experiments. Below is another record from the present study.

Sue, age 6, No. 24

Are there more children or more girls in your room? "There is just the same amount." Really just as many girls as children? "More children because I mean more girls, girls is better than boys always fight so got a new girl." What are children? "Boys and girls." Are there more girls or more children in your room? "More girls." And what are children? "Boys and girls."

Sue has just reached the second stage and says the girls and the children are the same amount. But when pressed she became confused like the first stage children saying there were more girls than children. The following two records are from children at the third stage. One child solves the problem logically, the other one solves it mathematically.

Mitch, age 8, No. 19

Are there more boys or more children in the room? "Looks like more children because the whole class is children and just the boys is not the whole class."

Paul, age 8, No. 92

How many children in your class? "Twenty-five." How many girls? "Thirteen." And how many boys? "Twelve." Are there more boys or more children in your room. "More children." Why is that? Because thirteen and twelve makes twenty-five and twenty-five is more than twelve."

As these examples indicate, children at the first and second stages as well as those at the third were able to give verbal definitions of children (besides boys and girls the most frequent were: little people, persons, kids) suggesting additive compositive of classes. Yet these same children were not able to dissociate and compare the part with the whole. Several factors probably account for this apparent contradiction: (*a*) verbal facility may advance more rapidly than the development of logical ability; (*b*) the copula "is" may have been used by the children only in the identity sense (children are the same as boys and girls) and not in the predicative sense (children have the property of being people) or in the inclusion sense (children are in the class of people or boys and girls are in the class of children). Because of this ambiguity of language success in comparing classes quantitatively is probably a better index of the ability to include classes than is a qualitative verbal definition.

D. Discussion

The results of the present study were in agreement with Piaget's finding of three age related stages in the development of the child's ability to additively compose classes. The discussion will briefly summarize Piaget's interpretation of these developmental stages.

According to Piaget the difficulty in composing classes experienced by the children at the first and second stages can be described in either of two ways. From the *extensive* point of view (considering the elements possessing the class property) the child's difficulty arises from his inability to think of the same set of elements in two classes at once. At the early stages the child's thought still reflects realism (Piaget, 1929) in the sense that the child takes his mental construction, a class, for a real spatial entity. In the present study, for example, when the child thought of some of his peers in the class of "boys" he used them up, so to speak, by putting them in one class and was not able to put them in another class which due to his realism constituted a second "place." This explains why so many of the children answered "more boys than girls" or the reverse even though the question asked was whether there were more boys (girls) or more children. After classifying some of the children as boys only girls remained (or boys if girls were classed) and so the subjects compared the two part classes.

From the *intensive* point of view (considering the class properties) the child's difficulty arises from his inability to think of a single element possessing two properties at once. At the early stages of class composition, conceptions of classes are not clearly differentiated from object conceptions. The child's realism is such that properties like "brown" and "boy" still have a concrete object connotation. For these children once something is *a* brown or *a* boy it cannot also be *a* wooden or *a* child just as a bead cannot be a block.

Piaget attributes the child's difficulties with extension and intension to the irreversibility of his thought. Once the child has conceived a set of objects as being in one class (or possessing one property) he cannot return to the starting point of his mental construction and re-conceive the same set of objects as being in a second class (or possessing a second property). Once, however, the child has developed the necessary mental structures he can return to the starting point of a mental problem and discover that the same elements can be conceived in two classes simultaneously and as possessing two properties at once.

It is also possible, according to Piaget, to formulate the class inclusion problem in logical terms and to make a logical reconstruction of the processes leading to the children's success and failure with including classes. From the logical point of view a class is a set of objects possessing a common property, and is capable of being symbolized and of being operated upon. To add classes is to form the smallest class which will contain all the elements in the constituent classes. This operation is symbolized $A + A' = B$. From this equation it follows logically that $A = B—A'$ and that $A < B$ (A is less than or included in B). These three operations form a group which leaves the total class invariant. Since a logical class remains invariant regardless of empirical events every logical class presupposes this group of operations.

By means of this logical paradigm it is possible to discover just where, in the logical sense, the first and second stage children met with difficulty. These children all had a conception of a general class made up of sub-classes. In Piaget's study the children knew the wooden beads were brown and white and in the present study the subjects knew that children were boys and girls. Implicitly they were capable of the operation $A + A' = B$. Likewise these children could easily judge one set of beads as greater than another or could tell if there were more girls or boys. So they were also capable, implicitly, of the operation $A < B$. The child's difficulty was therefore not in forming classes or in performing operations but rather in the grouping of the operations. Without a grouping of operations the whole does not remain the same when its relation to the parts changes.

The young children performed an operation and then stopped as if unaware of the implications of the proposition they had formed. They seemed unable, or not to feel the need, to coordinate one proposition or operation with the other. It was only when at the third stage children grouped operations "The children are more because it is boys and girls $(A + A' = B)$ and boys are not so many $(A < B)$" that the invariance of the whole class was retained.

In brief Piaget holds that psychologically the inability to include classes arises from the irreversibility of the child's thought while logically it derives from his inability to group operations so that the whole remains invariant whatever the relationship between whole and part.

E. Summary

One hundred children between the ages of five and eight were tested for their ability to additively compose classes in a systematic replication of one of Piaget's studies. The results agreed with Piaget's finding of three age related stages in the development of the ability to form class inclusions. Briefly presented was Piaget's interpretation that psychologically the inability to compose classes arises from the irreversibility of the child's thought while logically it derives from the child's inability to group operations so that the total class remains invariant despite changing relations with its parts.

References

1. ELKIND, D. The development of quantitative thinking. A systematic replication of Piaget's studies. *J. Genet. Psychol.*, 1961a, **98**, 37-46.
2. ———. Children's discovery of the conservation of mass, weight, and volume: Piaget replication study II. *J. Genet. Psychol.*, 1961b, **98**, 219-227.
3. PIAGET, J. The Child's Conception of the World. London: Kegan Paul, 1929.
4. ———. The Child's Conception of Number. London: Kegan Paul, 1952. (First French edition, 1942.)
5. WELCH, L. The genetic development of the associational structures of abstract thinking. *J. Genet. Psychol.*, 1940, **56**, 175-206.

Department of Psychology
Wheaton College
Norton, Massachusetts

EDITORIAL COMMENTS

This study is one in which time spent with each subject is very brief. The investigator may want to add one or two more series of questions paralleling those given in the procedure using different sets of objects, such as ten toy horses and four toy cows. The questions would then substitute "horses" for "girls," "cows" for "boys," and "animals" for "children." The same thing can be done with paper cutouts representing apples and bananas with fruit as the superordinate category. Another alternative for making full use of the subjects, once arrangements have been made, would be to have investigators working on different studies interview each subject after he or she had been questioned for purposes of this study.

The sample can be reduced by using three groups of subjects, ages five, seven, and nine, and the size of each group can be reduced to 20. This would call for 60 subjects instead of 100. Although Elkind does not indicate the sex distribution of his subjects, it would be advisable to use children of one sex throughout or to try to obtain the same distribution of males and females in each age group. If 20 subjects are used for each age group and the sexes are divided evenly, 10 males and 10 females, a comparison by sex can be made. If the number of subjects in each group is kept constant, then the information reported in Table 1 can be the actual number of cases in each of the stages rather than the percentage.

The student would be well advised to read the following articles on the same topic in order to obtain additional ideas on how to modify the study.

Suggestions for Further Reading

L. Welch, The genetic development of the associated structures of abstract thinking. *Journal of Genetic Psychology*, 1940, 56, 175–206.

J. F. Wohlwill, Response to class inclusion questions for verbally and pictorially presented items. *Child Development*, 1968, 39, 449–465.

Z. I. Youssef and C. J. Guardo, The additive composition of classes: The role of perceptual cues. *Journal of Genetic Psychology*, 1972, *121*, 197–205.

Offprinted from THE AMERICAN JOURNAL OF PSYCHOLOGY
June 1955, Vol. 68, No. 2, pp. 274-279

THE DISTANCE-EFFECT IN THE TRANSPOSITION OF INTERMEDIATE SIZE BY CHILDREN

By HAROLD W. STEVENSON and M. E. BITTERMAN, University of Texas

After learning to discriminate between two points on some afferent continuum, the inarticulate S is more likely to transpose the solution when the testing stimuli are close to the training stimuli than when the two pairs are far apart. This *distance-effect*, which has appeared repeatedly in experiments with rat, monkey, chimpanzee, and preverbal child, is of considerable theoretical significance.[1] While it can be deduced from the nonrelational theory of Spence,[2] it contradicts a strict relational interpretation of learning which suggests that transposition should not be affected by a change in the absolute properties of the training stimuli as long as their relational properties are unaltered. In the light of recent evidence, which gives rise to serious doubts about the validity of an absolute theory, and which points to some sort of relational determination in the discriminative performance of inarticulate Ss,[3] it is important to note that the distance-effect is not entirely incompatible with a relational view. In the course of a relational solution S may learn something about the absolute properties of the training situation, and transfer of the relational solution may be impaired to the extent that those absolute properties are changed.

To account for the results of experiments on the discrimination of size by children in simple two-choice problems, a distinction between verbal (abstract) and preverbal (absolute) modes of learning has been suggested.[4] Children who were unable to verbalize the principle of solution showed the distance-effect, but older, verbal children did not. This difference was considered to support the hypothesis that the absolute "mechanisms assumed by Spence to underlie" transposition "in animals are also operative in the young child, and that with the development in

---

* Accepted for publication May 1, 1954.

[1] Harold Gulliksen, Studies of transfer of response: I. Relative versus absolute factors in the discrimination of size by the rat, *J. Genet. Psychol.*, 40, 1932, 37-51; Heinrich Klüver, *Behavior Mechanisms in Monkeys*, 1933, 1-387; K. W. Spence, Analysis of the formation of visual discrimination habits in the chimpanzee, *J. Compar. Psychol.*, 23, 1937, 77-100; M. R. Kuenne, Experimental investigation of the relation of language to transposition behavior in young children, *J. Exper. Psychol.*, 36, 1946, 471-490; Elizabeth Alberts and David Ehrenfreund, Transposition in children as a function of age, *J. Exper. Psychol.*, 41, 1951, 30-38.

[2] Spence, The differential response in animals to stimuli varying within a single dimension, *Psychol. Rev.*, 44, 1937, 430-444.

[3] E. L. Saldanha and M. E. Bitterman, Relational learning in the rat, this JOURNAL, 64, 1951, 37-53; C. B. Elam and Bitterman, The effect of an irrelevant relation on discriminative learning, *ibid.*, 66, 1953, 242-250; E. C. Wortz and Bitterman, On the effect of an irrelevant relation, *ibid.*, 66, 1953, 491-493; R. C. Gonzalez, G. V. Gentry, and Bitterman, Relational discrimination of intermediate size in the chimpanzee, *J. Compar. & Physiol. Psychol.*, 47, 1954, 385-388.

[4] Kuenne, *op. cit.*, 471-490; Alberts and Ehrenfreund, *op. cit.*, 30-38.

older children of the capacity to employ verbal responses in such . . . situations, a shift occurs to the verbal type of control."[5] To be sure, the verbal ability of the older children together with their freedom from the distance-effect may be taken as evidence of an abstract level of functioning which is qualitatively distinct from the level displayed by younger children; there is, however, no need to conclude that the younger children (or even the infrahuman Ss with which they have been classed) function *solely* on an absolute basis, despite their lack of verbal ability and their dependence on distance. Instead, the somewhat general assumption may be made that, in the course of discriminative training, the younger child (or infrahuman S) may learn, not only the relation between positive and negative stimuli, but also something about the absolute properties of those stimuli (*e.g.* the region of the afferent continuum which they occupy), and the two sets of properties may be so linked that the stability of performance will be impaired in proportion to the extent of absolute change. From this point of view the difference in the behavior of older and younger children in previous experiments reflects, not a difference between an abstract, verbally-mediated relational process and a purely absolute one, but a difference between two relational processes—one that is abstract and one that is more closely bound up with the absolute properties of particular situations.

In the experiment to be reported, preschool children were trained to choose the intermediate member of a set of three stimulus-objects which differed in size. Then tests for transposition were made with new sets of objects either one or five steps removed from the training set. The appearance of a distance-effect in this experiment could be understood on the assumption that certain relative and absolute properties of the training stimuli were functionally linked in the original solution. The mere occurrence of transposition at the near point would indicate a relational process, since in the case of the intermediate-size problem the absolute theory predicts no transposition at all,[6] while a decline in transposition at the far point would indicate some dependence on absolute properties. The appearance of a distance-effect could not, on the other hand, be understood in terms of a theoretical dichotomy between verbal and absolute processes. With Ss capable of verbal solution, there should be as much transposition at the far point as at the near. With Ss incapable of verbal solution, there should be no transposition at either point.

METHOD AND PROCEDURE

Subjects. The Ss were 24 preschool children between the ages of 4 and 6 yr. Children of this age were selected because they can learn the intermediate-size problem with relative ease, although for the most part they are unable to verbalize the basis of solution.

Apparatus. The apparatus consisted of (1) a small, brightly colored 'Easter egg,' cut from paper, which served as the goal-object; (2) a series of eight blocks differing in size which served as the discriminanda; (3) a large tray on which the three blocks used on each trial could be arranged in a horizontal row; and (4) an opaque screen which could be interposed between S and the tray while the blocks were being arranged for each trial. The tray and screen were painted flat black. The eight blocks, designated in order of size by the numbers *1–8*, were unpainted

---

[5] Kuenne, *op. cit.*, 474.

[6] Spence, The basis of solution by chimpanzees of the intermediate size problem, *J. Exper. Psychol.*, 31, 1942, 257-271; Gonzalez, Gentry, and Bitterman, *op. cit.*, 385-388.

squares cut from $\frac{1}{4}$-in. Masonite. The area of the smallest block was 4 sq. in., and the area of each successive block increased by a factor of 1.4.

Procedure. S was seated before the tray on which the three blocks to be used in training were set in the first of a predetermined, random series of horizontal arrangements. E explained: "This is a game called 'Find the Easter Egg.' See the Easter egg? And see these blocks?" (pointing to the blocks). "Well, I'm going to hide the Easter egg under one of these blocks and I want to see if you can find it. I'll hide it under the same block every time. So let's see how often you can find it." E lowered the screen and hid the egg under the block of intermediate size. Then he raised the screen, exposing the blocks to S, and said: "You pick the one you think it's under." S was allowed only one choice on each trial. If the choice was incorrect, E lowered the screen and made some encouraging comment, such as "No, it wasn't under that one. But see if you can find it next time." After correct choices the procedure was the same except that E made some such comment as "Good. You found it. Now see if you can find it again." Training continued to a criterion of five consecutive correct choices.

Immediately after S had met the criterion of learning, a second E (who had been recording the data) attracted S's attention and asked him to complete a simple drawing of a 'little boy' or a 'little girl.' S was occupied in this manner while the blocks used for training were removed from the tray and those to be used for the first test of transposition (T_1) were arranged. Approximately 2 min. after the last training trial, it was suggested to S that the 'game' be continued, and the first transposition series was begun. It consisted of six differentially reinforced trials with a set of stimuli either one (*near-test*) or five (*far-test*) steps removed from the training set. The intermediate stimulus in the transposition set was reinforced. Following these trials, S was asked to do further work on his drawing for a period of about 2 min. while the blocks employed for T_1 were replaced with those to be used in the second transposition test (T_2). T_2 was identical to T_1, except that if T_1 was a far-test T_2 was a near-test, and vice versa.

At the conclusion of T_2, S's ability to verbalize the concept of *middleness* was explored. Indicating the set of blocks used for T_2, E asked S to identify the "middle-sized" or the "medium-sized" block (both terms were tried on the assumption that some Ss might be more familiar with one than the other) and then, in sequence, the biggest, the middle-sized, the smallest, and the middle-sized blocks. Identical questions were asked about a set of blocks at the opposite end of the series. Finally, S was asked: "How did you know which one the egg would be under?" This question was rephrased in several ways to give S every opportunity to verbalize the basis of solution.

The design of the experiment is summarized in Table I. Of the 24 Ss, 12 selected at random comprised Group I and the remaining 12 comprised Group II. Half of each group was trained with blocks *1-2-3*, while the remaining half was trained with blocks *6-7-8*. For Group I, T_1 (near-test) was made with a set of blocks one step removed from the training set—*2-3-4* in the case of Ss trained with *1-2-3*, and *5-6-7* in the case of Ss trained with *6-7-8;* T_2 (far-test) was made with a set of blocks five steps removed from the training set—*6-7-8* for Ss trained with the small set and *1-2-3* for Ss trained with the large set. For Group II, T_1 was the far-test and T_2 was the near-test.

RESULTS

The training problem was learned very rapidly; the mean number of trials (including the five criterion trials) was 12.7, and the corresponding median was 11.0. The small number of trials may be explained in part by the relatively uncomplicated training conditions, and in part by the fact that if any S failed to reach the criterion of learning in 30 trials training was discontinued and he was dropped from the experiment.[7] The instruction to S that the egg would be hidden under the "same" block every time may also have contributed to the ease of learning. It should be noted that this instruction may have been taken by S either in an absolute or a relative sense, although the question of whether S was biased absolutely or rela-

TABLE I

EXPERIMENTAL DESIGN

Group	N	Training	Test	
			1	2
I (a)	6	1–2–3	2–3–4	6–7–8
I (b)	6	6–7–8	5–6–7	1–2–3
II (a)	6	1–2–3	6–7–8	2–3–4
II (b)	6	6–7–8	1–2–3	5–6–7

tively by the instructions is not relevant to the results of the experiment. Neither bias could, in itself, contribute to the distance-effect; a relative bias would be expected to facilitate transposition equally at both points, and an absolute bias would preclude transposition at both points.

Four of the 24 Ss (one in each subgroup) were able to point without error to the largest, middle-sized, and smallest blocks in the two sets used in the naming tests. There was, however, not a single S who could explain the significance of the middle-sized block for the solution of the problem. With regard to the concept of middleness, therefore, these Ss may in general be considered 'preverbal.'

On the first trial of T_1, which was a near-test for Group I, 6 of the 12 Ss in this group chose the intermediate stimulus (Table II). Of the 12 Ss in Group II, only one chose the intermediate stimulus on the first trial of T_1, which for this group was a far-test. The difference between the two groups in this respect is significant beyond the 4% level by Fisher's exact method.[8] If the two Ss in each group who made no errors on the naming test are eliminated, the significance of the results is unchanged. Of the 10 remaining Ss in Group I, 5 transposed on the first trial T_1, while not one of the 10 Ss in Group II transposed. This difference, by the exact method, is significant beyond the 2-% level. On the first trial of T_2 (far-test for Group I and near-test for Group II), not a single S in either group transposed successfully. Thus, the usual distance-effect appeared in the data for T_1, but not in the data for T_2. If within-group comparisons are made instead of between-group comparisons for the first trial of each testing series, similar results are obtained. That is, a significant distance-effect (beyond the 2-% level) appears in Group I (near-test first) but not in Group II (far-test first).

---

[7] There were five Ss in this category.
[8] R. A. Fisher, *Statistical Methods for Research Workers*, 1950, 96-97.

The results for all six trials in each test (Table II) show the same pattern as do those for the first trials alone. On T_1, Group I (near-test) made a greater number of intermediate choices than did Group II (far-test), the difference being significant at the 2-% level by Wilcoxon's test for unpaired replicates.[9] On T_2, however, the performance of the two groups did not differ significantly. Within the data for Group I (near-test first), a significant distance-effect appeared (beyond the 2-% level by Wilcoxon's test for paired replicates)[10] The distance-effect did not, however, appear in the data for Group II (far-test first).

The absence of a distance-effect in the data for Group II may be due to the fact that, in one sense, both tests for this group were far-tests.' The first test was made with a set of stimuli 'far' from the training set, and the second test with a set of

TABLE II

FREQUENCY OF INTERMEDIATE CHOICE ON THE FIRST TRIAL OF EACH TEST
AND MEAN FREQUENCY OF INTERMEDIATE CHOICE
ON ALL SIX TRIALS OF EACH TEST

	First trial				All trials			
	Test 1	Test 2	Near −far	Sig.*	Test 1	Test 2	Near −far	Sig.†
Group I	6	0	6	1%	4.50	2.75	1.75	2%
Group II	1	0	1	—	3.08	3.42	0.34	—
Near−far	5	0			1.42	0.67		
Sig.‡	4%	—			2%	—		

* Fisher's exact method.
† Wilcoxon's nonparametric method for paired replicates.
‡ Fisher's exact method for the data of the first trial and Wilcoxon's nonparametric method for unpaired replicates in the case of the combined data for all trials.

stimuli 'far' from the first testing set. For Group I, by contrast, the first test was made with stimuli near the training set, while the second test was made with stimuli far from both the previous sets. In any event, the failure of transposition in the performance of Group II on the near-test provides further evidence for the inability of the Ss to grasp the concept of intermediate size; even after differentially reinforced experience with two sets of stimuli widely separated on the size-continuum there was no evidence of a generalized intermediate preference.

The relatively high frequency of transposition in the near-test for Group I may be traced in part to the fact that the difference in size among the stimuli was very small. The results of previous experiments suggest that when the differences in size among the stimuli to be discriminated are small, solution of the problem is more likely to require some sort of relational functioning, and the probability of transposition is increased. Furthermore, when the differences within a set of stimulus-objects are small, the differences between successive sets are also small. Transposition in a near-test may, therefore, be due to the fact that S is unable to discriminate between the successive sets of stimulus-objects and continues his old mode of response on the testing trials. It may be asserted that, under such conditions, transposition in the intermediate-size problem would be predicted by any theory. To criticize the absolute theory for failing to account for transposition when the difference between sets is small is like saying that a theory is erroneous because it does not explain why Ss fail to discriminate differences which are subliminal.

[9] Frank Wilcoxon, *Some Rapid Approximate Statistical Procedures*, American Cyanamid Co., Stamford, Conn., 1946, 1-16.
[10] *Ibid.*, 1-16.

The plausibility of this argument derives from the implicit assumption that the behavior of S may be determined by certain properties of a set of stimulus-objects as a whole. In fact, however, the absolute theory makes no such assumption. If, after training with the set *1-2-3*, S responds to 2 rather than 3 only because the net excitatory value of 2 is greater than that of 3, he cannot be expected to go to 3 rather than to 2 in the set *2-3-4*. This deduction holds irrespective of the absolute sizes of the stimuli.

SUMMARY AND CONCLUSIONS

Children between the ages of four and six years were trained to discriminate the intermediate member of a set of three stimulus-objects which differed in size, and then they were tested with sets one and five steps removed from the training set. Despite the inability of the children to verbalize the basis of solution, they transposed significantly to the near set, but there was no transposition to the far set. This distance-effect cannot be traced either to a purely absolute process or to a purely relational ('verbal') one. The solution must have been in part relational (as indicated by transposition to the near set, which, in the intermediate-size problem, cannot be dealt with in absolute terms) and in part absolute (as indicated by the lack of transposition to the far set). This outcome requires a change in the interpretation suggested by previous research on the distance-effect as a function of verbal ability. Available data can no longer be encompassed by a distinction between an abstract, verbally-mediated relational process and a purely absolute one. What is required instead is a distinction between two relational processes—one that is abstract and one that is more closely bound up with the absolute properties of specific situations.

EDITORIAL COMMENTS

This study can be placed within the context of a number of studies dealing with the issue of the effects of verbal mediation on learning and discrimination. It is hypothesized that children who do not rely on verbal mediation will not transfer (transpose) as effectively what they have learned in one situation to another situation. A mediator is defined by Kendler (1962) as follows: "a response, or series of responses, which intercede between the external stimulus and the overt response to provide stimulation that influences the external course of behavior. These [mediating] responses may be overt, but they are usually presumed to be covert" (page 34). The mediator being investigated here is the internal verbal response of middle-sizedness.

The following paraphrase of the first few sentences in the article may help the student follow the remainder of the introductory material. A subject learns to make a discrimination among a series of objects that differ in a particular dimension, for example, he learns to choose the larger of two objects. We then test his response on other series of objects. If he lacks the verbal mediator for "larger than," he will transpose more effectively what he has learned in the training sessions to a test series where the objects are close in size to those of the training task than if the test series' objects are far different in size from those of the training task. This distance effect (the less effective transposition to a series far different from the training series) has been demonstrated in a variety of animals and in preverbal children. The difference in performance on near-test tasks as compared to far ones can be interpreted in several ways. One way is to suggest that the *S* learns to make an absolute response to a particular object in a pair or a series and will transfer this response to another object if that object is closely similar to the original one but will not transfer to an object that is far different from the original. More recent evidence suggests that another interpretation is possible, namely, a relational interpretation. This would hypothesize that subjects lacking the appropriate verbal mediators may be learning to discriminate between objects on the basis of the relationship between them. For subjects who lack the verbal mediator the relationship holds only for sets of objects that are similar (near) to the original but would not be applied to sets of objects that are dissimilar (far).

Modifications of Sample and Procedure

In order to test for the effects of the presence of a verbal mediator we suggest the addition of a sample of children who could be presumed to have the verbal mediator—children between the ages of eight and ten. This sample would be treated in the same way as that described in the study. Comparisons could then be made between near and far transposition and between younger and older subjects. We would predict that the older subjects would make more successful transpositions on both near and far tests and that the difference in performance between the two transposition tasks would not be as great for the older subjects.

Analysis of Results

If the older sample of *S*s is added, Table II would be expanded to include rows for Groups III and IV, and the comparisons between older and younger subjects could be made by means of a chi-square analysis.

REFERENCE
T. S. Kendler, The development of mediating responses in children. In J. C. Wright and J. Kagan (Eds.), *Basic Cognitive Process in Children. Monographs of the Society for Research in Child Development*, 1962, *28*, No. 2, 33–52.

EXPERIMENTAL ANALYSIS OF THE DEVELOPMENT
OF THE CONSERVATION OF NUMBER [1]

Joachim F. Wohlwill* *and* Roland C. Lowe

Clark University

In Piaget's theory of intellectual development (8), a central role is assigned to the child's conceptualization of the principle of "conservation," i.e., his realization of the principle that a particular dimension of an object may remain invariant under changes in other, irrelevant aspects of the situation. For instance, children who lack conservation will assert that the relative weight of two objects has changed when the shape of one of them is altered or that numerical equality between two collections of objects no longer holds following a change in the length over which they extend. This phenomenon, which has been demonstrated for a variety of other dimensions, including those of volume, area and length, represents, according to Piaget, a manifestation of the immature level of functioning of the child's mental processes and of their failure to conform to the operational structures of logical thought.

Although Piaget has described some of the precursors of this notion of conservation in children who have not yet attained this level, little is known thus far about the specific ways in which the transition from lack of conservation to the presence of conservation takes place. It is apparent, however, that an adequate explanation of this problem ultimately requires a clearer understanding of the psychological processes at work in this transition phase.

One approach to this goal is to expose children presumed to be slightly below the age of onset of conservation to selected, systematically manipulated learning experiences, designed to call into play different factors believed to be important in the development of conservation. Any differential

* Department of Psychology, Clark University, Worcester 10, Massachusetts.

[1] This investigation was supported by a research grant to the senior author from the National Science Foundation (G-8608). Nelson Butters assisted in the collection of data.

changes in the children's tendency to give conservation responses should then reflect the role played by the particular factors manipulated. At the same time, a more detailed examination of the interrelationship among different tasks involving conversation and closely related concepts should likewise extend our understanding of the nature of this problem.

The domain of number lends itself particularly well to the investigation of the development of conservation, for several reasons. First of all, recent empirical work (3, 4, 12) has given strong support to the notion that the attainment of the level of conservation marks a clearly defined stage in the formation of the number concept. Secondly, in this domain the problem of conservation can be readily related to development in other aspects of the number concept (e.g., counting, arithmetical skills, etc.), rather than constituting the somewhat isolated, *sui generis* problem which conservation appears to represent for such dimensions as weight or volume. Thirdly, and most important, the number dimension occupies a unique position in regard to the question of conservation, insofar as the number of elements contained in a particular collection is exactly identifiable by the corresponding integer; by the same token, the *fact* of conservation—i.e., that the number of a collection remains invariant under changes in the spatial arrangement of its elements—is readily verifiable, through the operation of counting. This feature creates an opportunity for assessing the role of symbolic, mediational processes, as well as of reinforcement, in the development of conservation.

This very uniqueness of the number dimension represents of course a potential limitation, as regards the applicability of the results to the problem of conservation in general. It is of considerable interest, therefore, that a rather similar investigation of the acquisition of the conservation of weight has simultaneously been carried out by Smedslund (10); its results will thus provide us with a valuable basis for comparison, as we will note in the discussion section.

Three Alternative Theoretical Views of Number Conservation

If one looks closely at the problem confronting the child in the conservation situation, several different interpretations of the acquisition of this principle suggest themselves. We may label these alternatives the reinforcement hypothesis, the differentiation hypothesis, and the inference hypothesis.

The *reinforcement hypothesis* would propose that, as a child obtains increasing experience in counting numerical collections of different types and in different arrangements, he gradually learns that alterations in the perceptual dimensions of a set do not change its number, i.e., that the same number is obtained from counting the set after as before such a change. Accordingly, systematic reinforced practice in counting rows of elements prior and subsequent to changes in the length of the rows should promote conservation.

The *differentiation* hypothesis would interpret lack of conservation in the young child as a response to an irrelevant but highly visible cue (length) which typically shows substantial correlation with that of number. The child thus has to learn to differentiate the dimension of number from this irrelevant cue. Repeated experience designed to neutralize the cue of length, and thus to weaken the association between it and the dimension of number in the child's thinking, should be expected, then, to facilitate conservation responses.

The *inference* hypothesis, finally, is based in part on Piaget's own analysis of the role of learning in the development of logical operations (9). Piaget maintains that experiential factors can only become effective, in this realm of development, to the extent that it builds on the child's previously developed structures of thought, as through the activation of a reasoning process prior to, but logically related to the one to be developed. In the case of conservation, one possible implication might be that by dint of cumulative exposure to the effects of adding an element to a collection, or subtracting one from it, the child may be led to *infer* conservation as the result of a change involving neither addition nor subtraction. This implication is supported, incidentally, by the explanations frequently voiced by children who admit conservation, e.g., "it's still the same, because you haven't taken any away."

Prior work by the senior author also bears on this last alternative. First, in the course of a sequential analysis of the development of the number concept (12), it was found that success on tasks involving simple addition and subtraction not only regularly preceded success on a task embodying the principle of conservation, but appeared, in a certain number of subjects, to lead to the emergence of conservation responses. In a subsequent pilot study (11), it was found, furthermore, that subjects given a limited set of trials involving addition and subtraction subsequently made more conservation responses than subjects given equivalent training on conservation, though the difference did not reach significance.

The results of this pilot study suggested the possibility of a more extended investigation of the development of the conservation of number, by bringing to bear each of the above-mentioned theoretical interpretations in the context of a small-scale learning experiment and determining the effectiveness of the various conditions of learning in bringing about conservation, both in a limited and a generalized sense. This is the main aim of the study to be reported, a subsidiary purpose being to provide information regarding the cross-situational generality of number conservation and its relationship to other types of number skills.

METHOD

The experiment was conducted in two sessions over two successive days (except for two *S*s, for whom the interval between sessions was two and six days, respectively). The general design called for (a) a predominantly verbal pretest, partly of a diagnostic character, to reveal *S*'s ability to deal with

TABLE I

DESIGN OF THE STUDY

Order	First Day	Order	Second Day
1.	Diagnostic Questions	1.	Training Series (trials 10 to 18)
2.	Verbal Conservation Pretest	2.	Nonverbal Conservation Posttest
3.	Pretraining in Number Matching	3.	Verbal Conservation Posttest
4.	Nonverbal Conservation Pretest		
5.	Training Series (trials 1 to 9)		

number concepts, and partly dealing specifically with conservation; (b) a "nonverbal" test of conservation given in the form of a series of multiple-choice trials; (c) a training series on tasks presumed to be related to number conservation; and finally (d) a repetition of both the nonverbal and verbal tests of conservation to provide a measure of learning or change with respect to the understanding of this notion. This design is summarized in Table 1.

Procedure

Diagnostic Questions

1. *Number Production.* S was shown a pile of red poker chips and was told, "Give me six of them."

2. *Number Equivalence.* E laid out a row of seven red chips. S was told, "Put down just as many of your chips over here (indicating an imaginary row paralleling E's row), as I have here."

3. *Number vs. Length.* E laid out a row of six blue chips extending beyond the limits of his own row of seven red chips (S's row being longer than E's). S was asked, "Who has more chips, you or I?" If he answered that he had more, but without having counted the chips, he was asked, "How do you know?"

These three questions concerned, respectively, the child's ability to (a) reproduce a particular cardinal number, (b) establish a relationship of numerical equivalence between two collections, and (c) respond to the dimension of number independent of irrelevant perceptual cues (e.g., length).

Verbal Conservation Pretest

4. Two rows of seven chips each, one blue and the other red, were placed parallel to each other so that both rows were of the same length, and the chips in one row were directly opposite those in the other. S was asked, "Who has more chips, you or I?" This question, hereafter referred to as Q, was repeated for all the items in this part.

5a. *E* then extended the red row in both directions to a length about twice that of the blue row. (Q)

5b. The red row was subdivided into two rows of four and three chips placed parallel to *S*'s blue row. (Q)

5c. The red chips were placed in a vertical pile in front of the blue row. (Q)

5d. The red chips were inserted into an opaque tube. (Q)

Question 4 served chiefly a preparatory function, i.e., to set up the following questions of conservation. Question 5a represented the main criterion of number conservation, while 5b to 5d indicate the generalizability of conservation. Accordingly, questions 5a to 5d were cumulative: if a *S* did not assert equality at any point, the remaining questions were omitted.

6. Questions 4 and 5a were repeated with 12 chips in each row instead of seven.

The suggestive nature of the questions (Q) used above ("Who has more chips, you or I?") requires comment. It should be noted that its initial use (in question 4) is in a situation where perceptual cues mitigate against the child's following the suggestion of inequality implicit in the question: the matched rows of chips afford a strong cue for direct perception of equivalence.[2] Second, the suggestion applied both in the pre- and the posttests and thus may be presumed to have played a constant role on both occasions.

Pretraining in Number Matching

The apparatus used here, shown in Figure 1, consisted of an upright panel containing three windows which had the numerals 6, 7, 8 inscribed on them from left to right. The *S*s were told they were going to play a game, in which they would find a chip hidden behind one of the windows, and that the object of the game was to get as many chips as they could. For the pretraining phase, the procedure consisted in presenting singly a series of six 5 by 5 in. cards showing six, seven, or eight colored stars arranged in simple configurations. On each trial a colored chip was hidden behind the corresponding window. *S* was informed that the number of stars on the card would tell him behind which window the chip was hidden and urged to count the stars. When *S* opened the correct window, he was instructed to remove the chip and place it onto a board at his side. He was told to fill up the board with chips; if he found "a lot" of them, he would on the following day receive a toy. The purpose of this series was to create a set in the child to respond to number, as well as to familiarize *S*s with the specific numbers shown. A correction procedure was used which involved

---

[2] All but 14 of the *S*s did in fact resist *E*'s suggestion, usually through some such answer as "we both do" or "you and me." The 14 *S*s who failed to do so were made to count the two rows, whereupon the question was again put to them. If *S* persisted in following the suggestion of inequality, *E* confronted them with the results of their counting and, if necessary, told him outright "So we both have the same, don't we?" This procedure was necessary in order to proceed to the following part, where S's prior knowledge of the equivalence of the two rows had to be presupposed.

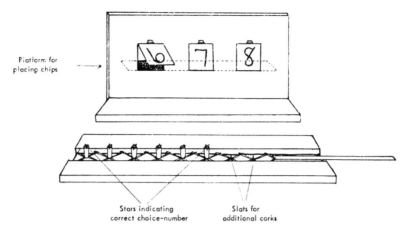

FIGURE 1—Apparatus for nonverbal conservation and training trials, showing device for presenting variable-length rows of sample numbers and display-board for choice numbers.

having Ss correct any mistakes made in counting the stars and guiding S to the correct window when, as occasionally happened, a S counted correctly but made an incorrect choice.

Nonverbal Conservation Pretest

This series consisted of three two-phase trials. Ss were presented with a row of colored stars, either six, seven, or eight in number, mounted on a set of corks which rested on a series of connected scissors-like slats. This apparatus, depicted in Figure 1, permitted lengthening or shortening the row while preserving the straight-line arrangement. E told S that he was to count the stars in order to find the chip behind the correct window. Following S's initial response, he was made to return the chip to E, who replaced it behind the same window, and then, depending on the trial, either extended or shortened the row of stars. S was allowed to count only on the first phase; he thus had to find the correct window on the second phase on the basis of the knowledge gained in the first and in the face of the perceptual changes in the row of stars.

Training

There were four conditions of training: Reinforced Practice, Addition and Subtraction, Dissociation, and Control. The three experimental conditions were designed to relate, respectively, to the reinforcement, inference, and differentiation hypotheses presented in the introduction. Each training series consisted of 18 trials, broken up into two sets of nine which were administered on successive days. The apparatus used was the same as in the conservation pretest trials.

a. *Reinforced Practice* (RP). The procedure here was the same as for the preceding conservation trials, with this modification: if *S* made an incorrect response on the second phase of the trial, he was told to count the stars, so as to find out which window he should have chosen. *E* then exposed the chip behind that window but did not allow *S* to remove the chip.

b. *Addition and Subtraction* (A&S). These trials were similar to the conservation trials, except that on two-thirds of the trials, following the *S*'s initial response after counting, *E* either added or subtracted a star at the end of the row before changing its length. The remaining third of the series consisted of straight conservation trials which were interspersed with the A&S trials.

c. *Dissociation* (Diss.). Unlike the above, these were single-phase trials, with the length of the row varying from one trial to the next over a range of four times the smallest length. *S* was urged to count the stars and open the corresponding window; if correct, he received the chip. Over the series of trials each number of stars appeared equally often at each of the different settings of length.

d. *Control*. This series of trials consisted likewise of single-phase trials as in the Dissociation condition, but the length of the row remained fixed throughout at its minimum spread.

Posttests

The *nonverbal* conservation posttest, consisting of three conservation trials as in the pretest, followed immediately upon the completion of the training trials. (For *S*s in groups Diss. and Control, *E* prefaced these trials with a remark to the effect that they would again have to find the chips twice in a row, the second time without counting.) Any *S* responding correctly on the last trial of this posttest was asked: "How did you know where to look for the chip that time?"

The *verbal* conservation posttest, consisting of a repetition of questions 4 through 6 as given in the pretest, concluded the experimental session.

At the end of the second session, each child was shown a variety of dime-store toys from which he picked one to take back with him as his "prize." Altogether, each of the sessions lasted about 20 to 25 minutes per child. The children's level of attention and motivation appeared to have remained high throughout these sessions, the "game" aspect of the situation apparently having proved effective in capturing their interest. This was reflected in their·universal eagerness to return to it when called for the second session.

Subjects

Subjects for this study were 72 kindergarten children, 35 boys and 37 girls, with a mean CA of 5 years, 10 months. (This age level was selected as one at which most children would still show lack of number conservation, while yet being old enough to be able potentially to profit from the learning experience; in other words, an interaction between learning and developmental level is presumed.) There were 18 Ss in each condition of training, Ss being assigned to their group according to a predetermined order. The four subgroups were closely matched as to their mean CA. (The range of the means was one month.)

The children were enrolled in the kindergarten classes of three public schools in Worcester, Massachusetts, located in predominantly lower-middle-class neighborhoods. They thus had been and were being exposed to a variety of activities in the area of number skills, consisting mainly of counting, number-matching, and identifying simple numerals.[3]

Results

The presentation of the results of the experiment is divided into three sections: the verbal pretest, including the diagnostic and verbal conservation questions; the learning of nonverbal conservation; and the transfer of training to the verbal posttest.

Verbal Pretest

Considering first the diagnostic questions, only one of the 72 Ss failed question 1, while four failed question 2. On question 3, however, only 20 Ss gave a correct response (i.e., based on counting the chips either before or in justification of their judgments). These results show that the Ss had adequate facility in counting and dealing with numbers symbolically in simple situations, such as producing a required number of elements and in matching two groups for number. Their success on these two tasks, however, contrasted sharply with their performance on question 3 where the task required the abstraction of number as independent from certain irrelevant perceptual cues. It should be noted that, since this question followed question 2 without a break, some Ss may have seen E take a chip from his row in setting up question 3. Thus, some of the correct responses may have been facilitated by this circumstance. In fact, nine Ss explicitly based their answers on this cue. (Control over this factor in a subsequent study did indeed result in lowering still further the number of Ss succeeding on this question, so as to equate it in difficulty with the conservation question, 5a.)

On the verbal conservation items, only nine of the 72 Ss answered correctly on question 5a. A breakdown of the incorrect responses shows that 41 Ss responded to the length of the rows, while 22 responded to the density

---

[3] The authors are greatly indebted to the principals and teachers of the Freeland, Columbus Park and Woodland Elementary Schools in Worcester, Massachusetts, for their splendid cooperation in providing subjects and facilities for this investigation. We also wish to acknowledge the assistance of the Worcester Country Day School in connection with a pilot study from which this investigation evolved.

of the elements. This tendency to regard the longer row as more numerous was also found on question 3 of the diagnostic questions.

As for the generality of the Ss' concept of number conservation, of the nine Ss who succeeded on question 5a, six extended their conservation to 5b, five to 5c, and four to 5d. On question 6, on the other hand, involving conservation for 12 elements, seven of these Ss showed conservation, in addition to one who had not responded correctly on question 5a. Thus, when conditions were qualitatively different, generalization was somewhat lower than it was when the new situation differed only in a.quantitative way.

Nonverbal Conservation Learning

Table 2 summarizes the performance of each group on the verbal and nonverbal tests of conservation, before and after the learning series.

TABLE 2

PERFORMANCE ON CONSERVATION BEFORE AND AFTER TRAINING

Condition of Training	Verbal Conservation*			Nonverbal Conservation†		
	Pretest	Posttest	Net Change	Pretest	Posttest	Net Change
A&S	1	3	+2	1.05	1.77	+.72
RP	2	3	+1	1.22	1.50	+.28
Diss.	4	2	−2	1.05	1.16	+.11
Control	2	4	+2	1.44	1.96	+.52

* Number of Ss giving correct responses on question 5a.
† Mean correct responses out of three trials.

An analysis of variance revealed no significant differences among training groups with respect to learning of nonverbal conservation ($F = 1.73$; $p > .05$ for 3 and 68 df). However, the mean over-all difference scores differed significantly from 0 ($t = 3.95$; $p < .01$), showing that for the total group as a whole conservation did increase from pre- to posttest.

A comparison between the responses of the A&S and RP groups on the conservation trials of their respective training series shows that the former Ss were correct on 48 per cent of their trials, while the latter were correct on 47 per cent. It will be recalled that only six conservation trials were given in the A&S series, while the RP series consisted wholly of 18 conservation trials for which, in addition, a correction procedure was used. Hence, direct training on conservation was no more effective than the more intermittent practice afforded on the A&S trials.

It was also found that the A&S group had greater success on the A&S trials than on the straight conservation trials: for the former, 59 per cent of the responses were correct, as compared to the 48 per cent for the conservation trials. This finding, which is consistent with the results of previous research (12), represents of course a prerequisite for the use of the A&S trials as a training experience.

The training trials under the control and dissociation condition, which involved only rote counting, were quite easy for these *S*s: a near perfect performance was the norm.

Transfer of Training to Verbal Posttest

With respect to verbal conservation, there were very few changes in any group. The number of *S*s showing conservation of number on the pretest was nine, while 12 *S*s showed it on the posttest. Two *S*s changed to conservation from the A&S group, two from the Control group, and one from the RP group. Two *S*s, in the Diss. group, who had shown conservation on the pretest, failed to do so on the posttest (cf. Table 2).

It is interesting to note that, whereas on the pretest of verbal conservation only four of the nine *S*s having conservation showed perfect extension of this concept on items 5b through 5d. on the posttest nine of the 12 *S*s showing conservation did show this extension, the remaining three *S*s belonging to the group of five who had not shown conservation on the pretest. This seems to indicate the unstable nature of the *S*s' conservation, as acquired in this situation.

Of the 12 *S*s showing conservation on question 5a of the posttest, 11 again showed conservation for 12 elements (question 6).

DISCUSSION

In this section we will consider some of the more specific implications of the results for the nonverbal conservation learning and for the transfer to the verbal test, leaving until a later section certain more general conclusions suggested by this investigation.

Nonverbal conservation learning. As regards the "learning" of conservation within the limited context of the training trials, a significant amount of improvement from pre- to posttest did take place for the group as a whole, but the lack of significant differential effects due to the conditions of training and the fact that the Control group gained more than either the Reinforced Practice or the Dissociation groups clearly prevents us from attributing beneficial effects to any specific learning condition.

The failure of the RP group to outperform the others nevertheless deserves comment. It had actually been anticipated that this group, which received essentially one continuous series of conservation trials, would as a result of this extended practice show the greatest amount of learning from pre- to posttest, although such learning might not necessarily transfer to the verbal posttest. The contrary results bear out the ineffectiveness of continued reinforced practice in bringing about conservation responses, even of a purely empirical sort (i.e., "pick the window where the chip was before"), which the above-mentioned pilot study (11) had already hinted at in a much shorter training series. Whether a still more extended series than that used in the present study might have yielded a greater amount of learning remains an open question, of course.

The greatest amount of improvement from the pre- to the posttest trials, on the other hand, took place in the A&S group, exposed to 12 addition and subtraction trials, set off against six conservation trials; these results are thus at least consistent with the possible role of a process of inference (i.e., conservation as the end-product of changes involving neither addition nor subtraction) to which the previous studies (11, 12) had pointed.[4]

Finally, as regards the virtual absence of learning in the Dissociation group, it might be suggested, in retrospect, that the very act of counting the stars interfered with directing the child's attention to the cue of length, which the condition was designed to neutralize. If so, no improvement on the conservation trials, based on explicit disregard of the biasing cue of length, would result.

Transfer to verbal conservation questions. Perhaps the major finding of the study is that none of the above procedures proved in any way effective in leading to an understanding of the principle of number conservation, such as the verbal posttest demanded. For instance, over the four training groups combined, a total of 10 Ss shifted from zero or one conservation responses on the nonverbal pretest to three on the posttest, yet these shifts did not bring with them a single change to conservation on the verbal posttest.

In explanation for this failure of the nonverbal conservation learning to transfer to the verbal posttest, one might suggest that the nonverbal learning situation favored the development of an essentially empirical rule, i.e., "the correct number remains the same as before after *E* shortens or lenthens the row," or simply "look for the chip behind the window where the chip was just previously." If this were the case, little if any transfer to the very different situation confronting the child in the verbal conservation questions would be expected. The verbalizations elicited from those Ss who made a correct response on the last posttest conservation trial lend some support to this argument: many of the Ss actually gave no meaningful explanation for their choice at all (e.g., "I just knew," or "I thought hard about the stars"), while most of the rest responded in such terms as "It was there before."

Interestingly enough, Smedslund (10), on the basis of his work on the learning of the conservation of weight, similarly argues for the very limited, nonconceptual nature of such learning. In his study, Ss were exposed to an extended series of judgments of the relative weight of two masses of plasti-

---

[4] It is worth noting that in a subsequent study, modeled closely after the present one, training with addition and subtraction again resulted in the greatest amount of improvement in (nonverbal) conservation, though the superiority over the control group still failed to be significant. In other respects, too, this study, in which the learning series was increased to 24 trials and the pre- and posttests of conservation to six trials each, yielded results which were closely comparable to those reported here.

cine, before and after one of these was deformed in shape; each judgment was reinforced by weighing the two objects on a balance. While Ss did learn to anticipate correctly the conservation of weight of the deformed object, the author feels that this learning was mainly that of an empirical fact, rather than of a logical principle, as shown both in the kind of explanations offered by the children, and in the lack of transfer of the learning to problems embodying logically equivalent principles (e.g., transitivity relationships).[5] Parenthetically, it is worth noting that in Smedslund's study a training procedure embodying addition and subtraction of matter, in a manner somewhat analogous to that of our A&S condition, yielded nearly as much learning as continued practice on conservation problems.

There remains, however, an alternative interpretation of our results. It is based on a major difference between the nonverbal and verbal tests of conservation, which might itself have accounted for the lack of transfer observed: while the nonverbal test involved a match between a given collection of elements and the corresponding, symbolically indicated number, the verbal test entailed rather the equivalence of the numerosity of two collections of elements. Thus, it is conceivable that the children did in fact learn, in their nonverbal training, that the *absolute* number of elements remained unchanged, without transfering this principle to the *relative* number of elements in two collections, in the verbal test. Implausible as this possibility may seem to a sophisticated adult, it is borne out by the total inefficacy of asking the children to count the two collections after a nonconservation response on the verbal posttest: of 23 Ss who were asked to do so, 19 persevered in their nonconservation responses when the question was repeated, immediately after ascertaining that there were seven chips in each row. Most recently, furthermore, Greco (5) has obtained clear evidence that children may show conservation in the first or absolute sense, without showing it in the second or relative sense.

Finally, the use of nonverbal methods in the investigation of children's thinking deserves brief comment. While the ineffectiveness of the nonverbal training procedures in our study may seem to cast doubt on the fruitfulness of such methods, they have been used to good advantage in several other recent studies (2, 12); moreover, the pitfalls of the verbal interrogation approach, at least as used by Piaget, have been persuasively analyzed (1,

---

[5] Perhaps more convincing evidence on this point comes from an ingenious "extinction" procedure which Smedslund (personal communication) has most recently utilized. This consisted in confronting Ss with apparent nonconservation, the weight of the deformed object being altered by surreptitiously adding or removing a small amount of plasticine. Under these circumstances Ss who had acquired conservation through their learning experience readily acceded to the lack of conservation which they seemed to be witnessing, i.e., abandoned their recently "learned" conservation. In contrast, Ss who had developed conservation spontaneously tended to invent explanations in order to reconcile this apparent contradiction, such as "we must have lost something on the floor."

Since the preparation of this paper portions of Smedslund's work (including the material of the personal communication referred to in the previous paragraph) have appeared in print (10). (Additional papers in this series, to be published in the same journal, are in press as of this writing.)

pp. 536f; 2).[6] Perhaps the central point is that it is incumbent on those applying nonverbal methods to determine, by varied and appropriate transfer tests, the breadth and depth of the child's understanding of the principles or concepts in question—a point which appears of special relevance to the application of automatic teaching methods to instruction in this and similar areas.

Conclusions

Although the predominantly negative outcome of this investigation does not allow us to give any definitive answer to the question posed at the outset, concerning the mechanisms involved in the child's acquisition of the concept of the conservation of number, a few general conclusions regarding this problem may be permissible.

First, the strong tendency of the children in this investigation to respond on the basis of differences in length in making numerical comparisons between two collections, even without the element of perceptual *change* introduced in the conservation situation (cf. question 3), lends some weight to the interpretation of lack of conservation as a failure to differentiate number from irrelevant perceptual cues, pointing to an aspect of the problem which appears to have received insufficient attention in Piaget's theoretical account of conservation.

Second, the consistent tendency across several studies for the A&S conditions to yield the most improvement in nonverbal conservation suggests that a process of inference may be operative in the development of number-conservation, even if this inference may be too limited in scope to lead to a generalized understanding of the principle. In view of the fact that children typically receive considerable experience in simple addition and subtraction in the very time period in which conservation generally appears (i.e., in late kindergarten and early first grade), this factor merits further attention.

Third, our investigation highlights the considerable gap separating the ability to *enumerate* collections by counting from a true understanding of the number concept, as it is reflected in the principle of conservation. In this respect the present results are entirely in agreement with those obtained in previous work on the development of the number concept (3, 12). Furthermore, even repeated identification of a collection with a particular number symbol, independent of length, appears to be relatively ineffective in bringing about conservation, thus raising the question of the adequacy of a mediation-theory approach to this particular aspect of concept formation.

---

[6] Relevant in this connection is a study most recently reported by Yost, Siegel, and McMichael (13), demonstrating considerable positive transfer from a nonverbal presentation of a probability-relationship problem to the corresponding verbal version of this problem as used by Piaget. These authors likewise found that by their nonverbal procedures the problem could be dealt with successfully at a much earlier age than Piaget had found, thus confirming the similar findings of Braine (2).

In a more positive vein, two suggestions for future attacks on this problem might be offered. The first is to construct a set of learning experiences which would not only be more extended but, more important, cover a wider variety of situations (i.e., stimulus materials, configurations, specific numbers involved, etc.). This would be in line with Harlow's (6) emphasis on *generalized* experience as a prerequisite for the learning of broad concepts and principles in primates as well as in man. It is plausible to suppose, in fact, that it is precisely such generalized experience—in the classroom, at play, and in other everyday activities of children of this age level—which represents the basis for the seemingly spontaneous appearance of conservation in the child.

The second suggestion is to undertake a thorough, intensive analysis of the ontogenesis of conservation in a selected number of children followed longitudinally. Special attention might be paid to the types of explanations given by the child at various stages, as well as to the stability and generalizability of conservation responses once they appear. Inhelder and Noelting, at the University of Geneva, have in fact already launched such a longitudinal project, with preliminary results that appear promising (cf. 7).

Summary

This study represents an attempt to determine more specifically the nature of the processes at work in the development of the notion of the conservation of number (invariance of number under changes in length or configuration of a collection), as studied by Piaget. The investigation was in the form of a nonverbal matching-from-sample type learning experiment, preceded and followed by verbal questions to measure the child's understanding of the conservation principle. There were four conditions of training, involving respectively the role of reinforced practice on conservation, of dissociation of biasing perceptual cues, and of inferential mechanisms based on the recognition of the effects of addition and subtraction of elements; a control group was also included. Subjects were 72 kindergarten-age children.

The results indicate an over-all increase in nonverbal conservation responses from a pre- to a posttest, within the limited context of the learning task, but they show no significant differences attributable to the conditions of training. Transfer of conservation learning to the verbal posttest was negligible under all conditions, indicating that whatever learning may have taken place was of a rather restricted type, representing perhaps more the formation of an empirical rule than the understanding of a general principle.

These results, together with additional findings pertaining to the relationship of certain number skills to conservation, are discussed in terms of their implications for the problem of the development of conservation.

REFERENCES

1. BERKO, J., & BROWN, R. *Psycholinguistic research methods.* In P. H. Mussen (Ed.), *Handbook of research methods in child development.* Wiley, 1960, Pp. 517-557.

2. BRAINE, M. D. S. The ontogeny of certain logical operations: Piaget's formulation examined by nonverbal methods. *Psychol. Monogr.,* 1959, 73, No. 4 (Whole No. 475).

3. DODWELL, P. C. Children's understanding of number and related concepts. *Canad. J. Psychol.,* 1960, 14, 191-203.

4. ELKIND, D. The development of quantitative thinking: a systematic replication of Piaget's studies. *J. genet. Psychol.,* 1961, 98, 37-46.

5. GRECO, P. Quotité et quantité. In J. Piaget (Ed.), *Structures numériques élémentaires.* Paris: Presses Univer. France, in press. (Etudes d'épistémologie génétique, XIII).

6. HARLOW, H. F. Thinking. In H. Helson (Ed.), *Theoretical foundations of psychology.* Van Nostrand, 1951. Pp. 452-505.

7. INHELDER, B., & NOELTING, G. Le passage d'un stade au suivant dans le développement des fonctions cognitives. *Proc. 15th Int. Congr. Psychol.,* Brussels, 1957, 435-438.

8. PIAGET, J. *The psychology of intelligence.* London: Routledge & Paul, 1950.

9. PIAGET, J. Apprentissage et connaissance. In J. Piaget (Ed.), *La logique des apprentissages.* Paris: Presses Univer. France, 1959. Pp. 159-188. (Etudes d'épistémologie génétique, X).

10. SMEDSLUND, J. The acquisition of conservation of substance and weight in children. *J. Scan. Psychol.,* 1961, 2, 71-87.

11. WOHLWILL, J. F. Un essai d'apprentissage dans le domaine de la conservation du nombre. In J. Piaget (Ed.), *L'apprentissage des structures logiques.* Paris: Presses Univer. France, 1959. Pp. 125-135. (Etudes d'épistémologie génétique, IX).

12. WOHLWILL, J. F. A study of the development of the number concept by scalogram analysis. *J. genet. Psychol.,* 1960, 97, 345-377.

13. YOST, P. A., SIEGEL, A. E., & McMICHAEL, J. E. Nonverbal probability judgments by young children. Paper read at Soc. Res. Child Develpm., Univer. Park, Pa., March, 1961.

EDITORIAL COMMENTS

This is the only study in this collection that involves "treatment"; that is, the subjects are provided with different kinds of training in order to determine whether the different treatments will have different effects. For the investigator this requires two sessions on two different days with each subject. Where such a pool of subjects is not available, this study will, of course, have to be passed up. However, where one can arrange for subjects who are willing to serve on two separate days, this study should prove of considerable interest.

Modifications of Sample and Procedure

It will be noted that there were four treatment groups: (1) Reinforced Practice, (2) Addition and Subtraction, (3) Dissociation, and (4) Control. Since these treatments did not result in significant improvement in the subjects' performance on conservation, the replication can be streamlined by eliminating one of the treatment groups, either the addition–subtraction or the dissociation. This will enable the investigator to examine the theoretical contrast of the reinforcement hypothesis and the inference hypothesis (if the dissociation group is eliminated) or the reinforcement hypothesis and the differentiation hypothesis (if the addition–subtraction treatment is eliminated).

The original groups consisted of 18 subjects each. This number can be reduced to 15 and the control group can be further reduced to 10. Thus the total of 72 subjects in the original study can be reduced to 40 and still allow meaningful comparisons. The addition of children one year older than those used in the original might produce some different results, since in the original study the number of subjects who showed verbal conservation on both the pretest and posttest was very small. An increase in the number of pretest conservation responses might allow for greater treatment effects.

The apparatus in Figure 1 can be readily built out of fiberboard. The part of the apparatus used in the nonverbal conservation test that permits the lengthening and the shortening of the row can be constructed out of sturdy cardboard strips, 3 to 4 inches in length and one-half inch in width, with brads to connect the strips. At each juncture where four strips come together, the cork can be affixed.

The most interesting aspect of carrying out this study is in the contact with children who, while they can count accurately, show lack of conservation of number and who are unduly influenced by the appearance of an array of objects.

Analysis of Results

The original investigators used analysis of variance to test for the significance of difference. A chi-square analysis would serve the same purpose and might be simpler for those carrying out the replication. On the verbal conservation the pretest and posttest columns would be the same as in Table 2. If the addition–subtraction or the dissociation condition has been eliminated, the data could be presented in a 3 × 2 table. On the nonverbal portion, the entries would consist of the total number of correct responses on the three trials for pretest and posttest, providing again a 3 × 2 table for chi-square analysis.

The Journal of Genetic Psychology, 1961, **98**, 37-46.

THE DEVELOPMENT OF QUANTITATIVE THINKING:
A SYSTEMATIC REPLICATION
OF PIAGET'S STUDIES*

Department of Psychology, Wheaton College, Norton, Massachusetts

DAVID ELKIND[1]

A. PROBLEM

One of the continuing needs in psychology is for the replication and refinement of significant experiments. This is especially true for the experiments of the Swiss psychologist, Jean Piaget. For over 30 years Piaget has been studying the development of children's thinking but many of his studies (Piaget, 1928; 1929; 1930) have been devoid of statistical methods and systematic design. The present replication study takes one of Piaget's later (1952) investigations as its starting point. It differs from other replications of Piaget's work (Dennis, 1940; Deutsche, 1937; Oakes, 1947) in being the first to systematically repeat Piaget's experiments on children's quantitative thinking.

Piaget assumes that the child's quantitative thinking develops and that the child's success in comparing quantity earmarks this development. By studying the child's responses to quantity comparisons of increasing difficulty Piaget sought to trace the developmental changes in the form and content of the child's quantitative thought.

In his work Piaget distinguishes three types of perceived quantity by which things can be compared without actual measurement. The simplest type of perceived quantity he speaks of as *gross*. Gross quantities are single perceived relations between objects (longer than, larger than) which are not coordinated with each other. A more complex type of quantity Piaget calls *intensive*. Intensive quantities are perceived quantity relations taken two by two (longer and wider, taller and thicker). The most complex type of perceived quantity Piaget calls *extensive*. Extensive quantities are unit relations between objects (X is half of Y, X is twice Y, etc.). Extensive quantities are logical constructs which must be attained by abstraction or

* Received in the Editorial Office on May 8, 1959.
[1] This study was carried out while the author was Research Assistant to David Rapaport at the Austen Riggs Center, and was supported by the Ford Foundation's Grant in Aid of Research.

reasoning but Piaget assumes that once attained, the subject perceives them directly as perceptually given properties of the object.

To test for success in comparing quantity Piaget had subjects of various ages compare two amounts of material several times. The two amounts were successively arranged so that sometimes a comparison of gross, sometimes a comparison of intensive, and sometimes a comparison of extensive quantity was the minimum requirement for a successful result. Experimenting with a variety of materials, including liquids, sticks, and beads, Piaget found three, age related, hierarchically ordered stages of success in comparing quantity.

Children at the first stage (usually age 4) succeeded only when a comparison of gross quantity was the minimum requirement for success. At the second stage (usually age 5) children succeeded when a comparison of gross or intensive quantity was the minimum requirement for success. Third stage children (usually age 6-7) succeeded when a comparison of gross, intensive, or extensive quantity was the minimum requirement for a successful result. Piaget reports his findings and interpretations with the aid of a great many illustrative experimental examples but without the aid of statistics.

In the present study the following hypotheses, derived from Piaget's findings, were tested: (*a*) that Age Groups (4, 5, 6-7) differ significantly in their success in comparing quantity; (*b*) that the Type of Quantity required (gross, intensive, or extensive) by the test significantly affects successful comparison; (*c*) that the Type of Material (sticks, liquids, or beads) significantly affects successful comparison; (*d*) that Age and Type of Quantity jointly affect successful comparison (the statistical test of Piaget's stages); (*e*) that Type of Quantity and Type of Material jointly affect successful comparison; (*f*) there is a positive correlation between performance on the three Types of Material; (*g*) there is a positive correlation between success in comparing quantity and performance on the W.I.S.C.

B. METHOD

1. *Subjects*

Eighty school and pre-school children living in Pittsfield, Mass., were tested. They were divided into three age groups and the number in each group was; Age four, 18, Age five, 40, Ages six and seven, 22. For each group the mean age and standard deviation were: Age four, 54.0 and 2.6 mos.; Age five, 64.9 and 2.7 mos.; Ages six and seven, 80.9 and 6.2 mos.

2. *Procedure*

All *S*s were tested on three types of material (sticks, liquids, beads) for three types of quantity. Each *S* compared two amounts of each material six times. The amounts were successively arranged[2] so that twice the minimum requirement for success was a comparison of gross quantity, twice the minimum requirement for success was a comparison of intensive quantity, and twice the minimum requirement for success was a comparison of extensive quantity. *E*'s directions were always phrased with general quantity terms like "number, amount, same," which could be taken either in the gross, intensive, or extensive sense. Because of this ambiguity in language, it was assumed that the verbal directions did not provide clues to the type of quantity that had to be compared.

The school age *S*s were tested on one material at a time àt weekly intervals. The pre-school *S*s were tested at hourly intervals in one morning. All *S*s took the tests in the same order; sticks, liquids, beads. The tests were structured as the games described below.

a. Sticks. Twenty-four wooden sticks, $\frac{1}{4}''$ square by $1\frac{1}{4}''$, were on the table. *E* "Let's pretend these sticks are candies. Your mother gives me this many candies." *E* takes six and puts them in a row at $1''$ intervals. *E* "You take just as many candies as I have, take the same number of candies as me." (Comparison of intensive quantity.)

After *S* took his "candies" *E* shortened his row and asked *S* to do the same. If *S* had taken more or less than six, shortening the rows made this immediately apparent and *E* asked him to "Make them the same." When the two rows were closed and of the same length, *E* asked "Do we both have the same number of candies?" (Comparison of gross quantity.)

E then spread his "candies" apart again but left *S*'s together so that *E*'s row was much longer but still equal in number of *S*'s row. *E* "Do we both have the same number of candies?" (Comparison of extensive quantity.)

The entire test was then repeated. The second time *E* arranged the sticks lengthwise and asked *S* to pretend the sticks were railroad cars and that they were making trains. The questions were phrased accordingly e.g., "Do we both have the same number of cars?" etc.

b. Liquids. Two 16 oz. and two 8 oz. drinking glasses were on the table beside a tall narrow glass and a pitcher of orange colored water. *E* "Let's

---

[2] Piaget's qualitative behavior analyses (Piaget, 1952) revealed what type of quantity comparison a particular arrangement required for a correct solution.

pretend we are at a party and this colored water is orangeade. Your mother pours this much for you," E fills one 16 oz. glass $\frac{3}{4}$ full, "and this much for me," E fills the outer 16 oz. glass $\frac{3}{4}$ full. E "Do we both have the same amount of orangeade to drink, do I have just as much as you?" (Comparison of gross quantity.)

Then, while S watched, E poured the "orangeade" from E's glass into the two 8 oz. glasses so that the levels in the two were equal but lower than the level in the 16 oz. glass. E "Now my drink is in these two glasses and yours is in this glass, do I have the same amount of drink as you?" (Comparison of extensive quantity.)

Next E poured all the orangeade back into the pitcher and took one 16 oz. glass and the narrow glass leaving the other containers aside. E filled the wide and narrow glasses to the same level and said "My drink is in here," pointing to the narrow glass, "and your drink is in there," pointing to the 16 oz. glass. E "Do we both have the same amount to drink, do I have as much to drink as you?" (Intensive comparison.)

E then repeated the entire procedure but the second time used the 8 oz. glass in the comparison with the narrow glass.

c. Beads. The procedures and containers used in this test were the same as those in the test with liquids. However, large wooden beads instead of colored water were used as the material. The diameter of the beads was such that only one could fit into the narrow glass at a time making a single column like an upturned necklace. The questions were phrased "Do we have the same amount of beads, do we both have the same number of beads?" etc.

d. Scoring. Each successful comparison was given a score of 1 and all failures were scored zero. For each S there was a total possible score of 18; for each type of material and for each type of quantity there was a total possible score of six.

e. Statistical analysis. To test the major hypotheses of this study—about the separate and combined effects of Age, Type of Quantity, and Type of Material on children's success in comparing quantity—a $3 \times 3 \times 3$ analysis of variance design was used (Lindquist, 1953, pp. 392-397). For two variables, Type of Quantity and Type of Material, between subject differences were controlled by testing all Ss on all types of quantity and all types of material.

C. Results[3]

1. *Age*

Piaget found that children's success in comparing quantity increased with age. In the present study the over-all F for the effects of Age was 56.88 and was significant beyond the .01 level. Table 1 gives the Age Group means, standard deviations, and t ratios. It shows that success in comparing quantities increased significantly with age in agreement with Piaget's finding.

TABLE 1

COMPARISON SCORE MEANS, STANDARD DEVIATIONS AND t RATIOS FOR THREE AGE GROUPS

Age group	N	Mean Score	SD	t
4	18	7.78	1.51	
				4.15*
5	40	9.98	2.46	
				7.87*
6-7	22	15.41	2.67	
				11.39*
4	—	—	—	

* Significant beyond the .01 level.

2. *Type of Quantity*

Piaget's illustrative examples indicated that other things being equal, the type of quantity required for a correct comparison affected children's success and failure. The same held true for the Ss of the present study. For the Type of Quantity means the over-all F was 480.90 and was significant beyond the .01 level. Statistics for the individual Type of Quantity means are given in Table 2. Gross quantities were the easiest to compare, intensive were

TABLE 2

COMPARISON SCORE MEANS, STANDARD DEVIATIONS AND t RATIOS FOR THREE TYPES OF QUANTITY
($N = 80$)

Type of quantity	Mean score	SD	t
Gross	5.98	0.71	
			3.80*
Intensive	3.51	1.83	
			5.12*
Extensive	1.47	2.47	
			5.82*
Gross	—	—	

* Significant beyond the .01 level.

[3] There was no reason to expect, from Piaget's findings, significant Age-Type of Material or Age-Type of Quantity-Type of Material interactions, and the F's for these interactions were NS.

intermediate, and extensive quantities were the hardest to compare. This result agreed with what Piaget reported.

3. *Type of Material*

In regard to the many types of material he used, Piaget concluded that success in comparing a given type of quantity of a certain type of material did not necessarily generalize to all materials. In the present study the F for Type of Material was 48.00 and was significant beyond the .01 level. Table 3, which gives the statistics for individual means, shows that liquids were the most difficult material to compare and produced the significant F. Piaget does not report this result with liquids as a specific finding but suggests

TABLE 3

COMPARISON SCORE MEANS, STANDARD DEVIATIONS AND t RATIOS FOR THREE TYPES OF
MATERIAL
($N = 80$)

Type of material	Mean score	SD	t
Stick	3.84	1.40	
			3.26*
Liquids	2.99	1.26	
			4.46*
Beads	4.15	1.50	
			1.19
Sticks	—	—	

* Significant beyond the .01 level.

comparison of a quantity of liquid may be more difficult because liquids are not broken up into perceivable units as are the sticks and beads. The present results support this assumption.

4. *Interaction of Age with Type of Quantity*

The stages Piaget reported suggested that success in comparing quantity depended jointly on age and the type of quantity comparison required by the test. In the study reported here, this joint effect was tested by the Interaction of Age with Type of Quantity. The F for this interaction was 35.57 and was significant beyond the .01 level. Table 4 shows that while the order of difficulty for types of quantity was the same at each age, the difference in difficulty decreased with age, and only the means at the four and five year levels were significantly different.

As indicated in Table 4, the majority of the four year group succeeded only with gross quantities, the majority of the five year group succeeded only with gross and intensive quantities, while most of the six and seven year group succeeded with all types of quantity. This agreed with Piaget's findings of age related, hierarchically ordered stages in the development of success in comparing quantity.

TABLE 4

COMPARISON SCORE MEANS AND F RATIOS FOR THREE TYPES OF QUANTITY FOR THREE AGE GROUPS

N	Age group	Gross	Quantity compared Intensive	Extensive	F
18	4	5.88	1.77	0.11	221.10*
40	5	6.0	3.20	0.75	220.76*
22	6-7	6.0	5.49	3.95	4.78

* Significant beyond the .01 level.

5. *Interaction of Type of Quantity with Type of Material*

The interaction F for Type of Quantity and Type of Material was 15.17 and was significant beyond the .01 level. Table 5 shows that the order of difficulty for types of quantity was the same for all materials. Table 5 also shows that the order of difficulty for types of material was the same for intensive and extensive quantities. However, the differences between the means of Type of Material were greater for intensive quantities than they were for extensive quantities. The intensive quantity of liquids, perceived in a narrow glass vs. perceived in wide glass, was unusually difficult for the Ss of this study to compare.

TABLE 5

COMPARISON SCORE MEANS AND F RATIOS FOR THREE TYPES OF QUANTITY FOR THREE TYPES OF MATERIAL
($N = 80$)

Material used in comparison	Gross	Quantity compared Intensive	Extensive	F
Sticks	1.99	1.38	.48	96.46*
Liquids	2.0	.66	.33	179.37*
Beads	1.99	1.48	.69	65.99*
F	.01	78.20*	13.20*	

* Significant beyond the .01 level.

6. *Correlations for Three Types of Material*

Implicit in Piaget's work on quantity was the assumption that the comparisons with different materials tapped the same conceptualizing ability. Table 6 gives the inter-correlations for the three materials used in the present study. The correlations were all high and significant. This result

supported Piaget's assumption that a common conceptualizing ability under-
lies children's success in comparing quantity with different materials.

TABLE 6
Comparison Score Correlations for Three Types of Material
(N = 80)

Material	Liquids	Beads
Sticks	.90*	.64*
Liquids		.76*

* Significant beyond the .01 level.

7. *Comparison and W.I.S.C. Score Correlations*

The Wechsler Intelligence Scale for Children was administered to the
62 school age children who took part in the study.[4] For each age group
(5 and 6-7) Z scores were computed for the quantity scores, and these were
used in the correlations with the IQs given in Table 7. In the sub-test correlations obtained comparison scores were used. The correlations were generally
positive, sometimes significant, and usually low. High correlations occurred
with Picture Arrangement, Arithmetic and Coding which, like the comparison of quantity, involve conceptual organizing.

TABLE 7
Quantity Comparison and W.I.S.C. Score Correlations
(N = 62)

Sub test correlations[a]			
Verbal		Performance	
Vocabulary	.31	Picture Completion	.13
Information	.47*	Picture Arrangement	.55*
Similarities	.29	Block Design	.26
Comprehension	.19	Object Assembly	.38*
Arithmetic	.35*	Coding	.42*
Digit Span	.20		

IQ Correlations[b]

Verbal	.47*
Performance	.29
Full Scale	.43*

a With obtained Comparison Scores.
b With transformed Comparison Scores.
* Significant beyond the .01 level.

D. Discussion

The results of the present study were in agreement with Piaget's finding
three, age-related, hierarchically ordered stages of success in comparing quan-

---

4 The author is indebted to Mrs. Jules Miller who administered the IQ tests.

tity. Piaget assumes that success in comparing quantity earmarks developmental changes in both the form and the content of children's quantitative thinking.

With regard to content Piaget's view is that stages of success in comparing quantity earmark steps in the development of an abstract quantity concept. Children at the first stage have only a general impression of quantity which Piaget calls a *global* conception. When forced to break down this impression and compare objects, first stage children make use of single perceived relations or gross quantity. Second stage children have a differentiated, relatively precise impression of quantity which Piaget speaks of as an *intuitive* conception. In comparing objects, second stage children deal with perceived relations two by two or with intensive quantity. At the third stage children have the impression of quantity as a logical whole which Piaget speaks of as an *abstract* conception. In comparing objects, third stage children do so in unit terms or by extensive quantity.

With regard to the form of thought Piaget assumes that stages of success in comparing quantity earmarks the development of internalized actions which he calls *mental operations*. It is the development of *logical multiplication* (the operation of coordinating two judgments of perceived relations) which makes possible the step from gross to intensive quantification and it is logical multiplication plus the development of *equation of differences* (the operation of coordinating judgments of the magnitude of differences between objects) which makes possible the step from intensive to extensive quantification.

The present study did not attempt to test Piaget's conception of the development of quantitative thinking in the child. It did seek to further substantiate some of those observations which Piaget reports and builds his conception upon.

E. Summary

Eighty school and pre-school children were divided into three Age Groups (4, 5, 6-7) and tested on three Types of Material for three Types of Quantity in a systematic replication of Piaget's investigation of the development of quantitative thinking. Analysis of variance showed that success in comparing quantities varied significantly with Age, Type of Quantity, Type of Material, and two of the interactions. Correlations for Types of Material were positive, high, and significant. Correlations of comparison scores and W.I.S.C. scores were positive, generally low, and sometimes significant.

The results were in close agreement with Piaget's finding that success in comparing quantity developed in three, age related, hierarchically ordered, stages. Piaget's conception of these stages as representing steps in the development of the form and content of children's quantitative thinking was briefly presented.

REFERENCES

1. DENNIS, W. Piaget's questions applied to Zuni and Navaho children. *Psychol. Bull.*, 1940, **37**, 520.

2. DEUTSCH, J. M. The development of children's concepts of causal relations. *Univ. Minn. Inst. Child Welf. Monog.*, 1937.

3. LINDQUIST, E. F. Design and Analysis of Experiments in Psychology and Education. Cambridge, Mass.: Riverside Press, 1953.

4. OAKES, M. E. Children's explanations of natural phenomena. *Teach. Coll. Contr. Educ.*, 1947.

5. PIAGET, J. Judgment and Reasoning in the Child. London: Routledge & Kegan Paul, 1928.

6. ———. The Child's Conception of the World. London: Routledge & Kegan Paul, 1929.

7. ———. The Child's Conception of Physical Causality. London: Routledge & Kegan Paul, 1930.

8. ———. The Child's Conception of Number. London: Routledge & Kegan Paul, 1952 (first French printing, 1941).

Department of Psychology
Wheaton College
Norton, Massachusetts

EDITORIAL COMMENTS

In this study three stages in the development of quantitative thinking are posited. Some may wish to investigate the thinking of children under age four, who are not yet thinking with quantitative concepts, even those involving *gross* quantities or single perceived relations.

Elkind lists seven hypotheses. Hypotheses (a), (b), and (d) can be combined into one hypothesis. The testing of hypothesis (g), involving the correlation between performance in comparing quantity and the score on the Wechsler Intelligence Scale, can be eliminated since the intelligence data would not be readily available and the hypothesis is only incidental to the main objectives of the study.

Modifications of Sample and Procedure

The number of subjects can be reduced to 16 in each age group. Elkind does not inform us as to the sex of his subjects. If a sex comparison is to be made it would be necessary to obtain at least 8 subjects of each sex for each age group.

In order to be able to test each subject in one sitting we would recommend that only two types of material be used, sticks and liquids. Elkind tested his school-age subjects on one material at a time at weekly intervals. Presumably this was done in order to avoid fatigue and boredom. By reducing the number of different materials this problem can be overcome. If it is possible, the subjects can be tested on one material at a time and when the group of subjects in the one location have all been tested, the investigator can start again testing each subject with the second material. If this is not possible then the twelve short tests can be administered in one sitting.

Treatment of Data

If, as suggested, only two kinds of material are used, then the mean scores obtained in the replication will be proportionately lower than those presented in the original study. The comparisons in Table 1 can also be made by a chi-square table, which would appear somewhat as follows:

Table A

Comparison of Successes for Three Age Groups

Age Group	No. of Successes						
	0	1–2	3–4	5–6	7–8	9–10	11–12
4 ($N=$)							
5 ($N=$)							
6–7 ($N=$)							

The degrees of freedom for this 7×3 table would be 14.

The information provided in Tables 2 and 4 can be presented in a different form, thus allowing for a chi-square analysis, as follows:

Table B

Comparison of Successes on Gross Quantity for Three Age Groups

Age Group	No. of Successes						
	0	1	2	3	4	5	6
4 ($N=$)							
5 ($N=$)							
6–7 ($N=$)							

Similar tables can be set up for extensive and intensive quantities.

In order to use a chi-square analysis for the different materials a table such as the following could be set up:

Table C

Comparison of Successes on Two Types of Material

	No. of Successes						
Type of Material	0	1	2	3	4	5	6
Sticks							
Liquid							

The degrees of freedom in this table would be 6.

In order to relate the performance on the three types of quantity to the two types of material a more complex table would be required, appearing somewhat as follows:

Table D

Relationship of Performance on Three Types of Quantity to Type of Material

		Type of Material	
Type of Quantity	Successes	Sticks	Liquid
Gross	0 1 2		
Extensive	0 1 2		
Intensive	0 1 2		

An analysis of sex differences could be done by tallying the number of successes without regard to type of quantity or material in a 2×2 table—success and failure against male and female.

THE DEVELOPMENT OF THE EXPECTATION OF THE NONINDEPENDENCE OF RANDOM EVENTS IN CHILDREN

GERALD GRATCH[*][1]

University of Minnesota

Many individuals, untrained in statistics, tend to predict that random events will *never* alternate regularly, e.g., HTHTHT will never occur. Further, they tend to expect that the relative frequency of a short sequence of random events will match the probability of the events, e.g., five heads will occur in 10 flips of a coin. Such observations have become salient because the recent emphasis upon statistical reasoning has led to a renewed interest in the problem of measuring "subjective" probabilities or "degrees of belief" with respect to probable events (2). In particular, many investigators have attempted to find order in how people react to random events by comparing their behavior with the statisticians' probability models, e.g., game theorists.

Working within this tradition, Lawlor (10) has impressively documented the anecdotal results mentioned in the previous paragraph. Using adolescents and young adults as Ss, he made a detailed study of their tendency to expect random events to be sequentially dependent. In one portion of his investigation, the Ss estimated the relative likelihood of occurrence of a number of sequences of heads and tails (there were 16 events in each sequence). He found that the Ss guessed that there would tend to be as many runs as possible, with the qualification that regularly alternating sequences, e.g., HTHT . . ., HHTTHHTT . . ., were very unlikely to occur. The sequences that the Ss judged to be the most probable

[*] Illinois Neuropsychiatric Institute, University of Illinois, Chicago.

[1] This study was adapted from a dissertation submitted to the University of Chicago in partial fulfillment of the requirements for the degree of Doctor of Philosophy. The author wishes to express his appreciation to Professors Helen L. Koch, Lyle V. Jones, and Frederick L. Strodtbeck for their advice and help in carrying out this research. Thanks are also due Robert A. Bassham, Prof. Raymond O. Collier, Prof. Henry W. Riecken, and Dr. William Rozeboom for their aid in the preparation of this manuscript. Finally the author wishes to thank Bernard Berkin for making it possible to study the subjects of this study.

were characterized by runs seldom longer than two, many runs, and approximately equal numbers of heads and tails. Lawlor's results are consistent with Skinner's (15) analysis of the Zenith experiments on mental telepathy in which a radio audience predicted the outcome of a sequence of five flips of a coin. Therefore, the patterns Lawlor describes would seem to characterize adults' expectations of sequences of binary events generated by a random device such as a coin.

Relatively few attempts have been made to ascertain children's ideas about probable events (1, 13). However, many psychoanalytic writers have commented upon the difficulty that children have in conceiving that events, particularly emotionally significant events, may have an uncertain frequency of occurrence. The present study investigates children's expectations about sequences of random binary events in two ways. First, it tests the simple hypothesis that, with increasing age, children will develop the kinds of sequential expectations that Lawlor found adolescents and young adults to have. Secondly, this study considers the possibility that there is a development with age in the tendency of children to utilize information about the composition of a population of binary events when they are guessing about samples of events being drawn from the population.

METHOD

Subjects. Eighty-four children from an urban public school served as subjects in the study. There were 28 who were in the first grade, 28, in the third grade, and 28, in the fifth and sixth grades. The ages of the children in the three grades were approximately 6, 9, and 11 years. Half the children at each grade level were boys. Only the age comparisons will be considered in this report because no differences were found between the sexes.

Materials. The experimental material consisted of 12 decks of nine cards each. There were two kinds of decks. Six will be referred to as the 5-4 because they were composed of five cards marked with a blue square and four cards marked with a blue diamond (the square and the diamond were equal in area). The other six decks will be referred to as the 7-2 because they were composed of seven cards marked with a blue square and two cards marked with a blue diamond. The cards were of ordinary playing card size. (Hereafter, square and diamond will be referred to by s and d.)

Procedure. Each child had the following experiences. The child was taken from his classroom and was escorted to a room in the basement of the public school by the experimenter. The child was then seated at a table with the E across from him. First, the E spread the 5-4 deck face-up in front of the child and then the 7-2 deck. The E then told the child how many ss and ds each deck contained. Next, the E showed the child how the decks generated events. He picked up the 5-4 deck and shuffled it well. He took the top card off and showed it to the child. In every case the first card shown was a d. The E repeated this demonstration four more times with the 5-4 deck. The pattern of events thus displayed to each child was *dssds*. The procedure was repeated with the 7-2 deck, and this time the sequence of events was *sssds*. Both decks were then spread face-up in front of the child again, and they remained there throughout the experiment.

The actual guessing task of the child proceeded in the following way. The *E* would take a deck of cards, tell the *S* how many *s*s and *d*s the deck contained, and would ask the child to say whether the top card would be a *s* or a *d*. (The order in which *s* and *d* was said in the instructions was alternated randomly from trial to trial.) After the child guessed, the top card was not shown but the deck was placed in front of the child, another deck was selected, and the procedure was repeated. First, the child guessed the top card in six successive 5-4 decks. Then, he guessed the top card in six successive 7-2 decks. The child recorded his guesses for himself on a sheet of paper. (The *E* did this for the *S*s of age 6.) Then, the child was asked why he guessed as he did, and finally, he was shown the 12 events.

TABLE I

THE NUMBER OF RUNS IN THE GUESSES OF THE CHILDREN WHO GUESSED
THREE SQUARES AND THREE DIAMONDS

| | NUMBER OF RUNS | | | | | |
| | 5-4 DECKS | | | 7-2 DECKS | | |
Age (years)	$r \geq 5$	$r < 5$	Total	$r \geq 5$	$r < 5$	Total
6	11	6	17	11	4	15
9	9	5	14	12	4	16
11	5	16	21	2	8	10
Total	25	27	52	25	16	41
	$\chi^2 = 8.31, p < .02, 2\,df$			$\chi^2 = 26.23, p < .001, 2\,df$		

RESULTS

Two kinds of results will be reported. Results based upon the sequential properties of the *S*s' guesses will be presented first, and then the frequency with which the *S*s guessed *s* will be reported.

Table I compares the sequences of guesses of the three age groups for those *S*s who chose *s* three times on either the 5-4 or the 7-2 decks.[2] The important

---

[2] There are some problems in the analysis of sequences of events that are introduced by the fact that the the probability of the number of the runs and the maximum run length varies with the number of events of each kind in the sequence. Because so many *S*s chose *s* three times, these problems can be by-passed by considering only those *S*s who chose *s* three times. A separate analysis will be performed upon those *S*s who chose *s* a different number of times.

comparison is the number of Ss at each age level who guessed many runs or few runs. (A run is a maximal subsequence of like events.) This comparison is made by dividing the Ss into those whose guesses, on a given kind of deck, contained at least five runs and those whose guesses contained less than five runs. (The maximum number of runs in the guesses on the 5-4 decks and on the 7-2 decks is six and the minimum number of runs is two.) The result of this comparison is highly significant. The Ss of ages 6 and 9 tended to alternate their guesses much more often than the Ss of age 11 on both the 5-4 and the 7-2 decks.

TABLE 2

A COMPARISON OF THE OBSERVED WITH THE EXPECTED NUMBER OF RUNS AMONG THE CHILDREN WHO GUESSED THREE SQUARES

		NUMBER OF RUNS					
		5-4 DECKS			7-2 DECKS		
Age (years)		$r \geq 5$	$r < 5$	Total	$r \geq 5$	$r < 5$	Total
6 + 9 ..	f(X) ...	20.0	11.0	31	23.0	8.0	31
	E(X) ..	9.3	21.7	31	9.3	21.7	31
11	f(X) ...	5.0	16.0	21	2.0	8.0	10
	E(X) ..	6.3	14.7	21	3.0	7.0	10
	P(r)* ..	0.3	0.7	1.0	0.3	0.7	1.0

$\chi^2_{(6+9)} = 17.6, p < .001, 1\ df$ $\chi^2_{(6+9)} = 28.8, p < .001, 1\ df$
$\chi^2_{(11)} = 0.35, 1\ df$

* P(r) is the probability that such a number of runs will occur by chance (5, p. 57).

Furthermore, the Ss of ages 6 and 9 alternated their guesses significantly more often than would be expected by chance on both kinds of decks whereas the Ss of age 11 did not do so on either kind of deck.[3] Table 2 shows these results. The Ss of ages 6 and 9 are treated as a single group because their choices were so similar, as can be seen from Table 1.

These results follow, in large part, from the fact that the Ss of ages 6 and 9 tended to alternate their guesses on each trial, i.e., six runs, whereas the Ss of age 11 did not. Thus, the guesses of the Ss of age 11 were like those of the Ss in Lawlor's study in that they did not alternate regularly whereas the younger Ss did. Only one S of age 11 ever alternated on each successive trial, and he did this only on the 5-4 decks. There were 10 Ss of ages 6 and 9 on the 5-4 decks and 14 Ss on the 7-2 decks who alternated their choices on each successive trial. On both kinds of decks, only 3.1

[3] The test is made by comparing the number of Ss whose guesses have five or more runs and the number of Ss whose guesses have less than five runs with the number of Ss in each category that would have been expected by chance.

Ss would have been expected to act in this way ($Z_{5-4} = 3.11$, $p < .002$; $Z_{7-2} = 4.61$, $p < .0001$).

Lawlor's results suggest the possibility that the maximum run length of children's guesses will tend to be short also. We have already seen from the previous analyses that the Ss of ages 6 and 9 tended to guess short runs, their maximum run length being either one (where there are six runs) or two (where there are five runs). The maximum run length of the Ss of age 11 was also short, but, unlike the guesses of the younger Ss, their maximum run length tended to be exactly two. On the 5-4 decks, 18 of the 21 Ss had a longest run of two; three Ss had maximum runs of three or one. The probability that the longest run will be exactly two is .60 and, therefore, since 12.6 Ss would be expected to guess a maximum run of two by chance, the observed results are significantly different from chance ($\chi^2 = 5.78$, $p < .02$, 1 df). The same trend is apparent on the 7-2 decks. Nine of the 10 Ss chose so that their maximum run length was two and six would be expected to do so by chance.

In summary, among those Ss who guessed s three times, the Ss of ages 6 and 9 tended to guess alternate events on each successive trial. The Ss of age 11 tended to guess that the events would alternate less often, but they did tend to predict that ss and ds would not occur in runs longer or shorter than two.

Most of the Ss who did not guess s three times, guessed either two or four ss. (The number of Ss who guessed zero, one, five, or six ss was five on the 5-4 decks and four on the 7-2 decks.) When the Ss who guessed some number of ss other than three are compared with respect to the number of runs in their guesses, it is found that there are no significant differences between the age groups on either the 5-4 and the 7-2 decks. Also, these Ss did not alternate the events they guessed more often than would be expected by chance. However, the longest run in their sequence of guesses also was short, i.e., the length was two. This result is obtained by

TABLE 3

MAXIMUM RUN LENGTH OF Ss WHO CHOSE SQUARE TWO OR FOUR TIMES

	MAXIMUM RUN LENGTH					
	5 - 4 DECKS			7 - 2 DECKS		
No. of Ss	$r = 2$	$r = 3, 4$	Total	$r = 2$	$r = 3, 4$	Total
f(X)	19.0	8.0	27	22.0	17.0	39
E(X)	10.8	16.2	27	15.6	23.4	39
P(r)*	.4	.6	1.0	.4	.6	1.0
	$\chi^2 = 10.38$, $p < .005$, 1 df			$\chi^2 = 4.38$, $p < .05$, 1 df		

* P(r) is the probability of the maximum run length when there are two or four ss and the six events are arranged randomly (4, p. 59).

comparing the number of Ss whose longest run was two and the number of Ss whose longest run was greater than the number expected by chance. Table 3 shows this analysis for the 5-4 and the 7-2 decks.

We are now ready to consider the frequency with which the Ss guessed *s* on the two kinds of decks. As one can anticipate from the sequential analyses, there is a significant age trend. The Ss of age 11 tended to guess *s* more often on the 7-2 decks than they did on the 5-4 decks, whereas the other two groups did not guess differentially on the two kinds of decks. Tables 4 and 5 show, respectively, the mean number of guesses of *s* of each age group on the two kinds of decks and the results of an analysis of variance of these guesses (11).

TABLE 4

THE MEAN NUMBER OF CHOICES OF SQUARE ON THE 5-4 AND 7-2 DECKS

	D E C K		
Age (years)	7 - 2	5 - 4	*Total*
6	3.25	3.32	3.28
9	3.03	3.21	3.12
11	3.43	2.82	3.12
Total	3.24	3.12	3.18

The scores in the analysis based upon error$_1$ are correlated, i.e., each S had a score based upon the number of times he guessed *s* on the 5-4 decks and another score based upon the number of times that he guessed *s* on the 7-2 decks. There is a significant interaction between deck and age. To evaluate the difference between the six means, a multiple range test was used (4, 9). Of the 15 possible pairs of comparisons, two were significant at the 5 per cent level: (a), the Ss of age 11 guessed *s* significantly more

TABLE 5

ANALYSIS OF VARIANCE OF CHOICES OF SQUARE

Source	*Sum of Squares*	*df*	*Mean Square*	*F*
Decks	0.60	1	0.60	1.02
Age Groups ✕ Decks	5.08	2	2.04	3.50*
Error$_1$	47.32	81	0.58	
Age Groups	0.96	2	0.48	
Between Ss (error$_2$)	52.68	81	0.65	
Total	106.64	167		

* Significant at the 5 per cent level.

often on the 7-2 decks than they did on the 5-4 decks; and (b), on the 5-4 decks, the *S*s of age 6 guessed *s* significantly more often than the *S*s of age 11. In the analysis based upon the "Between *S*s" error term (error₂), each *S*'s score is the sum of the number of times he chose *s* on both kinds of decks. There are no significant differences in this latter analysis.

Before discussing these results, we should note that the *S*s tended to guess *s* three times to a striking degree (as will be shown below). In the cases of the *S*s of ages 6 and 9, this "peakedness" in the distribution of their guesses of *s* follows directly from the fact that they tended to alternate their guesses of *s* and *d* on each successive trial. However, the *S*s of age 11 did not alternate more often than would be expected by chance, and yet, on the 5-4 decks, many of them guessed *s* three times. The possible implications of the behavior of the *S*s of age 11 will be discussed below. Table 6 shows that more *S*s did guess *s* three times than would be expected by

TABLE 6

THE NUMBER OF CHILDREN CHOOSING SQUARE THREE OR SOME
OTHER NUMBER OF TIMES

	NUMBER OF SQUARES					
	5 - 4 DECKS			7 - 2 DECKS		
Age (years)	$s = 3$	$s \neq 3$	Total	$s = 3$	$s \neq 3$	Total
6	17	11	28	15	13	28
9	14	14	28	16	12	28
11	21	7	28	10	18	28
Total	52	32	84	41	43	84
$P_1(s)$*	.31	.69	1.00	.31	.69	1.00
$P_2(s)$*	.30	.70	1.00	.10	.90	1.00

* $P_1(s)$ is the probability that a subject will choose square three times if he is choosing at random and is choosing *s* with a probability of one-half. $P_2(s)$ is the probability that a subject will choose square three times if he is choosing randomly and is choosing *s* with a probability equal to the probability of occurrence of square in the decks.

chance on either the assumption that they were guessing *s* and *d* equally often $[P(s_{7\text{-}2}) = P(s_{5\text{-}4}) = 0.5]$ or on the assumption that they were guessing *s* and *d* with the same probability with which they would tend to occur in the decks $[P(s_{7\text{-}2}) = 0.78; P(s_{5\text{-}4}) = 0.56]$.

With respect to the first assumption, that the *S*s were guessing *s* and *d* with the same probability, significantly more *S*s in all three age groups guessed *s* three times than would be expected by chance on the 5-4 decks. On the 7-2 decks, with the same assumption, more *S*s of ages 6 and 9 guessed *s* three times than would be expected by chance. But no more of the *S*s of age 11 guessed *s* three times than would be expected by chance, and the majority of the *S*s of age 11 chose *s* four times on the 7-2 decks. On the other hand, under the second assumption, that the *S*s were guessing *s* with the same probability with which it would occur in the two kinds of decks, more *S*s in all three age groups guessed *s* three times than would be expected by chance on both kinds of decks.

In summary, all the *S*s tended to guess so that their runs were short. However, the *S*s of ages 6 and 9 tended to alternate the events that they guessed on each successive trial on both kinds of decks. The *S*s of age 11 alternated their guesses of events less often than the younger *S*s. Secondly, the frequency of the latter *S*s' guesses of *s* and *d* tended to match the probabilities of *s* and *d* in the respective decks whereas the younger *S*s did not guess differentially on the two kinds of decks.

Finally, it should be noted that the *S*s did not seem to have any special preference for either the *s* or the *d* alternatives. If the *S*s as a group had "liked" one of the two choice-alternatives more, they would have manifested their preference on the first trial, for that deck had almost the same number of *s*s and *d*s, i.e., 5-4. On this first trial, the guesses of the three groups did not differ significantly from one another and there was no significant tendency for the *S*s to guess *s* more often than *d*. Moreover, the *S*s did not seem to display any special concern over the markings of the cards and they did not tend to say that they "liked" either *s*s or *d*s more.

Discussion and Conclusions

As a group, the *S*s of age 11 seem to have followed the "plan" of trying to guess as many *s*s and *d*s as there were in the two kinds of decks. Indeed, some of them explained their guesses in just that way. Of course, the *S*s' explanations showed that they were confusing sampling with replacement (the conditions of this experiment) with sampling without replacement (their explanation). That they were following the plan outlined above is supported by the distribution of their guesses. Considering the restrictions placed upon their guesses, namely, they had to make only six guesses on each kind of a deck and they had a tendency to choose *s* not more than twice in succession, we would expect the pattern observed: three *s*s on the 5-4 decks; four *s*s on the 7-2 decks. However, this explanation is clearly an incomplete account of the *S*s' behavior, for it does not clarify their tendency to have a maximum run length of two. The author can offer no explanation for this sequential tendency at the present time. He only can emphasize the fact that the *S*s of age 11 seem to have had the beliefs about random events that Lawlor and others have found characteristic of adults.

The remarks of the younger *S*s also suggest that, as a group, these *S*s thought they knew what was going to happen, and their comments provide a possible explanation of their behavior. Many of the *S*s of ages 6 and 9, particularly of age 6, explained that they chose in the way that they did because it was "fair." They would say such things as "the *s*s and *d*s ought to take turns," "the *s*s and *d*s take turns," etc., and we have already seen that they tended to alternate the events in this way, irrespective of the kinds of decks. Thus, it is possible that they were acting upon the basis of an expectation that the events would conform to a moral order, e.g., Piaget's view (12) that young children's thinking is "morally realistic" in the sense that they tend not to distinguish between moral rules and physical laws and to project the former upon physical events. This explanation is consistent with the fact that the older children had relatively more experience with numbers and the younger children were probably relatively more concerned with the problem of learning what is right and what is wrong. However, it is possible that their moralizing simply may have been their way of rationalizing what they did for quite different reasons (*see below*).

In support of the view that the Ss' guesses indicated how they thought the events would occur, it should be noted first that the Ss in all three groups gave every indication that they were expecting their guesses to match a set of events. The Ss frequently asked, both throughout the guessing sequence and at the end of it, about the number of guesses that they would get "right" and whether what they guessed would happen.

There are several general theories of learning and performance which deal with alternation of responses in a way which is consistent with the behavior of the Ss of ages 6 and 9. Walker's "reaction decrement" hypothesis (16), Hull's "reactive inhibition" assumption (5), and the Gestalt hypothesis that children and adults have a preference for balanced and repetitive actions and events (e.g., Koffka, 8) all predict that Ss will alternate binary responses on pairs of successive trials. These latter views would permit an interpretation of the Ss' behavior in less vague and "mentalistic" terms than have been used in the discussion above. Unfortunately, these views do not attempt to explain what will happen when Ss make longer sequences of choices. Further, they do not seem to afford any simple basis for understanding why the Ss of age 11 made different patterns of choices than the younger Ss.

Therefore, the principal conclusions of this study must be empirical rather than explanatory. Some developmental facts have been presented, and they do not appear to be isolated phenomena. For example, other studies have found that young children (1, 13) and adults (7, 10) tend to predict that binary events will alternate on successive trials. Secondly, these studies have utilized a variety of situations, e.g., which of two teams will win the game, which of two nonsense syllables will appear, which hole will the marble roll into. Further, these kinds of facts are relevant to a variety of choice situations in which Ss make sequences of choices, e.g., psychophysical experiments (e.g., 14), econometric studies, learning studies. Therefore, there would seem to be a need for further exploration of the sequences of choices of adults and children and for an incorporation of these facts into present theories of learning and performance, which for the most part have not attempted to account for such response contingencies, e.g., Estes (3).

SUMMARY

Children 6, 9, and 11 years old predicted what the top card would be of a sequence of decks of cards. The first six decks were composed of five cards marked with a blue square and four cards marked with a blue diamond. The next six decks each had seven squares and two diamonds. The children were told what the composition of each deck was. After they made all 12 guesses, they were shown what the top cards were. The Ss of ages 6 and 9 tended to alternate their choices on each successive trial on both kinds of decks. It was suggested that their behavior might have been a result of a belief on their part that the events should or would be "fair" and should or would "take turns." The Ss of age 11 did not tend to alternate their choices on each successive trial, but they did predict that *ss* and *ds* would never occur more than twice in succession. They responded to the cue of deck composition by tending to predict that *s* would occur three times on the 5-4 decks and four times on the 7-2 decks. It was suggested that their behavior could be explained in terms of their having made an attempt to match, with their predictions, the probability of *s* in the two kinds of decks. The relation between the behavior of the Ss of age 11 and adult Ss was discussed.

REFERENCES

1. COHEN, J., & HANSEL, C. E. M.   The idea of independence.   *Brit. J. Psychol.*, 1955, 46, 178-190.
2. EDWARDS, W.   The theory of decision making.   *Psychol. Bull.*, 1954, 51, 380-417.
3. ESTES, W. K., & BURKE, C. J.   A theory of stimulus variability in learning.   *Psychol. Rev.*, 1953, 60, 276-286.
4. DUNCAN, D. B.   Multiple range and multiple F tests.   *Biometrics*, 1955, 11, 1-42.
5. FELLER, W.   *An introduction to probability theory and its applications.*   New York: Wiley, 1950.
6. HULL, C. L.   *Principles of behavior.*   New York: D. Appleton-Century, 1943.
7. JARVICK, M. H.   Probability learning and a negative-recency effect in the serial anticipation of alternating symbols.   *J. exp. Psychol.*, 1951, 41, 291-297.
8. KOFFKA, K.   *The growth of the mind.*   New York: Harcourt, Brace, 1924.
9. KRAMER, C. Y.   Extension of multiple range tests to group correlated adjusted means.   *Biometrics*, 1957, 13, 13-18.
10. LAWLOR, W.   Subjective probability in sequential uncertainty situations.   Unpublished doctoral dissertation, Univer. of Chicago, 1956.
11. LINDQUIST, E. L.   *Design and analysis of experiments in psychology and education.*   Boston: Houghton Mifflin, 1953.

12. PIAGET, J. *The child's conception of the world.* London: Routledge & Kegan Paul, 1951.
13. PIAGET, J., & INHELDER, B. *La genese de l'idee de hasard chez l'enfant.* Paris: Presses Univer. De France, 1951.
14. SENDERS, V. L., & SOWARDS, A. Analysis of response sequences in the setting of a psychophysical experiment. *Amer. J. Psychol.*, 1952, 65, 358-374.
15. SKINNER, B. F. The processes involved in the repeated guessing of alternatives. *J. exp. Psychol.*, 1942, 30, 495-502.
16. WALKER, E. L. The duration and course of reaction decrement and the influence of reward. *J. comp. physiol. Psychol.*, 1956, 49, 167-175.

EDITORIAL COMMENTS

This study, along with several others (Brackbill, Kappy, & Starr, 1962; Stevenson & Hoving, 1964; Stevenson & Weir, 1959), has investigated the responses of individuals to the probability of occurrences. Each of the studies examines a different aspect of the development of expectation in a probability situation. They each document that the younger child's expectations differ from those of the older child and the adult. In this study by Gratch the younger subjects' expectations seemed to conform to a belief that "events should or would be 'fair,'" and they thus alternated their responses even when they were informed that the probability of events was not 50 percent. The older subjects seemed to attempt to match their predictions to the probability of events.

Modifications of Sample and Procedure

Since no differences were found between the sexes in Gratch's study, it is not essential to maintain the equality in the number of male and female subjects at each age level. Nevertheless, the distribution of subjects by sex at each age level should be kept roughly comparable. The number of subjects at each level could be reduced from 28 to 20.

In the experimenter's (*E*'s) demonstration of how the decks generated events Gratch indicated that the *E* picked up the 5–4 deck and shuffled it well. He took the top card off and showed it to the child. In every case the first card shown was a diamond. In a personal communication Gratch explains how he managed to show a diamond (or any other desired card) in every case. He writes: "I shuffled the cards so that the top of the cards faced *S* and the squares and diamonds faced me. Thus I could always see the bottom card and after several vigorous shufflings (4 or 5) the appropriate card was at the bottom and I would shuffle for the last time, placing the bottom card at the top in that last shuffle. It's easy to do, both in the case where you grasp the last card alone or grasp several cards along with the last one." The student investigator is advised to rehearse the whole procedure so that shuffling and the showing of the cards appear natural.

Analysis of the Data

It is possible to simplify the analysis of the data by setting up two tables presenting the number of alternations for each deck. A table combining data from the two sets of alternations would look as follows:

Age (years)	No. of alternations 5–4 decks			No. of alternations 7–2 decks		
	0–1	2–3	4–5	0–1	2–3	4–5
6						
9						
11						

The significance of the chi square would be read as having 4 degrees of freedom for each table.

The type of analysis presented in Table 2 does not contribute a great deal to the interpretation of the results. In our judgment the report would be adequate without such an analysis.

REFERENCES

Brackbill, Y., M. S. Kappy, and R. H. Starr, Magnitude of reward and probability learning. *Journal of Experimental Psychology*, 1962, *63*, 32–35.

Stevenson, H. W. and K. L. Hoving, Probability learning as a function of age and incentive. *Journal of Experimental Child Psychology*, 1964, *1*, 64–70.

Stevenson, H. W. and M. W. Weir, Variables affecting children's performance in a probability learning task. *Journal of Experimental Psychology*, 1959, *57*, 403–412.

FOUR

STUDIES IN LANGUAGE DEVELOPMENT

THE CHILD'S LEARNING OF ENGLISH MORPHOLOGY

JEAN BERKO

In this study[1] we set out to discover what is learned by children exposed to English morphology. To test for knowledge of morphological rules, we use nonsense materials. We know that if the subject can supply the correct plural ending, for instance, to a noun we have made up, he has internalized a working system of the plural allomorphs in English, and is able to generalize to new cases and select the right form. If a child knows that the plural of *witch* is *witches*, he may simply have memorized the plural form. If, however, he tells us that the plural of *gutch* is *gutches*, we have evidence that he actually knows, albeit unconsciously, one of those rules which the descriptive linguist, too, would set forth in his grammar. And if children do have knowledge of morphological rules, how does this knowledge evolve? Is there a progression from simple, regular rules to the more irregular and qualified rules that are adequate fully to describe English? In very general terms, we undertake to discover the psychological status of a certain kind of linguistic description. It is evident that the acquisition of language is more than the storing up of rehearsed utterances, since we are all able to say what we have not practiced and what we have never before heard. In bringing descriptive linguistics to the study of language acquisition, we hope to gain knowledge of the systems and patterns used by the speaker.

In order to test for children's knowledge of this sort, it was necessary to begin with an examination of their actual vocabulary. Accordingly, the 1000 most frequent words in the first-grader's vocabulary were selected from Rinsland's listing.[2] This listing

[1] This investigation was supported in part by a fellowship from the Social Science Research Council. During the academic year 1957-58 the writer completed the research while holding an AAUW National Fellowship. A dissertation on this subject was presented by the writer to Radcliffe College in April, 1958. I am indebted to Professor Roger W. Brown for his inspiration and his help in the conduct of this study.

[2] H. D. Rinsland, *A Basic Vocabulary of Elementary School Children*, New York, MacMillan, 1945.

Reprinted from WORD, Vol. 14, No. 2/3, August-December, 1958

contains the most common words in the elementary school child's vocabulary, as taken from actual conversations, compositions, letters, and similar documents.   This list was then examined to see what features of English morphology seem to be most commonly represented in the vocabulary of the first-grade child.   From this we could decide what kind of extensions we might expect the child to be able to make.   All of the English inflexional morphemes were present.

The areas that seemed to be most promising from this examination were the plural and the two possessives of the noun, the third person singular of the verb, the progressive and the past tense, and the comparative and superlative of the adjective. The pronouns were avoided both because of the difficulty involved in making up a nonsense pronoun, and because the pronouns are so few in number and so irregular that we would hardly expect even adults to have any generalized rules for the handling of new pronouns.   Moreover, we do not encounter new pronouns, whereas new verbs, adjectives, and nouns constantly appear in our vocabularies, so that the essential problem is not the same.   The past participle of regular or weak verbs in English is identical with the past tense, and since the regular forms were our primary interest, no attempt was made to test for the past participle.   A number of forms that might suggest irregular plurals and past tenses were included among the nouns and verbs.

The productive allomorphs of the plural, the possessive, and the third person singular of the verb are phonologically conditioned and identical with one another.   These forms are /-s ᴗ -z ᴗ -əz/, with the following distribution:

/-əz/ after stems that end in/s z š ž č ǰ/, e.g. *glasses, watches;*
/-s/ after stems that end in /p t k f θ/, e.g. *hops, hits;*
/-z/ after all other stems, viz. those ending in /b d g v ð m n ŋ r l/, vowels, and semivowels, e.g. *bids, goes.*

The productive allomorphs of the past are /-t ᴗ -d ᴗ -əd/, and they are also phonologically conditioned, with the following distribution:

/-əd/ after stems that end in /t d/, e.g. *melted;*
/-t/ after stems that end in /p k č f θ š/, e.g. *stopped;*
/-d/ after stems ending in voiced sounds except /-d/, e.g. *climbed, played.*

The progressive *-ing* and the adjective *-er* and *-est* do not have variants.   It might also be noted that the possessive has an additional allomorph /-ø/ ; this occurs after an inflexional /-s/ or /-z/, so that if the form *boy* is made plural, *boys*, the possessive of that plural form is made by adding nothing, and indicated in writing only by the addition of an apostrophe: *boys'*.

The children's vocabulary at the first-grade level also contains a number of words that are made of a free morpheme and a derivational suffix, e.g. *teacher*, or of two free morphemes, e.g. *birthday*. The difficulties encountered in this area are many. First, it might be noted that there are not many contrasts, i.e., not many cases of the same derivational suffix being added to different bases to produce forms of like function. Although *beautiful* and *thankful* both appear on the list, it does not seem that these examples are numerous enough for us to expect a young child to be able to append *-ful* to a new noun in order to produce an adjective. Word derivation and compounding are furthermore often accompanied by changes in stress and pronunciation, so that the picture is additionally complicated. There seemed to be enough examples of the stress pattern ′ ‵, as in *bláckboàrd* as against *bláck boárd*, and of the diminutive-affectionate *-y*, the adjectival *-y*, and the agentive *-er* to warrant testing for these forms.

So far as the general picture is concerned, all speakers of the language are constrained to use the inflexional endings and apply them appropriately to new forms when they are encountered. We are not so often called upon to derive or compound new words, although by the time we are adults we can all to some extent do this. From the children's actual vocabulary we were able to make an estimate of the kind of morphological rules they might be expected to possess, and from these items a test could be constructed. It was noted, moreover, that in the child's vocabulary there are a number of compound words, like *blackboard* and *birthday*. It is entirely possible to use a compound word correctly and never notice that it is made of two separate and meaningful elements. It is also possible to use it correctly and at the same time have a completely private meaning for one or both of its constituent elements. In order to see what kind of ideas children have about the compound words in their vocabularies, it was decided to ask them directly about a selected number of these words.

Within the framework of the child's vocabulary, a test was devised to explore the child's ability to apply morphological rules to new words. He was called upon to inflect, to derive, to compound, and, lastly, to analyse compound words.

MATERIALS AND PROCEDURE

In order to test for the child's use of morphological rules of different types and under varying phonological conditions, a number of nonsense words were made up, following the rules for possible sound combinations in English.   Pictures to represent the nonsense words were then drawn on cards.   There were 27 picture cards, and the pictures, which were brightly colored, depicted objects, cartoon-like animals, and men performing various actions.   For reasons that will be discussed later, several actual words were also included.   A text, omitting the desired form, was typed on each card.   An example of the card to test for the regular plural allomorph in /-z/ can be seen in figure 1.

The subjects included 12 adults (seven women and five men), all of whom were college graduates.   Many of these adults had also had some graduate training.   All were native speakers of English.

The child subjects were obtained at the Harvard Preschool in Cambridge and the Michael Driscoll School, in Brookline, Massachusetts.   At the Preschool, each child was brought to the experimenter, introduced, and told that now he was going to look at some pictures.   The experimenter would point to the picture and read the text.   The child would supply the missing word, and the item he employed was noted phonemically. After all of the pictures had been shown, the child was asked why he thought the things denoted by the compound words were so named.   The general form of these questions was "Why do you think a blackboard is called a blackboard?" If the child responded with "Because it's a blackboard", he was asked, "But why do you think it's called that?" The children at the preschool ranged between four and five years in age.   Twelve girls and seven boys were asked all items of the completed test, and two groups, one of three boys and three girls and one of five boys and three girls, were each asked half of the inflexional items in preliminary testing.

At the Driscoll School, the experimenter was introduced to the class and it was explained that each child was going to have a turn at looking at some pictures.   The procedure from this point on was the same as for the Preschool.   All children in the first grade were interviewed.   There were 26 boys and 35 girls in this group. Ages ranged from five and one half to seven years.

Figure 1.   The plural allomorph in /-z/.

The following is the order in which the cards were presented. Included is a statement of what was being tested, a description of the card, and the text that was read. Pronunciation is indicated by regular English orthography; a phonemic transcription is included for first occurrences of nonsense words.

1. Plural. One bird-like animal, then two. "This is a wug /wʌg/. Now there is another one. There are two of them. There are two ———·"

2. Plural. One bird, then two. "This is a gutch /gʌč/. Now there is another one. There are two of them. There are two ———·"

3. Past tense. Man with a steaming pitcher on his head. "This is a man who knows how to spow /spow/. He is spowing. He did the same thing yesterday. What did he do yesterday? Yesterday he ———."

4. Plural. One animal, then two. "This is a kazh /kæž/. Now there is another one. There are two of them. There are two ———·"

5. Past tense. Man swinging an object. "This is a man who knows how to rick /rik/. He is ricking. He did the same thing yesterday. What did he do yesterday? Yesterday he ———."

6. Diminutive and compounded or derived word. One animal, then a miniscule animal. "This is a wug. This is a very tiny wug. What would you call a very tiny wug? This wug lives in a house. What would you call a house that a wug lives in?"

7. Plural. One animal, then two. "This is a tor /tɔr/. Now there is another one. There are two of them. There are two ———·"

8. Derived adjective. Dog covered with irregular green spots. "This is a dog with quirks /kwərks/ on him. He is all covered with quirks. What kind of dog is he? He is a ——— dog."

9. Plural. One flower, then two. "This is a lun /lʌn/. Now there is another one. There are two of them. There are two ———·"

10. Plural. One animal, then two. "This is a niz /niz/. Now there is another one. There are two of them. There are two ———·"

11. Past tense. Man doing calisthenics. "This is a man who

knows how to mot /mat/.   He is motting.   He did the same thing yesterday.   What did he do yesterday?   Yesterday he ———·"

12. Plural.   One bird, then two.   "This is a cra /kra/.   Now there is another one.   There are two of them.   There are two ———·"

13. Plural.   One animal, then two.   "This is a tass /tæs/.   Now there is another one.   There are two of them.   There are two ———·"

14. Past tense.   Man dangling an object on a string.   "This is a man who knows how to bod /bad/.   He is bodding.   He did the same thing yesterday.   What did he do yesterday?   Yesterday he ———·"

15. Third person singular.   Man shaking an object.   "This is a man who knows how to naz /næz/.   He is nazzing.   He does it every day.   Every day he ———·"

16. Plural.   One insect, then two.   "This is a heaf /hiyf/.   Now there is another one.   There are two of them.   There are two ———·"

17. Plural.   One glass, then two.   "This is a glass.   Now there is another one.   There are two of them.   There are two ———·"

18. Past tense.   Man exercising.   "This is a man who knows how to gling /gliŋ/.   He is glinging.   He did the same thing yesterday.   What did he do yesterday?   Yesterday he ———·"

19. Third person singular.   Man holding an object.   "This is a man who knows how to loodge /luwdž/.   He is loodging.   He does it every day.   Every day he ———·"

20. Past tense.   Man standing on the ceiling.   "This is a man who knows how to bing /biŋ/.   He is binging.   He did the same thing yesterday.   What did he do yesterday?   Yesterday he ———·"

21. Singular and plural possessive.   One animal wearing a hat, then two wearing hats.   "This is a niz who owns a hat.   Whose hat is it?   It is the —— hat.   Now there are two nizzes.   They both own hats.   Whose hats are they?   They are the —— hats."

22. Past tense.   A bell.   "This is a bell that can ring.   It is ringing.   It did the same thing yesterday.   What did it do yesterday?   Yesterday it ———·"

23. Singular and plural possessive.   One animal wearing a hat, then two.   "This is a wug who owns a hat.   Whose hat is it?   It is the —— hat.   Now there are two wugs.   They both own hats.   Whose hats are they?   They are the —— hats."

24. Comparative and superlative of the adjective.   A dog with a few spots, one with several, and one with a great number. "This dog has quirks on him.   This dog has more quirks on him. And this dog has even more quirks on him.   This dog is quirky. This dog is ——· And this dog is the ——·"

25. Progressive and derived agentive or compound.   Man balancing a ball on his nose.   "This is a man who knows how to zib /zib/.   What is he doing?   He is ——·   What would you call a man whose job is to zib?"

26. Past tense.   An ice cube, then a puddle of water.   "This is an ice cube.   Ice melts.   It is melting.   Now it is all gone. What happened to it?   It ——·"

27. Singular and plural possessive.   One animal wearing a hat, then two.   "This is a bik /bik/ who owns a hat.   Whose hat is it?   It is the —— hat.   Now there are two biks.   They both own hats.   Whose hats are they?   They are the —— hats."

28. Compound words.   The child was asked why he thought the following were so named.   (No pictures were used for these items.)

a. afternoon	h. handkerchief
b. airplane	i. holiday
c. birthday	j. merry-go-round
d. breakfast	k. newspaper
e. blackboard	l. sunshine
f. fireplace	m. Thanksgiving
g. football	n. Friday

It took between ten and fifteen minutes to ask a child all of these questions.   Even the youngest children have had experience with picture books, if not actual training in naming things through pictures, and no child failed to understand the nature of the task before him.   It was, moreover, evident that a great number of these children thought they were being taught new English words.   It was not uncommon for a child to repeat the nonsense word immediately upon hearing it and before being asked any questions. Often, for example, when the experimenter said "This is a *gutch*", the child repeated, "*Gutch*".   Answers were willingly, and often insistently, given.   These responses will be discussed in the following section.

RESULTS

Adult answers to the inflexional items were considered correct answers, and it was therefore possible to rate the children's answers.   In general, adult opinion was unanimous—everyone said the plural of *wug was *wugs, the plural of *gulch was *gulches; where the adults differed among themselves, except in the possessives, it was along the line of a common but irregular formation, e.g. *heaf became *heaves in the plural for many speakers, and in these cases both responses were considered correct. If a child said that the plural of *heaf was *heafs or *heaves /-vz/, he was considered correct.   If he said *heaf (no ending), or *heafès /-fəz/, he was considered incorrect, and a record was kept of each type of response.

SEX DIFFERENCES

The first question to be answered was whether there is a sex difference in the ability to handle English morphology at this age level.   Since it seemed entirely possible that boys entering the first grade might be on the whole somewhat older than girls entering the first grade, it was necessary to equate the two groups for age.

TABLE 1. DISTRIBUTION OF CHILDREN AT EACH AGE LEVEL
FOR COMPARISON OF THE SEXES

Age	Boys	Girls	Total
4	2	2	4
4:6	1	1	2
5	2	2	4
5:6	2	2	4
6	10	10	20
6:6	6	6	12
7	5	5	10
Total:	28	28	56

The children were divided into seven age groups.   Since at each of these levels there were more girls than boys, a random selection of the girls was made so that they would match the boys in number.   The distribution of these ages and the number in each group can be seen in Table 1.   This distribution was utilized only in comparing the performance of the boys with that of the girls; in all other instances, the responses of the entire sample were considered.

The groups of 28 boys and 28 girls thus selected were compared with one another on all inflexional items.   The chi square criterion with Yates' correction for small frequencies was applied to each item, and on none was there a significant difference between the boys' and girls' performance; boys did as well as girls, or somewhat better, on over half the items, so that there was no evidence of the usual superiority of girls in language matters. From this it would appear that boys and girls in this age range are equal in their ability to handle the English morphology represented by these items.

AGE DIFFERENCES

Having ascertained that there was no difference between boys' and girls' answers, we combined the sexes and went on to compare the younger with the older children.   The oldest children at the Preschool were five years old, and the youngest at the Driscoll School were five and one half years, so that the dividing line was made between the schools.   Chi square corrected for small frequencies was again applied to all inflexional items.   First graders did significantly better than preschoolers on slightly less than half of these.   The differences can be seen in Table 2.

TABLE 2. AGE DIFFERENCES ON INFLEXIONAL ITEMS

Item	Percentage of correct pre-school answers	Percentage of correct first-grade answers	Significance level of difference
Plural			
glasses............	75	99	.01
wugs.............	76	97	.02
luns.............	68	92	.05
tors.............	73	90	—
heafs............	79	80	—
cras.............	58	86	.05
tasses............	28	39	—
gutches...........	28	38	—
kazhes............	25	36	—
nizzes............	14	33	—

Item	Percentage of correct pre-school answers	Percentage of correct first grade answers	Significance level of difference
Progressive			
zibbing..........	72	97	.01
Past Tense			
binged............	60	85	.05
glinged..........	63	80	—
ricked...........	73	73	—
melted...........	72	74	—
spowed..........	36	59	—
motted..........	32	33	—
bodded..........	14	31	.05
rang.............	0	25	.01
Third Singular			
loodges..........	57	56	—
nazzes...........	47	49	—
Possessive			
wug's............	68	81	—
bik's............	68	95	.02
niz's............	58	46	—
wugs'...........	74	97	.02
biks'...........	74	99	.01
nizzes'..........	53	82	.05

FORMATION OF THE PLURAL.

The nature of the children's answers can best be seen through a separate examination of the noun plurals, the verbs, and the possessives. The percentage of all children supplying correct plural endings can be seen in Table 3. The general picture indicates that children at this age have in their vocabularies words containing the three plural allomorphs $/\text{-s} \infty \text{-z} \infty \text{-əz}/$, and can use these words. The real form *glasses* was included here because we knew from a pretest that children at this age generally did not make correct application of $/\text{-əz}/$ to new forms, and we wanted to know if they used this form with a common English word. Evidently they have at least one actual English model for this contingent plural. In uncomplicated cases children at this age can also extend the use of these forms to new words requiring

/-s/ or /-z/, as indicated by the high percentage of right answers for *wug* and *bik*, a form used in the pretest and answered correctly by a correspondingly high number of children.   For the items *wugs* and *glasses* there is, moreover, a significant difference between the younger and older groups.   For *glasses* they progress from 75 % right to 99 % right in the older group, a change that is significant at the 1 % level.   The few wrong answers in these cases were either a complete failure to respond, or a repetition of the word in its singular form.

TABLE 3. PERCENTAGES OF CHILDREN SUPPLYING CORRECT PLURAL FORMS

Item	*Allomorph*	*Per Cent Correct*
glasses	/-əz/	91
wugs	/-z/	91
luns	/-z/	86
tors	/-z/	85
heáfs, -ves	/-s/ /-z/	82
cras	/-z/	79
tasses	/-əz/	36
gutches	/-əz/	36
kazhes	/-əz/	31
nizzes	/-əz/	28

From this it is evident that however poorly children may do on extensions of the rule for forming the plural of *glass*, they do have this item in their vocabulary and can produce it appropriately.   During the period from preschool to the first grade, those who do not have this item acquire it.   They can also extend the rule for the addition of the /-s/ or /-z/ allomorph where the more general rules of English phonology dictate which of these forms must be used.   During this period they perfect this knowledge.

The ability to add /-z/ to *wug* and /-s/ to *bik* does not alone prove that the child possesses the rule that tells which allomorph of the plural must be used: English phonology decrees that there cannot be a consonant cluster */-kz/ or */-gs/.   The final consonant determines whether the sibilant must be voiced or unvoiced.   The instances in English where there is a choice are after /l/ /n/ and /r/, and after a vowel or semivowel.   Thus we have minimal pairs like: *ells : else ; purrs : purse ; hens : hence ; pews : puce.*   In forming the plural of *wug* or *bik*, the child has only to know that a dental sibilant must be added; which one it is is determined by the invariant rules of combination that govern English consonant clusters.   If, however, he is faced with a new word ending in a vowel, semivowel, /-l/, /-n/, or /-r/, he himself must make the choice, because so far as English phonology is concerned he could add either a /-z/ or an /-s/ and still have a possible English word. We would expect him, therefore, to have more difficulty forming the plural of a new word ending in these sounds than in cases where phonology determines the form of the sibilant.   These problems are represented by the forms *cra, *tor, and *lun.   As table 3 indicates, the percentages correct on these items were respectively 79, 85, and 86.   The difference between performance on *wug and *cra is significant at the 5 % level.

During the period from preschool to the first grade, they improved markedly in their handling of *cra and *lun.   The differences between the younger and older groups were significant at the 5 % level.   The case of adding /-s/ to these forms did not, however, arise.   The child here, as in so many other stages of language learning, answered complexity with silence: the wrong answers were invariably the unaltered form of the singular.

The only other case to be answered correctly by the majority of the children was *heaf.   Since adults responded with both *heafs and *heaves /-vz/, both of these answers were considered correct.   It must be noted that although 42 % of the adults gave *heaves as the plural of this item, employing what would amount to a morphophonemic change along the lines of: *knife: knives; hoof: hooves*, only three children out of a total of 89 answering this item said *heaves; 9, or 10 % added nothing, and an additional four formed the plural with the wrong allomorph, i.e. they said /hiyfəz/, treating the /-f/ as if it belonged to the sibilant-affricate series.   /f/ is, of course, phonetically very similar to /s/, and one of the questions suggested by this problem was whether children would generalize in the direction of phonetic similarity across functional boundaries—/f/ is distinguished phonetically from /s/ only in that it is grave and /s/ is acute. It is, so to speak, no more different from /s/ than /z/ is, and it is as similar to /s/ as /ž/ is to /z/.   It does not, however, so far as English phonology is concerned, function like /s š z ž č ǰ/, none of which can be immediately followed by another sibilant within the same consonant cluster.   The high percentage of correct items indicates that /f/ had already been categorized as belonging to the consonant class that can be followed by /-s/, and the phonetic similarity between /f/ and the sibilants did not lead the children to generalize the rule for the addition of the /-əz/ allomorph in that direction.   Nor could any irregular formation be said to be productive for children in this case, although for adults it apparently is.

The proportion of children's right answers suddenly drops when we come to the form *lass.   As table 3 shows, 91 % of these children when given the form *glass* could produce the form *glasses*.   When given the form *lass, a new word patterned after *glass*, only 36 % could supply the form *lasses.   The picture becomes progressively worse with the other words ending in sibilants or affricates, and by the time we reach the form *niz, only 28 % answered correctly.   *Niz of these four, is the only one that ends in a sound that is also the commonest plural allomorph, /-z/, and the children did the worst on this item.   What is of additional interest, is that on these four items there was no significant improvement from the preschool to the first grade. The difference between performance on *cra, the worst of the other items, and *lass, the best of these, was significant at the .1 % level. Again, the wrong answers consisted in doing nothing to the word as given.   It must be noted, however, that in these items, the children delivered the wrong form with a great deal of conviction: 62 % of them said "one *lass, two *lass" as if there were no question that the plural of *lass should and must be *lass.   From this it is evident that the morphological rules these children have for the plural are not the same as those possessed by adults: the children can add /-s/ or /-z/ to new words with a great deal of success.   They do not as yet have the ability to extend the /-əz/ allomorph to new words, even though it has been demonstrated that they have words of this type in their vocabulary.

The form "kazh" /kæž/ was added here once again to see in what direction the children would generalize.   /ž/, although it is in the sibilant-affricate group, is very rare as a final consonant in English: it occurs only in some speakers' pronunciation of *garage*, *barrage*, and a few other words.   As table 3 indicates, the children treated this word like the others of this group.   It might also be noted here that for the forms *gutch and *kazh, some few children formed the plural in /-s/, i.e., /gʌčs/ and /kæžs/.   10 % did this for *gutch, and 5 % for *kazh, errors that indicate that the phonological rules may not yet be perfectly learned.   What is clearest from these answers dealing with the plural is that children can and do extend the /-s/ and /-z/ forms to new words, and that they cannot apply the more complicated /-əz/ allomorph of the plural to new words.

VERB INFLEXIONS

The children's performance on the verb forms can be seen in Table 4. It will be observed that the best performance on these items was on the progressive, where they were shown a picture of a man who knew how to *zib and were required to say that he was *zibbing. The difference between *zibbing and the best of the past tense items, *binged, was significant at the 5 % level. The improvement from the younger to the older group was significant at the 1 % level; fully 97 % of the first graders answered this question correctly. Here, there was no question of choice, there is only one allomorph of the progressive morpheme, and the child either knows this -ing form or does not. These results suggest that he does.

The results with the past tense forms indicate that these children can handle the /-t/ and /-d/ allomorphs of the past. On *binged and *glinged the percentages answering correctly were 78 and 77, and the older group did significantly better than the younger group on *binged.

TABLE 4. PERCENTAGES OF CHILDREN SUPPLYING
CORRECT VERB FORMS

Item	Allomorph	Percentage Correct
Progressive		
zibbing	/-iŋ/	90
Past Tense		
binged, bang	/-d ∽ æ ← (i)/	78
glinged, glang	/-d ∽ æ ← (i)/	77
ricked	/-t/	73
melted	/-əd/	73
spowed	/-d/	52
motted	/-əd/	33
bodded	/-əd/	31
rang	/æ←(i)/	17
Third Singular		
loodges	/-əz/	56
nazzes	/-əz/	48

Actually, the forms *gling and *bing were included to test for possible irregular formations.   A check of English verbs revealed that virtually all in -ing form their past tense irregularly: *sing: sang; ring: rang; cling: clung*, and many others.   The only -ing verbs that form a past tense in -ed are a few poetic forms like *enringed, unkinged,* and *winged,* and onomotopoeias like *pinged* and *zinged.*   Adults clearly felt the pull of the irregular pattern, and 50 % of them said *bang or *bung for the past tense of *bing, while 75 % made *gling into *glang or *glung in the past.   Only one child of the 86 interviewed on these items said *bang.   One also said *glang, and two said *glanged—changing the vowel and also adding the regular /-d/ for the past.

The great majority on these forms, as well as on *ricked which requires /-t/, formed the past tense regularly.   There was a certain amount of room for variation with the past tense, since there is more than one way of expressing what happened in the past. A number of children, for example said "Yesterday he was *ricking".   If on these occasions the experimenter tried to force the issue by saying "He only did it once yesterday, so yesterday once he—?"   The child usually responded with "once he was *ricking".   Taking into account this possible variation, the percentages right on *rick, *gling and *bing represent a substantial grasp of the problem of adding a phonologically determined /-t/ or /-d/.

With *spow the child had to choose one or the other of the allomorphs, and the drop to 52 % correct represents this additional complexity.   Several children here retained the inflexional /-z/ and said /spowzd/, others repeated the progressive or refused to answer.   No child supplied a /-t/.

On *motted, the percentage correct drops to 33, although the subjects were 73 % right on the real word *melted,* which is a similar form.   On *bodded they were 31 % right, and on *rang* only 17 % right.   The older group was significantly better than the younger on *rang* and *bodded.   What this means is that the younger group could not do them at all—not one preschool child knew *rang—* and the older group could barely do them.   What emerges here is that children at this age level are not able to extend the rule for forming the past tense of *melted* to new forms.   They can handle the regular /-d/ and /-t/ allomorphs of the past in new instances, but not /-əd/.   Nor do they have control of the irregular past form *rang,* and consequently do not form new pasts according to this pattern, although adults do.   They have the /-əd/ form in actual words like *melted*, but do not generalize from it. With *ring*, they do not have the actual past *rang*, and, therefore no model for generalization. In the children's responses, the difference between *spowd*, the worst of the items requiring /-t/ or /-d/, and *motted*, the best requiring /-əd/ is significant at the 2 % level. For *mot and *bod, the wrong answers, which were in the majority, were overwhelmingly a repetition of the present stem: "Today he* *bods; yesterday he *bod.* " To the forms ending in /-t/ or /-d/ the children added nothing to form the past.

The third person singular forms require the same allomorphs as the noun plurals, /-s ⌢ -z ⌢ -əz/, and only two examples were included in the experiment. These were *loodge and *naz, and required the /-əz/ ending. 56 % of the children supplied the correct form *loodges, and 48 % supplied *nazzes. The wrong answers were again a failure to add anything to the stem, and there was no improvement whatsoever from the younger to the older group on these two items.

FORMATION OF THE POSSESSIVE

The only other inflexional items statistically treated were the regular forms of the possessive. The percentages of children supplying right answers can be seen in Table 5. In the singular, the problem was the same as for the noun plurals, and the children's difficulty with the /-əz/ form of the allomorph is mirrored in the low percentage who were able to supply *niz's /-əz/ when told "This is a *niz* who owns a hat. Whose hat is it? It is the ————?" For *bik's there was a significant improvement at the 2 % level between the younger and older groups. For *niz's the younger group did no worse than the older group.

In the plural possessives the problem is somewhat different: since these words are already regularly inflected, the possessive is formed by adding a morphological zero. The children did not add an additional /-əz/ to these forms, and in the case of *nizzes', they erred on the side of removing the plural *-es*, e.g. for the plural possessive they said simply *niz in those cases where they gave the wrong answers.

It was the adults who had difficulty with the plural possessives: 33 % of them said *wugses /-zez/ and *bikses /-sez/, although none said *nizeses /-əzəz/. This is undoubtedly by analogy with proper nouns in the adults' vocabulary, i.e., no adult would say that if two dogs own hats, they are the *dogses /-zəz/ hats. However an adult may know a family named *Lyons*, and also a family named *Lyon*.   In the first instance, the family are the *Lyonses* /-zəz/ and if they own a house, it is the *Lyonses'* /-zəz/ house; in the second instance, the family are the *Lyons* and their house is the *Lyons'* /-nz/.   The confusion resulting from competing forms like these is such that some speakers do not make this distinction, and simply add nothing to a proper noun ending in /-s/ or /-z/ in order to form the possessive—they say "it is Charles' /-lz/ hat".   Some speakers seem also to have been taught in school that they must use this latter form.   It seems likely that the children interviewed had not enough grasp of the /-əz/ form for these niceties to affect them.

TABLE 5. PERCENTAGES OF CHILDREN' SUPPLYING
CORRECT POSSESSIVE FORMS

Singular	*Allomorph*	*Percentage Correct*
wug's	/-z/	84
bik's	/-s/	87
niz's	/-əz/	49
Plural		
wugs'	/-ø/	88
biks'	/-ø/	93
nizzes'	/-ø/	76

ADJECTIVAL INFLEXION

The last of the inflexional items involved attempting to elicit comparative and superlative endings for the adjective *quirky. The child was shown dogs that were increasingly *quirky and expected to say that the second was *quirkier than the first, and that the third was the *quirkiest.   No statistical count was necessary here since of the 80 children shown this picture, only one answered with these forms.   Adults were unanimous in their answers.   Children either said they did not know, or they repeated the experimenter's word, and said "*quirky, too".   If the child failed to answer, the experimenter supplied the form *quirkier, and said "This dog is *quirky.   This dog is *quirkier.   And this dog is the ——?"   Under these conditions 35 % of the children could supply the -*est* form.

DERIVATION AND COMPOUNDING

The children were also asked several questions that called for compounding or deriving new words. They were asked what they would call a man who *zibbed for a living, what they would call a very tiny *wug, what they would call a house a *wug lives in, and what kind of dog a dog covered with *quirks is.

Adults unanimously said that a man who *zibs is a *zibber, using the common agentive pattern -er. Only 11 % of the children said *zibber. 35 % gave no answer. 11 % said *zibbingmàn and 5 % said *zíbmàn, compounds that adults did not utilize. The rest of the children's answers were real words like *clown* or *acrobat*.

For the diminutive of *wug, 50 % of the adults said *wuglet. Others offered *little* *wùg, *wuggie, *wugelle, and *wugling. No child used a diminutive suffix. 52 % of the children formed compounds like *bàby* *wùg, *teény* *wùg, and *little* *wùg. Two children, moreover, said a little *wug is a *wig, employing sound symbolism—a narrower vowel to stand for a smaller animal. For the house a *wug lives in, 58 % of the adults formed the asyntactic compound *wúghoùse. Others said *wuggery, *wúgshoùse, and *wúghùt. Again, no child used a suffix. The younger children did not understand this question, and where the older children did, they formed compounds. 18 % of the first graders said *wughoùse. Others suggested *birdcage* and similar forms. What emerges from this picture is the fact that whereas adults may derive new words, children at this stage use almost exclusively a compounding pattern, and have the stress pattern ′‵ at their disposal: the adults unanimously said that a dog covered with *quirks is a *quirky dog. 64 % of the children formed the compound *quírk dòg for this item, and again, no child used a derivational suffix.

ANALYSIS OF COMPOUND WORDS

After the child had been asked all of these questions calling for the manipulation of new forms, he was asked about some of the compound words in his own vocabulary; the object of this questioning was to see if children at this age are aware of the separate morphemes in compound words. The children's explanations fall roughly into four categories. The first is identity: "a blackboard is called a *blackboard* because it is a blackboard." The second is a statement of the object's salient function or feature: "a blackboard is called a *blackboard* because you write on it." In the third type of explanation, the salient feature happens to coincide with part of the name: "a blackboard is called a *blackboard* because it is black;" "a merry-go-round is called a *merry-go-round* because it goes round and round". Finally, there is the etymological explanation given by adults—it takes into account both parts of the word, and is not necessarily connected with some salient or functional feature: "Thanksgiving is called *Thanksgiving* because the pilgrims gave thanks."

Of the children's answers, only 13 % could be considered etymological. Most of their answers fell into the salient-feature category, while the number of identity responses dropped from the younger to the older group. Many younger children offered no answers at all; of the answers given, 23 % were identity. Of the older children, only 9 % gave identity answers, a difference that was significant at the 1 % level.

As we might expect, the greatest number of etymological responses—23 %—was given for *Thanksgiving*, which is an item that children are explicitly taught. It must be noted, however, that despite this teaching, for 67 % of the children answering this item, Thanksgiving is called *Thanksgiving* because you eat lots of turkey.

The salient feature answers at first seem to have the nature of an etymological explanation, in those instances where the feature coincides with part of the name—72 % of the answers, for instance, said that a fireplace is called a fireplace because you put fire in it. When the salient feature does not coincide with part of the name, however, the etymological aspects also drop out. For *birthday*, where to the child neither the fact that it is a day nor that it is tied to one's birth is important, the number of functional answers rises: it is called *birthday* because you get presents or eat cake. Only 2 % said anything about its being a day.

The child approaches the etymological view of compound word through those words where the most important thing about the word so far as the child is concerned coincides with part of the name. The outstanding feature of a merry-go-round is that it does, indeed, go round and round, and it is the eminent appropriateness of such names that leads to the expectation of meaningfulness in other compound words.

Although the number of etymological explanations offered by the children was not great, it was clear that many children have what amounts to private meanings for many compound words. These meanings may be unrelated to the word's history, and unshared by other speakers.   Examples of this can be seen in the following.

"An airplane is called an *airplane* because it is a plain thing that goes in the air."

"Breakfast is called *breakfast* because you have to eat it fast when you rush to school."

"Thanksgiving is called that because people give things to one another." (Thingsgiving?)

"Friday is a day when you have fried fish."

"A handkerchief is a thing you hold in your hand, and you go 'kerchoo'."

These examples suffice to give the general nature of the private meanings children may have about the words in their vocabulary. What is of additional interest, is that the last explanation about the handkerchief was also offered by one of the college-graduate adult subjects.

We must all learn to handle English inflexion and some of the patterns for derivation and compounding.   So long as we use a compound word correctly, we can assign any meaning we like to its constituent elements.

CONCLUSION

In this experiment, preschool and first grade children, ranging from four to seven years in age, were presented with a number of nonsense words and asked to supply English plurals, verb tenses, possessives, derivations and compounds of those words.   Our first and most general question had been: do children possess morphological rules?   A previous study of the actual vocabulary of first graders showed that they know real items representing basic English morphological processes.   Asking questions about real words, however, might be tapping a process no more abstract than rote memory.   We could be sure that our nonsense words were new words to the child, and that if he supplied the right morphological item he knew something more than the individual words in his vocabulary: he had rules of extension that enabled him to deal with new words.   Every child interviewed understood what was being asked of him.   If knowledge of English consisted of no more than the storing up of many memorized words, the child might be expected to refuse to answer our questions on the grounds that he had never before heard of a *wug, for instance, and could not possibly give us the plural form since no one had ever told him what it was. This was decidedly not the case. The children answered the questions; in some instances they pronounced the inflexional endings they had added with exaggerated care, so that it was obvious that they understood the problem and wanted no mistake made about their solution. Sometimes, they said "That's a hard one," and pondered a while before answering, or answered with one form and then corrected themselves. The answers were not always right so far as English is concerned; but they were consistent and orderly answers, and they demonstrated that there can be no doubt that children in this age range operate with clearly delimited morphological rules.

Our second finding was that boys and girls did equally well on these items. Sometimes the girls had a higher percentage of right answers on an item, and more often the boys did somewhat better, but no pattern of differences could be distinguished and the differences were never statistically significant. These findings are at variance with the results of most other language tests. Usually, girls have been shown to have a slight advantage over boys. In our experiment, girls were no more advanced than boys in their acquisition of English morphology. Since other language tests have not investigated morphology *per se*, it is easy enough to say that this is simply one area in which there are no sex differences. A reason for this lack of difference does, however, suggest itself: and that is the very basic nature of morphology. Throughout childhood, girls are perhaps from a maturational point of view slightly ahead of the boys who are their chronological age mates. But the language differences that have been observed may be culturally induced, and they may be fairly superficial. Some social factor may lead girls to be more facile with words, to use longer sentences, and to talk more. This can be misleading. A girl in an intellectual adult environment may, for instance, acquire a rather sophisticated vocabulary at an early age. This should not be taken to mean that she will learn the minor rules for the formation of the plural before she learns the major ones, or that she will necessarily be precocious in her acquisition of those rules. What is suggested here is that every child is in contact with a sufficiently varied sample of spoken English in order for him to be exposed at an early age to the basic morphological processes. These processes occur in simple sentences as well as in complex ones. Practice with a limited vocabulary may be as effective as practice with an extensive vocabulary, and the factors that influence other aspects of language development may have no effect on morphological acquisition. Since, moreover, this type of inner patterning is clearly a cognitive process, we might expect it to be related to intelligence more than to any other feature. Unfortunately, there were no IQs available for the subjects, so that a comparison could not be made, and this last must remain a speculation.

Our next observation was that there were some differences between the preschoolers and the first graders. These were predominantly on the items that the group as a whole did best and worst on: since no child in the preschool could supply the irregular past *rang*, and a few in the first grade could, this difference was significant. Otherwise, the improvement was in the direction of perfecting knowledge they already had—the simple plurals and possessives, and the progressive tense. The answers of the two groups were not qualitatively different: they both employed the same simplified morphological rules. Since this was true, the answers of both groups were combined for the purpose of further analysis.

Children were able to form the plurals requiring /-s/ or /-z/, and they did best on the items where general English phonology determined which of these allomorphs is required. Although they have in their vocabularies real words that form their plural in /-əz/ in the age range that was interviewed they did not generalize to form new words in /-əz/. Their rule seems to be to add /-s/ or /-z/, unless the word ends in /s z š ž č ǰ/. To words ending in these sounds they add nothing to make the plural—and when asked to form a plural, repeat the stem as if it were already in the plural. This simplification eliminates the least common of the productive allomorphs. We may now ask about the relative status of the remaining allomorphs /-s/ and /-z/. For the items like *lun or *cra, where both of these sounds could produce a phonologically possible English word, but not a plural, no child employed the voiceless alternant /-s/. This is the second least common of the three allomorphs. The only places where this variant occurred were where the speaker of English could not say otherwise. So far as general English phonology is concerned a /-z/ cannot in the same cluster follow a /-k-/ or other voiceless sound. Once the /-k-/ has been said, even if the speaker intended to say /-z/, it would automatically devoice to /-s/. The only morphological rule the child is left with, is the addition of the /-z/ allomorph, which is the most extensive: the /-əz/ form for him is not yet productive, and the /-s/ form can be subsumed under a more general phonological rule.

What we are saying here is that the child's rule for the formation of the plural seems to be: "a final sibilant makes a word plural". The question that arises is, should we not rather say that the child's rule is: "a voiceless sibilant after a voiceless consonant and a voiced sibilant after all other sounds makes a word plural." This latter describes what the child actually does.   However, our rule will cover the facts if it is coupled with a prior phonological rule about possible final sound sequences.   The choice of the voiceless or voiced variant can generally be subsumed under phonological rules about final sound sequences; the exceptions are after vowels, semivowels, and /l- n- r-/.   In these places where phonology leaves a choice, /-z/ is used, and so the child's conscious rule might be to add /-z/.   It would be interesting to find out what the child thinks he is saying—if we could in some way ask him the general question, "how do you make the plural?"

Another point of phonology was illustrated by the children's treatment of the forms *heaf* and *kazh.*   It was demonstrated here that the children have phonological rules, and the direction of their generalizations was dictated by English phonology, and not simple phonetic similarity.   /-ž/ is a comparatively rare phoneme, and yet they apparently recognized it as belonging to the sibilant series in English, and they rarely attempted to follow it with another sibilant.   The similarity between /f/ and the sibilants, did not, on the contrary cause them to treat it as a member of this class.   The final thing to be noted about *heaf* is that several children and many adults said the plural was *heaves.*   This may be by analogy with *leaf: leaves.*   If our speculation that the /-z/ form is the real morphological plural is right, there may be cases where instead of becoming devoiced itself, it causes regressive assimilation of the final voiceless consonant.

The allomorphs of the third person singular of the verb and the possessives of the noun are the same as for the noun plural, except that the plural possessives have an additional zero allomorph. These forms were treated in the same way by the children, with one notable exception: they were more successful in adding the /-əz/ to form possessives and verbs than they were in forming noun plurals.   They were asked to produce three nearly identical forms: a man who *nazzes;* two *nizzes;* and a *niz's* hat.   On the verb they were 48 % right; on the possessive they were 49 % right, and on the noun plural they were only 28 % right.   The difference between their performance on the noun plural and on the other two items was significant at the 1 % level. And yet the phonological problem presented by these three forms was the same. For some reason the contingent rule for the formation of the third person singular of the verb and for the possessive is better learned or earlier learned than the same rule for the formation of noun plurals. The morphological rule implies meaning, and forms that are phonologically identical may be learned at different times if they serve different functions. These forms are not simply the same phonological rule, since their different functions change the percentage of right answers. Perhaps the child does better because he knows more verbs than nouns ending in /s z š ž č ǰ/, and it is possible that he has heard more possessives than noun plurals. It is also possible that for English the noun plural is the least important or most redundant of these inflexions. This is a somewhat surprising conclusion, since nouns must always appear in a singular or plural form and there are ways of avoiding the possessive inflexion: it is generally possible to use an *of* construction in place of a possessive—we can say *the leg of the chair* or *the chair's leg*, or *the chair leg* although in cases involving actual ownership we do not say *of*. A sentence referring to *the hat of John* sounds like an awkward translation from the French. And no child said it was *the hat of the *niz*. The children's facility with these forms seems to indicate that the possessive inflexion is by no means dying out in English.

Of the verb forms, the best performance was with the present progressive: 90 % of all the children said that a man who knew how to *zib* was *zibbing*. Undoubtedly, children's speech is mostly in the present tense, and this is a very commonly-heard form. Explanations of what is happening in the present all take this form. "The man is *running*" — or *walking* or *eating* or *doing* something. The additional point is that the *-ing* forms are not only very important; this inflexion has only one allomorph. The rules for its application are completely regular, and it is the most general and regular rules that children prefer.

The children's handling of the past tense parallels their treatment of the plurals, except that they did better on the whole with the plurals. Again, they could not extend the contingent rule. Although they have forms like *melted* in their vocabulary, they were unable to extend the /-əd/ form to new verbs ending in /t d/. They treated these forms as if they were already in the past. They applied the allomorphs /-d/ and /-t/ appropriately where they were phonologically conditioned, and only /-d/ to a form like *spow*, where either was possible.   This suggests that their real morphological rule for the formation of the past is to add /-d/, and under certain conditions it will automatically become /-t/. Many adult speakers feel that they are adding a /-d/ in a word like *stopped;* this may be because of the orthography, and it may be because they are adding a psychological /-d/ that devoices without their noticing it.

Whereas the children all used regular patterns in forming the past tense, we found that for adults strong pasts of the form *rang* and *clung* are productive.   Since virtually all English verbs that are in the present of an *-ing* form make their pasts irregularly, this seemed a likely supposition.   Adults made *gling* and *bing* into *glang* and *bang* in the past.   New words of this general shape may therefore be expected to have a very good chance of being treated according to this pattern — real words like the verb *to string* for instance, have been known the vacillate between the common productive past and this strong subgroup and finally come to be treated according to the less common pattern.   The children, however, could not be expected to use this pattern since we could not demonstrate that they had the real form *rang* in their repertory.   They said *ringed*.   At one point, the experimenter misread the card and told the child that the bell *rang*. When the child was asked what the bell did, he said, "It *ringed*." The experimenter then corrected him and said, "You mean it *rang*."   The child said that was what he had said, and when asked again what that was, he repeated, "It *ringed*," as if he had not even heard the difference between these two allomorphs.   Perhaps he did not.

The adults did not form irregular pasts with any other pattern, although a form was included that could have been treated according to a less common model.   This was the verb *mot*, which was of the pattern *cut* or *bet*.   There are some 19 verbs in English that form their past with a zero morpheme, but this group does not seem to be productive.

The cases of *gling*, which became *glang* in the past and *mot*, which became *motted* suggest some correlates of linguistic productivity.   About nineteen verbs in English form their past tense with a zero allomorph.   About 14 verbs form their past like *cling*, and seven follow the pattern of *ring*.   Within these last two groups there are words like *win*, which becomes *won* and *swim*, which becomes *swam*.   We can also find words similar to *win* and *swim* that are quite regular in the past: *pin* and *trim*. But virtually all of the verbs that end in *-ing* form their past in *-ang* or *-ung*.   There are approximately 10 of these *-ing* verbs.

The productivity of the *-ang* and *-ung* forms proves that new forms are not necessarily assimilated to the largest productive class.   Where a small group of common words exist as a category by virtue of their great phonetic similarity and their morphological consistency, a new word having the same degree of phonetic similarity may be treated according to this special rule.   *Ox* : *oxen* is not similarly productive, but probably would be if there were just one other form like *box* : *boxen*, and the competing *fox* : *foxes* did not exist.   With **mot*, the zero allomorph is not productive because although it applies to more cases than are covered by the *-ing* verbs, it is not so good a rule in the sense that it is not so consistent.   The final /-t/, which is the only common phonetic element, does not invariably lead to a zero allomorph, as witness *pit* : *pitted*, *pat* : *patted*, and many others.

Although the adults were uniform in their application of *-er* and *-est* to form the comparative and superlative of the adjective, children did not seem to have these patterns under control unless they were given both the adjective and the comparative form. With this information, some of them could supply the superlative.

Derivation is likewise a process little used by children at this period when the derivational endings would compete with the inflexional suffixes they are in the process of acquiring.   Instead, they compound words, using the primary and tertiary accent pattern commonly found in words like *bláckboàrd*.

The last part of the experiment was designed to see if the children were aware of the separate elements in the compound words in their vocabulary.   Most of these children were at the stage where they explained an object's name by stating its major function or salient feature: a blackboard is called a *blackboard* because you write on it.   In the older group, a few children had noticed the separate parts of the compound words and assigned to them meanings that were not necessarily connected with the word's etymology or with the meaning the morphemes may have in later life. Not many adults feel that Friday is the day for frying things, yet a number admit to having thought so as children.

These last considerations were, however, tangential to the main problem of investigating the child's grasp of English morphological rules and describing the evolution of those rules.   The picture that emerged was one of consistency, regularity, and simplicity.   The children did not treat new words according to idiosyncratic pattern.   They did not model new words on patterns that appear infrequently.   Where they provided inflexional endings, their best performance was with those forms that are the most regular and have the fewest variants.   With the morphemes that have several allomorphs, they could handle forms calling for the most common of those allomorphs long before they could deal with allomorphs that appear in a limited distribution range.

Massachusetts Institute of Technology.

EDITORIAL COMMENTS

GLOSSARY OF TECHNICAL TERMS

Morphology: An aspect of grammar dealing with the modifications of words to signal changes in meaning.

Morphemes: The smallest significant or meaningful element in speech. Words, as ordinarily understood, are free morphemes, for example, house, run, red. Prefixes and suffixes are bound morphemes.

Allomorphs: Two or more morphemes that have different phonetic structure but which signal the same meaning. In Berko's article the three allomorphs in English that signal the plural are /-əz/ /-s/ and /-z/ and the three allomorphs that signal past tense are /-əd/ /-t/ /-d/.

Modifications of Sample and Procedure

The adult sample can be smaller than 12 subjects and can be used both to obtain a standard measure and to train the investigator to listen carefully for the different sound patterns (phonemes) that are critical in the study.

From our experience the section of the investigation dealing with the child's understanding of the derivation of the compound words is the least revealing and can be dropped from the investigation.

Berko used 19 subjects (12 girls and 7 boys) who were in preschool, and 61 subjects (35 girls and 26 boys) in the first grade. It would be well to increase slightly the group of preschoolers—12 boys and 12 girls would be adequate. The first-grade population could be reduced to a sample of the same size. If several investigators work together, the sample could be increased to 15 or 20 in each age-sex group or, if preferred, three age groups could be tested: 3½–4½, 5½–6½, and 8–9.

If the number of subjects is kept the same in each sex group it would not be necessary to eliminate any subjects, as Berko did, in order to make a comparison of the performance of boys and girls. Also if the samples are of the same size in each group, Table 2 can be set up with simple frequencies instead of percentages. Totals for each of the subclasses, namely, plural, progressive, past tense, and so on, could be tallied, thus emphasizing the possible subclass differences.

A further variation could be introduced if a population of adults or children learning English as a second language is available. These subjects can reveal the particular difficulties encountered by speakers of different native languages in learning English. These subjects could be compared with the various age groups of English-speaking children or adults.

Stages in Language Development and Reading Exposure*

CAROL CHOMSKY

Harvard University

This study of language acquisition in children between the ages of six and ten investigates their linguistic competence with respect to complex aspects of English syntax. Thirty-six children were tested for knowledge of nine complex syntactic structures. Five of the structures proved to be acquired in sequence, revealing five developmental stages in acquisition of syntax. The nature of specific disparities between adult grammar and child grammar are discussed, and the gradual reduction of these disparities as the children's knowledge of their native language increases is traced. Of particular interest is the regular order of acquisition of structures, accompanied by wide variation in rate of acquisition in different children.

The author then examines the relationship between the children's exposure to the written language and the rate of linguistic development. The relations between linguistic development, a variety of reading measures, IQ, and socioeconomic status are discussed. The results show a strong correlation between a number of the reading exposure measures and language development.

* The work reported on here was performed under Office of Education Grant No. OEG-1-9-090055-0114 (010), Project No. 9-A-055, while the investigator was a Scholar at the Radcliffe Institute. This article was prepared from the final report to the Office of Education. The full report, "Linguistic Development in Children from 6 to 10," is available through the Educational Resources Information Center (ERIC) Document Reproduction Service (EDRS), as described in a forthcoming issue of *Research in Education*.

This article summarizes a study of linguistic development in elementary school children. We investigated children's knowledge of specific aspects of the syntax of English by testing their comprehension of a number of complex structures. Thirty-six children between the ages of six and ten were in the experiment.

Because the study deals with only a few structures, it does not attempt a general description of children's grammar within the age group. Rather it traces the acquisition of specific structures, revealing interesting aspects of the children's construction of implicit grammatical rules. In addition, the results demonstrate a common order of acquisition of syntactic structures among the different children though there is considerable variation in age of acquisition. This shared order of acquisition of structures defines a developmental sequence of linguistic stages through which all of the children apparently pass. The ages at which different children reach the stages vary, but the sequence of stages appears to be the same for all.

A second aspect of the study investigated the children's exposure to the written language through independent reading and through listening to books read aloud. We examined the relation between rate of linguistic development and exposure to written materials as a source of complex language inputs. Our results show a strong correlation between a number of the reading exposure measures and language development. A description of the reading study is presented in the second half of this paper, along with a discussion of the relations between language development, the reading measures, IQ, and socioeconomic status (SES).

This article is a brief and fairly condensed description of a detailed study of several years duration, and it attempts to present only the highlights of the methods employed and the experimental results.

Framework for the Linguistic Study

The approach and methods of the linguistic study, described in detail in an earlier work,[1] demonstrate the feasibility of dealing with the learning of complex syntactic structures in children beyond age five through psycholinguistic experimentation. This is the period of life when a major portion of the task of language acquisition has already been accomplished. The child of six exhibits

[1] C. Chomsky, *The Acquisition of Syntax in Children from 5 to 10* (Cambridge, Mass.: M.I.T. Press, 1969).

competence with his* native language that appears to approach adult competence. Discrepancies between his grammar and adult grammar are rarely revealed in spontaneous speech.

Our purpose is to explore areas in which the six-year-old's knowledge of his language falls short of adult knowledge, and to gain information about the course of the acquisition of this knowledge as the child matures. In order to deal with these questions, we must first characterize what we mean by knowing one's language. In effect, we must answer the question, "What is the nature of the information that is acquired by the child?"

Clearly, speakers of a language do not draw from a memorized list of all possible sentences in their language each time they wish to say something. Rather, they can understand and produce sentences they have never before heard. Indeed, a major portion of language usage consists of sentences that have never been spoken or written before, for example, this sentence or the closing sentence of any article in today's *New York Times*.

Given any sequence of words we care to devise, speakers can recognize whether or not the sequence constitutes a sentence in their language. This creative aspect of language use rests on the fact that we have learned the system of rules for making sentences. This system is called the grammar of the language.

Our knowledge of these rules is implicit. We are not taught them, and we would be hard put to state even the smallest fraction of them. Yet they govern our speech.

Because these rules are implicit, they cannot be observed directly. While the linguist is interested in the speaker's *competence* (the underlying system of rules), he has access only to a speaker's *performance* (the way he uses the rules). Thus, various aspects of performance are used to reveal the nature of underlying competence.

What the child learns, then, as he acquires his language is a complex system of rules that enables him to understand and produce the sentences of his language. He internalizes these rules from what he hears by a process of active construction as yet little understood. His earliest utterances, even at the stage when he begins to put two words together to make sentences, are innovative and rule-governed. The evidence shows he is not just repeating fragments of sentences he has heard, but is creating his own sentences according to grammatical rules

* The masculine form of pronoun is used here for convenience; children of both sexes were included in the study. [Ed.]

that he continually constructs and revises. The acquisition of syntax, then, means developing the rule system, restructuring it with increasing maturity as new evidence is added, and eventually producing an internalized grammar which accords with the facts of the language.

How do we employ this framework in studying knowledge of syntax in children between six and ten? The problem is that by age six, a child's grammar, as revealed in his spontaneous speech, does not appreciably differ from adult grammar. In order to identify areas in which child and adult grammar are different, we must actively probe the child's linguistic performance. We can do this by selecting complex grammatical structures—structures that we consider difficult and, therefore, likely to be acquired relatively late. Children's comprehension and interpretation of these complex structures yield evidence of the syntactic rules employed and the way in which these rules diverge from adult grammar. As we gain information about these child/adult discrepancies, we may contribute to existing notions about language complexity.

On the basis of current linguistic work we are able to select a variety of complex structures that appear to be likely candidates for late acquisition. Potential structures would include those "which deviate from a widely established pattern in the language, or whose surface structure is relatively inexplicit with respect to grammatical relationships, or even simply those which the linguist finds particularly difficult to incorporate into a thorough description." . . .[2] Some candidate structures turn out to be difficult for the children; some do not.

In order to be useful in this study, a structure must also lend itself to testing with young children. We must be able to devise an operational test of comprehension that even six-year-olds can handle. This requirement sharply limits the selection. The structures and tests finally decided upon are the result of much planning and revision, a good bit of pilot testing, and many discards.

Altogether, we tested nine structures with the children. Of these, only the five that turned out to be relevant to an overall developmental sequence will be discussed here. The other four were either too easy (all the children knew them), too hard (known by only one or two of the children), or they elicited scattered responses not relevant to the sequence. Almost twice as many structures were tested as turned out to be relevant to the developmental sequence. Thus, we proceeded by collecting a range of structures, testing them all, and leaving it up to the experimental results to reveal a sequence, if any.

---

[2] Chomsky. p. 4.

We did have some theoretical and practical guidelines to aid in selecting structures. For example, the relation between two structures, *promise* and *ask*, is such that a given order of acquisition is implied on theoretical grounds. *Promise* is simpler than *ask* along a particular scale of complexity, and ought therefore to be acquired first. And, in fact, evidence of this predicted order was found in an earlier experiment with *promise* and *ask*.[3] These two structures, then, were useful to include because of their strong potential for yielding developmental data. Another construction, *easy to see*, is recognized as a good indicator of grammatical development from the work of several different researchers[4] although no experimental work has yet suggested a relationship to other constructions in terms of order of acquisition. This construction was included because of its stability as a measure. Use of the measure led to identical conclusions in three separate experiments. Beyond considerations of this sort, there was little to go on. In fact all of the constructions tested with children for the first time here resulted from a fortuitous intersection of complex structures and experimental techniques that could measure them.

Our experimental procedure elicited information from the children by direct interview. By age six, the children are willing to be questioned, play games, carry out tasks, manipulate toys, identify pictures, and engage in conversation. The interview was carried out informally and, for the children, was interesting play.

Our test group ranged in age from five years old, when many of the children gave evidence of not yet knowing the constructions, up to ten years old, when a number of the children exhibited an adult command of the structures. For some structures there was considerable variation in age of acquisition in different children. Of particular interest is that this variation in *age* of acquisition does not seem to affect *order* of acquisition of different structures. For the structures reported here, the evidence is that linguistic development, whether it occurs earlier or later, nevertheless proceeds along similar paths. This has been a basic and repeated finding of longitudinal studies with younger children at earlier stages of language development. It is encouraging that the same principle is demonstrable on the basis of cross-sectional studies with older children at much later stages of linguistic development.

[3] Chomsky.
[4] R. F. Cromer, " 'Children are nice to understand':Surface Structure Clues for the Recovery of a Deep Structure." *British Journal of Psychology*, 61, 1970, pp. 397-408; F. S. Kessel, "The Role of Syntax in Children's Comprehension from Ages Six to Twelve," *Monographs of the Society for Research in Child Development*, Ser. no. 139, 35, (September, 1970); C. Chomsky. 1969.

We drew children from an elementary school in Cambridge, Massachusetts, which is predominantly middle-class, but has nevertheless some range in the socioeconomic background of the children. Thirty-six children from kindergarten through fourth grade were selected to ensure a representative sample in terms of age and reading level. The children were interviewed individually at school by the author and an assistant over a period of several months in the fall of 1969, with each interview lasting about a half hour.

The Test Constructions

1.   The construction *Easy to See* in the sentence *"The doll is easy to see"*

In this interview we tested the child's ability to determine the grammatical relations which hold among the words in sentences of the form *The doll is easy to see*.

The complexity of this construction derives from the fact that the grammatical relations among its words are not expressed directly in its surface structure. Of the two constructions

  (a) The doll is eager to see.
  (b) The doll is easy to see.

which look alike on the surface, only (a) retains in its surface structure the relations of subject and verb which are implicit in the meaning of the sentence; i.e., not only is *doll* the subject of sentence (a), but it is also the implicit subject of the complement verb *see*. The surface structure of (a) expresses this by normal word order of subject precedes verb. In (b), however, the word order is misleading. *Doll* is actually the implicit *object* of the complement verb *see*, for in (b) it is easy for someone else to see the doll. The implicit subject of *see* is omitted in (b)'s surface structure, and the listener must fill it in for himself as "someone else." The child who has not yet learned to recognize the underlying difference in structure of these two superficially similar sentences will interpret them both according to surface structure, and report that in (b), as well as (a), it is the doll who is doing the seeing. Such a child would interpret (b) incorrectly to mean "It is easy for the doll to see," instead of "It is easy for someone else to see the doll."

The interview was opened by placing a doll, with eyes that close, lying down with eyes closed on a table in front of the child. The child was then asked to say whether the doll was easy to see or hard to see. After responding, he was asked the question "why?" Then he was asked to make the doll either easy to see or hard to see, depending on his response to the first question.

The child who interprets the sentence correctly will answer that the doll is easy to see and support this interpretation when asked by answering that the doll is right there in front of him. When asked to make the doll hard to see he will hide the doll under the table or cover his own eyes or make a similar meaningful response.

The child who misinterprets the sentence and answers that the doll is hard to see will support this interpretation by indicating that her eyes are closed so she can't see and when asked to make her easy to see will open the doll's eyes.

This construction was fairly easy for the children. Everyone over age 7.1[5] succeeded with it, and below this age there was mixed success and failure. Five of the children below 7.1 failed, approximately half of this age group. Our sample did not include children young enough for us to observe onset of acquisition. Below we will see that lack of competence in this construction constitutes Stage 1 in our developmental sequence.

2. The construction *Promise* as in
   "*Bozo promises Donald to stand on the book.*"

Here we examined the child's knowledge of a particular syntactic structure associated with the world *promise*. His ability to identify the missing subject of a complement verb following *promise* was tested, a task which is relatively complex for the following reasons. Consider the sentences

   (a) Bozo promised Donald to stand on the book.
   (b) Bozo told Donald to stand on the book.

In these sentences the subject of the verb *stand* is not expressed, but must be filled in by the listener. Although the two sentences are superficially alike, differing only in their main verbs *promise* and *tell,* in (a) it is Bozo who is to stand on the book, and in (b) it is Donald who is to stand on the book. Since this information is not given anywhere in the surface structure of these sentences, the listener must, in order to interpret them differently, draw on his underlying knowledge of the verbs *promise* and *tell* and the structures associated with them.

Sentence (b) is a very common structure in English. The missing subject of a

---

[5] 7.1 is used to indicate 7 years, 1 month.

complement verb is almost always the first noun phrase preceding it. If Bozo tells Donald to stand on the book, it is Donald who is to do the standing. This is true for almost all verbs in English that can substitute for *tell* in this sentence, for example, *persuades, urges, expects, wants, orders, hires, likes,* etc. We learn this rule early and we learn it well. *Promise,* however, is an exception. With *promise* the missing subject is not the closest noun phrase, but a noun phrase farther away. This is a rare construction in English found with only a very few verbs. In order to interpret sentence (a) correctly, we must have learned in dealing with *promise* to discard the general rule and to substitute the special rule for *promise.*

Our expectation was that children who have not yet learned this exceptional feature of the verb *promise* will use their well-learned general principle and interpret sentence (a) according to the structure of (b). They will report that in (a) it is Donald who is to stand on the book; Bozo promises Donald that he, Donald, can stand on the book. In a previous experiment carried out by this writer, this was found to be the case; some children still misinterpreted the construction up to the age of eight and one-half, and uniform success was achieved only above this age.[6]

To test knowledge of this construction we had the child manipulate two toy figures to illustrate the action of a series of test sentences. The figures used were Bozo the Clown and Donald Duck, and a book was provided for them to stand on.

First it was determined that the child knew the meaning of the word *promise* by asking questions such as: Can you tell me what you would say to your friend if you promise him that you'll call him up this afternoon? What do you mean when you make somebody a promise? What's special about a promise?

Then the child was asked to name the two figures. Practice sentences were given to familiarize the child with the actions and with the "intentional" nature of the test sentences. The child has to illustrate how the stated intention of the sentence is carried out because in "Bozo promises Donald to stand on the book," the child shows who stands on the book. The practice sentences introduce this notion: Bozo wants to do a somersault—Make him do it. Bozo wants Donald to do a somersault—Have him do it. Donald decides to stand on the book—Make him do it.

This was followed by five test sentences of the form "Donald promises Bozo to hop up and down—Make him hop."

[6] Chomsky.

In general the children easily understood what they were to do, and appeared to enjoy the task. The sentences were repeated freely for those children who required repetitions or who seemed to hesitate.

The children who interpreted the sentences correctly selected the more distant noun phrase as subject of *stand*. For "Bozo promised Donald to stand on the book—Make him do it," they picked up Bozo and placed him on the book. The children who misinterpreted the construction selected the closest noun phrase as subject of *stand*. In response to this same sentence, they picked up Donald and placed him on the book.

We found the children to be highly consistent in their responses. The most common response was to assign the missing subject the same way in all five sentences, whether correct or incorrect, and to do so rapidly and with assurance. Only a very few children varied their responses, and generally these were the ones who hesitated and appeared confused.

Our results indicate that this construction was relatively easy for the children. Criterion for success was four correct out of five. Two thirds of the thirty-six children succeeded with the construction. The failers, with one exception, were all under eight years old, with failure being the rule for the five-year-olds, as likely as success for the six-year-olds, and the exception for the seven-year-olds. Lack of competence in this construction with the verb *promise* distinguishes children in Stage 2 in our developmental sequence from those in Stage 3.

3. The construction *Ask* as in
   "The girl asked the boy what to paint."

This interview examined the child's knowledge of a particular syntactic structure associated with the verb *ask*. This construction, or the child's handling of the verb *ask* in general, proves to be a particularly good indicator of syntactic development. The child must identify the missing subject of a verb following *ask* in a complement clause, introduced by a question word such as *when* or *what*, for example, the subject of *paint* in

The girl asked the boy what to paint.

The verb *ask* breaks a general structural rule of English as does *promise*. The nature of the complexity of this construction has been treated at length elsewhere,[7] and will be reviewed only briefly here.

---

[7] Chomsky.

Consider the sentences

(a) The girl asked the boy what to paint.

(b) The girl told the boy what to paint.

The missing subject of *paint* in (a) is *the girl.* The correct paraphrase of (a) is *The girl asked the boy what she should paint.* In (b), as in most other sentences of this form in English, the missing subject is *the boy,* that is *the girl told the boy what he should paint.* Since the weight of evidence in the language as a whole favors the (b) interpretation, children who have not yet learned this exceptional feature of the verb *ask* will interpret sentence (a) according to the structure of (b). They will report that in (a) the girl is asking the boy what he is going to paint. This interpretation persists in some children until age ten or later.

The actual interview consisted of a conversational portion and a picture identification test. In the conversational portion, two children who knew each other well carried out a number of tasks according to instructions. Only one child was being tested, the second child serving as a conversational partner. The two children were seated at a table on which were placed toy food, and figures of Donald Duck, Pluto Pup, and Bozo. We explained to the child that he was going to play some games with the things on the table; he would feed the dog, for example, and so on.

The instructions themselves were then given. *Ask* instructions were interspersed with *tell* instructions, but the opening instruction was always *ask.* The interview proceeded as follows:

Interviewer: Ask Bruce what to feed the dog.

Child: THE HAMBURGER.

Interviewer: Tell Bruce what food to put back in the box.

Child: THE HOT DOG.

                etc.

The interview was carried out in an informal conversational manner, with repetitions, extra instructions at the child's point of difficulty, discussion of confusions and inconsistencies, and with special attempts to draw the child's attention to his "errors." Maximum help was given the child to express what he knew.

Errors were of two kinds. Some children told their partner what to do in response to an *ask* instruction, rather than asking him. *The hamburger* above would be a correct response if the instruction had been "Tell Bruce what to feed the dog." Children who respond in this manner have failed to interpret *ask* as requiring a question response, and respond as if instructed to tell. This response error indicated the least competence with the verb *ask*.

When making the other error, children asked their partner a question, but assigned the wrong missing subject to the key verb, responding to "Ask Bruce what to feed the dog" with "What are you going to feed the dog?" The child who answers in this manner understands that he is to ask a question, but has not yet learned that *ask* signals an exception to his well-learned general rule of English for picking missing subjects. He picks his missing subject incorrectly, according to the general rule, which says to choose your partner rather than yourself. He may ask a variety of questions, all with the subject *you* following *ask;* for example,

What do you want to feed the dog? or
What are you going to feed the dog?

This response indicates greater competence with *ask* than the preceding response, but still reveals lack of knowledge of *ask* as signalling an exceptional structure.[8]

Only one third of the children were able to give the correct response, asking a question and assigning the correct subject to the key verb, responding to "Ask Bruce what to feed the dog," with the question "What should I feed the dog?" This response indicates mastery of the construction, and was the only one accepted as correct for our purposes. Criterion for success was correct response to at least four-fifths of the instructions given.[9]

After the conversational portion of the interview was concluded, the partner left, and the subject was shown two pairs of pictures (Figs. 1 and 2). For Pair 1 he was asked: "Which picture shows the girl asking the boy what to paint?" and "What is she saying to him?"; for Pair 2 he was asked: "Which picture shows the boy asking the girl what shoes to wear?" and "What is he saying to her?" The child was instructed to look at both pictures of a pair before deciding on an answer. In each case, the correct choice is Picture a. For Picture 1a, the girl should be quoted as saying, "What should I paint?" and for Picture 2a, the boy should be quoted as saying, "What shoes should I wear?"

Here again, we find the same two kinds of error as with the conversational

---

[8] The children's performance with *ask* in general reveals a number of levels of competence, which the present discussion only touches on. Since the various degrees of competence short of total mastery do not contribute to our developmental sequence, they are referred to only peripherally here.

[9] The actual number of instructions given varied from child to child because of the informal nature of the interview.

1a. Correct interpretation   *1b. Incorrect interpretation*

Test Pictures 1a. and 1b.
Test sentence: The girl asks the boy what to paint.

   Subject is shown both pictures simultaneously and asked

      1. Which picture shows the girl asking the boy what to paint?
      2. What is she saying to him?

FIGURE 1

2a. Correct interpretation   *2b. Incorrect interpretation*

Test Pictures 2a. and 2b.
Test sentence: The boy asks the girl which shoes to wear.

   Subject is shown both pictures simultaneously and asked

      1. Which picture shows the boy asking the girl which shoes to wear?
      2. What is he saying to her?

FIGURE 2

test of *ask*. Some children choose the wrong picture (b), giving a quote in which one child *tells* the other what to do, e.g., "Wear those shoes." This would be a correct response if the cue had been "Which picture shows the girl telling the boy what shoes to wear?" As before, children who respond in this manner have failed to interpret *ask* as requiring a question response. They respond as if instructed to tell. This response indicates the least competence with the verb *ask*.

The second error is to choose the wrong picture, quote the picture child as asking a question, but the wrong question: "What are you going to paint?"; "What shoes are you going to wear?" Again, the child who answers in this manner understands that he is to ask a question, but has not yet learned the exceptional nature of *ask*. He picks his missing subject incorrectly and proceeds to choose a picture and question consistent with his hypothesis. As before, this response indicates greater competence with *ask* than the preceding response, but falls short of total mastery.

In each of the above errors the picture choice and quoted command or question are consistent with each other. Given the way the child interprets the cue sentence, his response is logical and "correct." He is not confused nor is he guessing. This was true also for the conversational test, where the child's actions supported his words in almost all cases. He is operating successfully according to rule; it is just that his rule differs from the standard. This is a common observation in this type of linguistic testing, where children are often confident when operating with well-entrenched, though inappropriate, rules. Indeed, confusion or hesitation, or recognition that a construction is problematic, may signal progress on the child's part, usually indicating that he has begun the process of restructuring his rule system.

An interesting feature of the results is that the picture test for *ask* was easier for some children than the conversational test. Five children succeeded with the pictures and failed the conversational test, and only one child reversed this pattern. Criterion for success with the *ask* construction as a whole was success with both the pictures and the conversation test.[10]

An analysis of our results showed that this construction was considerably more difficult for the children than our preceding ones, and exhibited strong vari-

---

[10] This scoring procedure simplifies the stages of our developmental sequence, and was adopted for this reason. Separating the children who passed only the picture test would add one stage to the sequence, which might be useful for some purposes but seemed superfluous here.

ability in age of acquisition. Only one third of the children, ranging in age from 7.2 years to 10.0, succeeded at both the conversational interview and the picture test. The ages of those who failed ranged from 5.9 to 9.9. No child under 7.2 succeeded. From 7.2 up, we find the children fairly evenly divided among passers and failers. The mean age of the failers was six months under that of the passers, 8.2 as compared to 8.8.

The striking feature of these results is the high variability in age of acquisition of the structure, and the persistence of lack of knowledge right up to the top age in our sample. Clearly after age seven, individual rate of development is a stronger factor than is age in acquisition of the *ask* construction. Below we will see that knowledge of this construction distinguishes Stage 3 from Stage 4 in our developmental sequence.

It is interesting that the ability to assign a missing subject correctly following *ask* appears later in the child than the ability to carry out what appears to be the same task with the verb *promise*. Both verbs require that a general rule of subject assignment be broken and replaced with a rule specific to these two words. If the specific rule is the same for both *ask* and *promise*, why then does the child consistently learn to apply it first with *promise*?

The answer appears to lie in the greater simplicity of the verb *promise* as compared to *ask*. *Promise* is a consistent verb, whereas *ask* evidences inconsistency when used in two different senses as follows. Consider (a) Seymour asked Gloria to leave, (b) Seymour asked Gloria when to leave. In (a) Gloria is to leave; *ask* behaves as the majority of verbs in English. In (b) Seymour is to leave; *ask* behaves according to the special rule. The child must learn conflicting rules for these two structures with *ask,* whereas no such problem exists with *promise*. *Promise* always requires the special rule—there is no structure such as (a) to complicate matters.

4. Constructions following *And* and *Although*

Here we tested the children's ability to identify a missing verb differently in two sentences which differ only in the use of *and* and *although* as clause introducers. Consider the sentences:

(a) Mother scolded Gloria for answering the phone, and I would have done the same.

(b) Mother scolded Gloria for answering the phone, although I would have done the same.

These sentences do not say what I would have done; the listener must fill it in for himself. There are two candidate verbs preceding *done the same* which might serve as referent: *scolded* and *answered*. Following *and,* the referent is *scolded;* following *although,* the referent is *answered;* in (a) I would have scolded Gloria, and in (b) I would have answered the phone.[11]

No careful experimental technique was devised for testing these constructions. We simply read the sentences to the children and asked for each one: "What does this sentence say I would have done?" There was some question in our minds about the effectiveness of this direct approach, but it appears to have been adequate in this case. The results show interesting developmental patterns, and they fit in very well with the rest of our data.

The examples mentioned above were used as well as the sentences: "The cowboy scolded the horse for running away, and I would have done the same—What would I have done?" "The cowboy scolded the horse for running away, although I would have done the same—

What would I have done?"

These sentences were usually read several times to the children, particularly the younger children, before they were able to formulate an answer. Those who could read were given the sentences typed on cards to follow as we read aloud.

We determined in an earlier portion of the interview that all of the children could correctly interpret the shorter sentence, "The cowboy scolded the horse for running away—Who ran away?" None of the children had any trouble assigning *horse* as subject of *running away*.

We also determined earlier in the interview session which children were competent in the use of *although* in simpler sentences where no deletions were involved. All but eight of the children performed successfully on an oral sentence-completion task with sentences such as "Although my favorite TV program was on, I..." and "I wore a heavy jacket although...." Those who failed were under seven years of age, and not among the passers of our *and* and *although* test.

This experiment turned out to be more interesting than anticipated. During the planning stage we considered the *although* sentences to be the difficult ones, and had included *and* sentences only for contrast. As it turned out, not only was the *although* construction very difficult for the children (only four children succeeded with it), but the *and* sentence, surprisingly enough, proved to be inter-

---

*This interesting and rather unusual aspect of the word *although* was brought to the author's attention by Adrian Akmajian.

esting in its own right. Unexpectedly, twenty-three children failed the *and* sentence. Whereas we had set out to test *although, and* itself proved to be a useful test construction as discussed below.

Scoring was as follows. In the *although* sentences the child had to choose the referent of *done the same* from two candidate verbs preceding it in the sentence: *scolded,* the far candidate, and *answering,* the near candidate. The correct choice is the near candidate, *answering.* Scoring, however, requires caution, for some children will choose the near candidate from lack of knowledge. As we have seen in the constructions of *promise* and *ask,* the child tends to always choose the *near* candidate to fill in a deletion when he works from general principles of English. In our test sentence the near candidate (*answering*) is the correct one, the one the child would choose also from specific knowledge of the *although* construction. Since both general principles and specific knowledge of *although* yield the same answer, how can we determine on what basis the child is choosing? Fortunately, our *and* sentence provides the means for distinguishing. It presents what appears to be the same construction differing only in the replacement of *although* by *and,* and requires the *far* candidate, *scolded,* as referent of *done the same.*

By correctly choosing the far candidate (*scolded*) for *and* the child shows that he has learned to discard general principles in dealing with this surface structure. When this child then chooses the near candidate for *although* we can assume that he does so not from general principles but because he recognizes the different function of *although* in the sentence.

And indeed we find a pattern of development which supports this hypothesis. The younger children selected the near candidate for both *and* and *although;* apparently they worked from general principles for both words. As age increases children began to select the far candidate for both words; they have learned the exceptional nature of the surface structure, but not the specific *although* rule. In the most advanced stage, children have also learned the specific *although* rule and distinguish the two cases.

The criterion for success with *although,* then, was choosing the near candidate verb as referent of *done the same,* while at the same time choosing the far candidate verb for *and.* Children were scored correct only if all four test sentences were judged correctly. Only four children, ages 7.6, 8.3, 8.11, and 9.9. achieved this success. Clearly age is a poor predictor of success with this construction, and knowledge of it is strongly dependent on individual rate of development.

The relation between our simple use of *although* in the sentence completion task and its more complex use with verb deleted shows the expected course of development. There are children who know neither construction, children who know both, and many intermediate children who know the simple construction but not the complex one. No children reverse this order, and know the complex construction without knowing the simple one.

In summary, all children seven and older succeeded with *although* in its simple construction. The more complex *although* construction was very difficult for the children and only four succeeded at it. Knowledge of the simple construction precedes knowledge of the complex one.

This *although* construction was the most difficult of the constructions reported here, and we will see below that success at it constitutes the highest stage in our developmental sequence.

Considered separately, the *and* construction yielded interesting results. Above we pointed out that the youngest children dealt with *and* according to general principles of English and selected the near candidate to fill in the missing verb.

The parallel of these *and* results with our results for *ask* is remarkably close. Their main feature is the high variability in age of acquisition of the structure, and the fact that we find children up to the oldest failing. After age seven, age is less of a factor in acquisition of the construction than individual rate of development. We will see below that, with only minor exceptions, the same children succeeded with both *ask* and *and*. Accordingly, joint knowledge of *ask* and *and* serves to distinguish Stage 3 from 4 in our developmental sequence.

Overall Developmental Sequence

By measuring children's competence in dealing with individual grammatical constructions, we gain information about patterns of acquisition characteristic of the different constructions. If we are fortunate this information may shed some light on the nature of the constructions themselves. It is far more interesting, however, to deal with a number of related structures. With a variety of structures, we hope to observe developmental sequences in the acquisition of the different constructions.

Thus, for a set of related constructions, with the verb *ask,* for example, we find that an individual child's successes and failures on test questions always assume the same pattern. Consider for the moment two separate *ask* constructions, the one

TABLE 1

Stages in Acquisition of Ask Constructions

	Task 1	Task 2	Task 3
Stage A	—	—	—
Stage B	+	—	—
Stage C	+	+	—
Stage D	+	+	⊤

+ Success
— Failure

discussed earlier and another, simpler one: (a) Ask Harry what time it is; (b) Ask Harry what to feed the dog.

Sentence *a* is simpler than *b* in that there is no missing subject in the clause —all information is given and nothing has to be filled in by the listener. To interpret (a) or (b) correctly, the child must recognize that *ask* signals a question. To interpret (b) correctly, the child must, in addition, select the missing subject correctly. In effect, the child must carry out the following three tasks:

1. Recognize that *ask* signals a question before the simple construction (a);
2. Recognize that *ask* signals a question before the complex construction (b);
3. Assign a correct missing subject in the complex construction (b).

Now when we test children on these two structures, we find the pattern of successes and failures shown in Figure 3.

Task (3) implies (2), which in turn implies (1).[12]

Given this pattern, we conclude that the children attain competence on these tasks in the order listed. The grammatical development is observed to take place in an orderly fashion, from simple to complex, according to an invariant sequence.

[12] Children who can do Task 3 can always do 2 and 1, and children who can do 2 can always do 1. There are no children who break this pattern, who can do 3, for example, and not 2 and 1; or who can do 2 without being able to do 1; or 1 and 3 without 2. On the other hand we do find children who can do 1 but not 2 or 3; and children who can do 1 and 2, but not 3. When our data are of this sort, when the operations can be arranged into a Guttman scale such that 3 presupposes 2 which in turn presupposes 1, then we have information about order of acquisition. Although we have not observed children over time as they progress from 1 to 2 to 3, we can nevertheless conclude that this is the order of acquisition and that we have an invariant developmental sequence.

That we can find such sequences when testing closely related structures is not very surprising. Sometimes, however, we find a stage we did not expect (such as the first two lines of Table 1 above). This is more interesting because we have learned something about how individual syntactic rules are adjusted in children's grammatical systems as their linguistic competence increases and they approach the adult linguistic system. This is the heart of the matter in linguistic work of this sort, for in this way we find out what the rules look like, how they change, what steps the child has to go through, what progress actually looks like step by step, what is hard and what is easy.

It is most interesting of all, of course, when structures that are related to each other only loosely reveal this same orderly developmental sequence. The five structures discussed exhibit this sequential relationship, in the order presented: *easy to see, promise, ask, and,* and *although.*

These structures appear to be quite divergent, and one would not ordinarily group them together as candidates for a developmental sequence, nor predict a specific order of acquisition. Yet our results show that they are acquired in the order listed. The children's performance on these constructions divides them into five stages as shown in Table 2.

TABLE 2

Developmental Stages in Children's Acquisition of Five Test Structures

		easy to see	promise	ask	and	although
STAGE 1:	age 5.9-7.1 n=4	−	−	−	−	−
STAGE 2:	age 5.9-9.5 n=9	+	−	−	−	−
STAGE 3:	age 6.1-9.9 n=12	+	+	−	−	−
STAGE 4:	age 7.2-10. n=7	+	+	+	+	−
STAGE 5:	age 7.6-9.9 n=4	+	+	+	+	+

+ Success
− Failure

Children who fail all five constructions are at Stage 1; Stage 2 children pass *easy to see* and fail the others; Stage 3 children pass *easy to see* and *promise* and fail the others; Stage 4 children pass all but *although;* Stage 5 children pass all five constructions.

What is interesting in the data is the uniformity of the results. The amount of divergence from this sequence of acquisition is extremely small, the children's individual responses deviating from the observed pattern at the rate of 4 responses per 100.[18]

How do we account for this striking orderliness in the children's acquisition of these seemingly diverse structures? A closer look at the structures themselves reveals that they do have one feature in common. They all require the listener to fill in a missing item in order to understand the sentence. The surface form of these sentences lacks either a noun phrase or a verb phrase which is crucial to its understanding, and the listener must know how to fill it in if he is to understand the sentence correctly. In each case it has to be filled in in a manner at variance with the general tendency of the language, which accounts for the difficulty. More technically, the listener, given only the surface structure of the sentence, must recreate its underlying form. To do this he has to know, among other things, the rules governing deletions from underlying to surface structure. If a child has not yet mastered the rules for these constructions, he will make mistakes in filling in the missing items, and end up with wrong interpretations.

The general rule in English for filling in deletions such as in the above constructions is to choose the nearest preceding candidate item in the sentence. The child has learned this as a general principle of the language very early on. These five constructions, though very different from each other, all require that this principle be abandoned. They require instead the rather unusual principle: don't choose the nearest preceding candidate item in the sentence, keep looking. In a sense the child has to be freed from a deeply entrenched constraint in order to interpret each one of these constructions. He has specifically to learn in each of the above cases that his general principle does not apply. Evidently the relative complexities of these five structures are such that children tend to master them in the order listed, with surprisingly little variation.

Table 3 summarizes our test constructions. It illustrates the five structures, with the correct and incorrect interpretations given. Children who do not know a construction respond with the incorrect interpretation (near candi-

---

[18] When the stages are considered as a Guttman scale, the coefficient of reproducibility is .96.

TABLE 3

Correct and Incorrect Interpretations of 5 Test Structures

	to be filled in	near candidate incorrect	other candidate correct
EASY TO SEE	subject of *see*	doll	somebody else
PROMISE	subject of *lie down*	Donald	Bozo
ASK	subject of *paint*	boy	girl
AND	referent of *done the same*	answered the phone	scolded
ALTHOUGH	referent of *done the same*	scolded*	answered the phone

* likely candidate by analogy with AND sentence, once learned

STRUCTURES: EASY TO SEE: The doll is easy to see.
      PROMISE : Bozo promises Donald to lie down.
      ASK : The girl asks the boy what to paint
      AND : Mother scolded Gloria for answering the phone, and I would have done the same.
      ALTHOUGH : Mother scolded Gloria for answering the phone, although I would have done the same.

date); those who know the construction respond with the "other" candidate.

Several interesting observations may be noted in connection with the sequence of acquisition outlined here.

First, *easy to see,* which was tested along with *promise* and *ask* by the author in an earlier experiment[14] did not precede *promise* in that experiment as it does in this one. The reason for this may be faulty experimental technique in the first experiment, which introduced extraneous cues and made the construction too difficult for the children. The current experiment, with improved technique, may reflect the children's competence more accurately.

Second, *promise* precedes *ask* in this experiment as in the 1969 experiment, confirming the earlier results. Only the final stage in the acquisition of *ask* (Table 1, Stage D) is relevant to this overall developmental sequence.

And finally, *and* and *ask* appear to "come in" together if *ask* is scored from

[14] Chomsky.

both the conversational portion of the interview and the picture test. Apparently the child learns the *and* construction at about the time he masters *ask*; if this result is borne out by future experimentation, it would suggest that the two constructions are of approximately the same degree of complexity.

In summary, the five constructions tested in this study can be ordered in a Guttman scale, indicating a developmental sequence in children's acquisition of these structures. The five structures, though quite diverse, all require that the child apply a specific principle of sentence analysis that is uncommon in English. Apparently, the child's ability to apply this principle progresses in a regular fashion from simple structures to more complex ones.

Reading

A second portion of this study surveyed the children's reading background and current reading activity. We wished to consider the relation of the amount and complexity of what children read to rate of linguistic development, along with other factors such as IQ and SES. To do this we used the five linguistic stages outlined above as the measure of rate of linguistic development and a variety of information on reading and listening.

Reading information was gathered through questionnaires to both children and parents, and through daily records kept at home of all reading (and listening to books read aloud) engaged in by the child over a one-week period. We calculated amount and complexity of independent reading (and listening), background in children's literature, and recall and recognition of books read and heard. In order to judge the extent of the children's reading at different complexity levels, we applied our own formula for measuring syntactic complexity to the books and magazines reported by the children in their week's record of day-to-day reading.

Our records thus contain a variety of measures of each child's reading exposure which together yielded a general picture of some interest. We have information on books read over a week's time, books that the child named in the course of a half-hour interview, parent reports of reading aloud, and so on. By assessing how much and what is read to him, and how much and what he reads on his own, we attempted to characterize each child's independent reading and get a picture of how reading functions in his background and current life. As mentioned above, both the amount read and the complexity of the material were taken into consideration.

EDITORIAL COMMENTS

One of the interesting findings in this study is that though the sequence of acquisition of different syntactic structures is stable and invariant, the age at which they are acquired is variable. Thus, we observe in Table 2 that the overlap of ages in each of the stages is considerable. It might appear that the selection of subjects by age in order to compare one age level with another would not be indicated. However, we would suggest that the sample be constituted with similar numbers of children in each of the age groups from kindergarten through fourth grade. If a large enough sample can be obtained (10 subjects at each of 5 age levels) an additional analysis can be made and presented in a table showing the numbers of children of each age level found in each of the stages. The analysis would more clearly show the degree of relationship between ages and stages.

In the section testing for comprehension of the construction *ask*, Chomsky used two children in order to conduct an informal conversation. It would be possible to eliminate the conversational portion of the interview and to restrict the testing for this construction to the picture test. According to Chomsky's finding the picture test for *ask* was easier for some children than the conversational test. This should be kept in mind when interpreting the results and in comparing findings with those of Chomsky.

The original article contained a section devoted to establishing the relationship of children's reading background to the rate of linguistic development. The procedures for conducting this part of the investigation go beyond the kind of investigative activities called for in this collection of readings. It would be well, however, for the student to consult the original article to learn how linguistic development is related to the child's background.

The Journal of Genetic Psychology, 1968, **112**, 275-286.

RELATION OF AGE TO CHILDREN'S EGOCENTRIC AND COOPERATIVE COMMUNICATION* [1]

KERBY T. ALVY, *State University of New York at Albany*

A. INTRODUCTION

This study is concerned with two forms of verbal communication, egocentric and cooperative, which are assumed to be functions of the absence and presence of underlying cognitive abilities or operations. The study is based on certain assumptions from Piaget's developmental theory.

Piaget views the child's cognitive development as a continuous process of child-environment interactions which lead to the attainment and elaboration of cognitive operations. He theorizes that a child at an early stage of development will engage in a form of verbal communication that reflects his not having attained the one cognitive operation upon which all socialized speech is based (8, 9). That form of communication is egocentric communication, and the cognitive operation which it lacks is the ability to shift mental perspective in order to consider the hearer's point of view. Egocentric communication may give the impression of being socialized, but it is not because the speaker fails to appreciate that what he sees, thinks, or understands may not be what the hearer sees, thinks, or understands. When the child develops this ability to shift mental perspective, when he becomes able to view a situation or issue from other than his own viewpoint, his verbal communications become potentially cooperative. That is, having attained this basic operation, it is now possible for the child to engage in an exchange of ideas and viewpoints. He now can appreciate that there are other perspectives and he can take these into consideration during a verbal exchange. From this point on, cooperative communication begins to dominate the child's verbal exchanges and egocentric communication diminishes.

* Accepted by Editorial Board Member Richard J. Havighurst; and received in the Editorial Office, Provincetown, Massachusetts, on April 20, 1967. Copyright, 1968, by The Journal Press.

[1] The author would like to acknowledge his gratitude to Drs. Morris Eson and Shirley Brown for their counsel on this project and to Dr. James Mancuso for his helpful comments. A note of appreciation is also extended to Frank Austin and his staff at Grout Park School for their cooperation.

The present study seeks to add to the empirical substantiation of these notions by creating a situation that requires one child to assume another's viewpoint in order to cooperate successfully over a commonly shared task. The situation consists of two same-aged children, who are separated by an opaque screen, each having before him identical sets of pictures. The task consists of one child (the listener) having to choose the picture which the other child (the speaker) is describing. The type of verbal exchange which the children engage in should reflect whether or not they have assumed each other's perspective. Specifically, if a speaker uses a description which could refer to two pictures, this ambiguous description would be classified as an egocentric communication because it fails to reflect the speaker's having considered that, from the listener's standpoint, such a description is insufficient to differentiate between the two pictures. This communication is egocentric regardless of whether or not the speaker has actually distinguished the pictures in terms of some differentiating characteristic. The point is that his description fails to reflect an awareness that what is sufficient subjective description may not be sufficient description for an objective presentation of differences, and such a lack of awareness is what one would expect from a child who has not attained the ability to take the hearer's view into consideration. Also, if the speaker persists in using this type of ambiguous description even after he is presented with evidence that his descriptions have been insufficient to allow the listener to differentiate the pictures (evidence derived from either the listener's requesting additional description or by being shown that the listener is choosing the wrong picture), this would be further evidence that he is unable to shift perspective in order to accommodate the listener's problems. Descriptions that refer to only one picture (unambiguous descriptions), or descriptions which could refer to more than one picture but which the speaker changes after receiving evidence that they are insufficient, would be classified as cooperative communications because they presumably reflect the speaker's having shifted perspective in consideration of the listener's problems.

The present study has certain features in common with other laboratory investigations which were explicitly concerned with egocentric and cooperative communications (1, 2, 3). But the present study differs in two important ways. (*a*) The specific task over which the children are to communicate has not been used previously. (*b*) The youngest age group in the present study (6 year olds) was not used previously in the other laboratory investigation that dealt with communications between pairs of same aged children. In that study (1), the youngest age group was an 8-year-old group. The other studies (2, 3) investigated communications between different aged children and adults, and communications between different aged children and hypothetical listeners. Thus, the present study differs from other studies in this area mainly in terms of the nature of the task employed and the age and pairings of the subjects utilized.

In addition to the above-mentioned reason, two other considerations support the use of a 6-year-old group. (a) A laboratory study by Glucksburg, Krauss, and Weisberg (5), which was not explicitly concerned with egocentric and cooperative communications, showed that children under five could not complete a task similar to the one used in the current experiment. (b) Piaget's field investigation of conversations between same aged children (8) led him to hypothesize that, when the content of the communication is of a concrete nature (visually immediate or commonly shared activities), the age at which cooperative communications appears is between 5 and 7.

Since the present study consists of same aged children conversing over a visually immediate and commonly shared activity, it would be expected from Piaget's hypothesis that the 6-year-old children will show some cooperative communications and that the older children will show increasing amounts of cooperative communications. The reverse would be true of egocentric communications: the 6 year olds will show the greatest amount of egocentric communication, and the older children will show decreasing amounts of egocentric communications. Therefore it is predicted that egocentric communications will decrease with age. Also, since egocentric communication implies not having shifted perspective, and since successful completion of the task requires having to shift perspective, it is also predicted that successful completion of the task will vary inversely with the amount of egocentric communications.

B. Method

1. *Subjects*

The Ss were 96 students from Schenectady, New York. There were 16 boys and 16 girls in each of three age groups, 6, 8, and 11. All Ss were assigned partners randomly; the boys were paired with the same aged boys, the girls with the same aged girls. The mean age for the eight pairs of 6-year-old boys was 6:02 and for the eight pairs of 6-year-old girls, 6:06. The mean age for both the 8-year-old boys and girls was 8:07, and for both the 11-year-old boys and girls the mean age was 11:06.

2. *Materials*

Two identical sets of nine drawings from a children's book were used (see Figure 1). The drawings were traced from the book, photostatically copied, and pasted on 3" × 4" index cards. These drawings, showing the facial expression of various affective states, were chosen on the basis of the range and nuance of affective expression. The experimentation took place in a room usually used

FIGURE 1
PICTURES USED IN PRACTICE MATCHING PROCEDURE AND TESTING PROCEDURE

for speech therapy which contained a small table and three small chairs. A 2′ ×
2½′ opaque screen was used to separate the Ss during the testing procedure. A
portable tape recorder was used to record each session.

3. *Procedure*

E spoke to the Ss before the experiment began. He told them that they were
going to be called out of class two at a time to play a game.

a. Practice matching procedure. After a pair of Ss entered the experimental
room, *E* told them they were going to play two games. The *E* spread a set of
nine pictures on the table. *E* then told Ss that he was going to hand them a picture which was exactly the same as one of the pictures on the table. Ss were instructed to place the picture next to the one on the table that was exactly the
same. After *S* had matched one picture, *E* handed *S* another until all nine pictures were matched. After the first *S* had matched all nine pictures, the other *S*
went through the same matching procedure. If in the course of the matching
procedure either of the Ss mismatched a picture and subsequently noticed the
mismatch, the *S* was allowed to correct the error. If the *S* did not notice the error, *E* brought it to his attention, allowing the *S* to correct the error.

b. Testing procedure. Upon completion of the matching procedure, Ss were
told they were going to play another game. They were seated at opposite ends of
the small table. *E* placed a set of nine pictures in front of each *S*, spreading each
set in two parallel rows of five and four pictures. Although each *S* had the same

nine pictures, the pattern of the pictures differed for each S, since E shuffled each set before spreading them in the two rows. E emphasized that one S had the same nine pictures in front of him as did the other S. E then placed the opaque screen between the Ss, saying that the screen was being used so that neither S could see each other's pictures. The Ss, who were three feet apart, could not see each other but they could see E. The arrangement was such that the Ss and the E formed the angles of a triangle. E turned on the tape recorder which was in full view of the Ss. E spoke to the S on his left (Speaker) and instructed the speaker to pick up one of the pictures (the speaker was allowed to pick up any picture and he was allowed to describe the set of pictures in any order he cared to). The speaker was told to look at the picture, ask himself "what is the boy feeling," then tell the other subject (Listener) what the boy was feeling. Both speaker and listener were informed that, from what the speaker told the listener, the listener had to pick out the picture to which the speaker referred. The listener was informed that, if from what the speaker told him he could not tell which picture was being referred to, he could ask the speaker for additional information to help him decide which picture was being discussed. If in the initial description of the picture the speaker referred to other characteristics than what the boy was experiencing emotionally, he was instructed to refer to affective characteristics. For example, if the speaker originally interpreted "feeling" as a tactile notion (saying, for example, "the boy is feeling a horse") he was told, "Not what the boy may be touching, you're to say what he is feeling." The listener was allowed to ask any type of question that would help him identify the picture being discussed. After the speaker described a picture and the listener made a choice from the pictures before him, they handed their respective pictures to E. E recorded whether a match had occurred and then showed both pictures to the Ss, indicating verbally as well as visually whether a match had occurred. E told Ss to continue playing the game. At least once during a trial, which was defined by an attempted matching of all nine pictures, the E reminded the listener that he could ask questions if he was not being told enough about a picture to allow him to be sure of his choice. After the first trial the Ss were told that they were going to play the same game again. E reshuffled the pictures, spread a set in front of each S, reminded the speaker to tell the listener "what the boy was feeling," and reminded the listener that he could ask questions. The same procedure was followed after the Ss had completed the second trial except that they were informed that this was to be the last time they would play the game. In all, each pair of Ss went through three trials. At the end of the third trial E asked the Ss not to tell any of their fellow classmates about the games they had played.

C. RESULTS

Table 1 contains a summary of the percentages for the first four dependent measures per age group, sexes combined, and the z scores for comparisons of percentages.

TABLE 1

PERCENTAGES FOR DEPENDENT MEASURES PER AGE GROUP, AND z SCORES FOR COMPARISONS OF PERCENTAGES BETWEEN 6 AND 8 YEAR OLDS AND BETWEEN 8 AND 11 YEAR OLDS
(Sexes combined)

	Age group			z scores for comparisons of percentages	
Dependent measure	6	8	11	6 *vs.* 8	8 *vs.* 11
1. Total matched pictures $(N = 432)$[a]	34	47	67	3.9*	6.0*
2. Total speakers using ambiguous descriptions $(N = 48)$[b]	98	77	52	3.1*	3.9*
3. Total speakers not changing ambiguous descriptions $(N = 32)$[c]	91	63	13	2.9*	4.6*
4. Total listeners asking for additional description $(N = 48)$[d]	21	61	73	4.4*	1.1 (n.s.)

* Significant at .01 level.
[a] $N = 432$: 16 (pairs) $\times$ 9 (pictures) $\times$ 3 (trials).
[b] $N = 48$: 16 (speakers) $\times$ 3 (trials).
[c] $N = 32$: 16 (speakers) $\times$ 2 (trials).
[d] $N = 48$: 16 (listeners) $\times$ 3 (trials).

1. *Percentage of Total Matched Pictures*

To see if the three age groups differed on overall performance on the experimental task, the percentages of total pictures matched on the three trials were computed. With the sexes combined, the percentage of matched pictures for the 6-year-old group was 34 per cent, for the 8-year-old group it was 47 per cent, and for the 11-year-old group, 67 per cent. As shown in Table 1, the differences in percentages between the 6 and 8 year olds, and between the 8 and 11 year olds were significant at the .01 level.

In a breakdown according to sex, the percentage of matches for the 6-year-old boys was 37 per cent as compared to 32 per cent for the same aged girls; 50 per cent for the 8-year-old boys as compared to 42 per cent for the same aged girls; and 63 per cent for the 11-year-old boys as compared to 71 per cent for the same aged girls. With a z test statistic, it was shown that these differences between the percentages of the sexes at the same age level were not significant at the .05 level, indicating that sex was not a significant variable underlying the overall differences in performance.

2. *Percentage of Total Speakers Using Ambiguous Descriptions*

The second measure was designed to get at one of the assumed indicators of egocentric communications, the speaker's use of ambiguous descriptions, descriptions that reflect his not having shifted perspective in order to accommodate the listener's point of view. An ambiguous description was defined as the use of the exact same description to describe two or more pictures on any given trial. A speaker who used the description "feeling mean" to refer to two or more pictures on any given trial would be counted as a speaker who used ambiguous descriptions. The measure employed was the percentage of total speakers, trials combined, using ambiguous descriptions. The percentage of total 6-year-old speakers using ambiguous descriptions was 98 per cent; for the 8-year-old speakers it was 77 per cent; and for the 11 year olds 52 per cent of the total speakers used ambiguous descriptions. Thus, an inverse relationship exists between the percentage of matched pictures and the percentage of total speakers using ambiguous descriptions. As shown in Table 1, the differences in percentages of total speakers using ambiguous descriptions for the 6 year olds *vs.* the 8 year olds and for the 8 year olds *vs.* the 11 year olds were significant at the .01 level.

3. *Percentage of Total Speakers Persisting in the Use of Ambiguous Descriptions*

The third measure was designed to get at the other assumed indicator of egocentric communications, the persistence in the use of ambiguous descriptions after receiving information that these descriptions were not leading to matches. Specifically, the percentage of total speakers using ambiguous descriptions on the second and third trial after these exact same ambiguous descriptions had not led to a match on the first and second trial were computed. For example, if the speaker's originally ambiguous description of picture No. 5 on the first trial did not bring about a match, and the speaker used the exact same description to refer to picture No. 5 on the second trial, he would be counted as a speaker who persisted in using ambiguous descriptions. Descriptions were considered ambiguous in terms of the criterion put forth in the last measure. The percentage of total speakers on the second and third trials persisting in the use of ambiguous descriptions was 91 per cent for the 6-year-old group, 63 per cent for the 8 year olds, and for the 11 year olds 13 per cent of the speakers persisted in using ambiguous descriptions. Thus, an inverse relationship exists between percentage of matched pictures and the percentage of total speakers persisting in the use of ambiguous descriptions. As shown in Table 1, the differences in percentages of total speakers persisting in ambiguous descriptions for the 6 year olds *vs.* the 8 year olds and for the 8 year olds *vs.* the 11 year olds were significant at the .01 level.

4. *Percentage of Total Listeners Requesting Additional Description*

In the previous measures listener behavior was implicitly tapped. An explicit measure of listener behavior is the percentage of total listeners, trials combined, who asked the speakers for additional description. The percentage of total 6-year-old listeners was 21 per cent, for the 8-year-old group it was 61 per cent, and for the 11 year olds it was 73 per cent. Thus, a positive relationship exists between percentage of matched pictures and percentage of listeners asking for additional description. As shown in Table 1, the difference in percentages of total listeners requesting additional description for the 6 year olds *vs.* the 8 year olds was significant at the .01 level, but the difference in percentages for the 8 year olds *vs.* the 11 year olds was not significant.

Although all were encouraged to ask for additional description, only four of the 16 six-year-old listeners asked questions. Of these four, two of them asked questions that were the mere repetitions of the descriptions offered by the speaker. For example, the speaker described a picture as "happy" and the listener asked, "Happy?" "Yes," was the speaker's reply and the listener went ahead and made his choice. Examples of the questions asked by the other two 6-year-old listeners were "Does he have his eyes closed?" "The one with the big mouth open?" and "Would I see the side of his face?" Their 6-year-old counterpart speakers often gave "incorrect" answers to these questions. For example, when one of the listeners asked, "Would I see the side of his face?" referring to a profile shot, the speaker said "Yes" even though the picture to which the speaker was addressing himself was one which showed a front view of the boy's face.

5. *Percentage of Total Verbal Exchanges Consisting of More than One Question and One Answer*

This measure was designed as a further index of the amount of verbal exchange between the speakers and listeners. The measure was the percentage of total verbal exchanges over any given picture that consisted of more than one question from the listener and more than one answer from the speaker. An example of this type of exchange, which was taken from an exchange between 11 year olds who were discussing picture No. 4, would be as follows: speaker describes the picture as "This boy looks happy"; listener asks, "Is he facing a certain direction?"; speaker answers, "Facing the front direction"; listener asks,

"Are his eyes open or closed?"; speaker answers, "Closed, like squinting." The percentage of total 6 year olds engaging in this type of exchange was 20 per cent ($N = 26$), for the 8 year olds 39 per cent ($N = 107$), and for the 11 year olds 48 per cent ($N = 216$). Thus, a positive relationship exists between the percentage of matched pictures and the percentage of total verbal exchanges consisting of more than one question and one answer. With a z test statistic, the difference in percentages of this type of verbal exchange for the 6 year olds *vs.* the 8 year olds was significant at the .05 level, but the difference in percentages for the 8 year olds *vs.* the 11 year olds was not significant.

D. Discussion

The results of the present study confirm the predictions that (a) egocentric communications decrease with age and that (b) successful completion of the experimental task, which was a function of the ability to shift mental perspective, varies inversely with the amount of egocentric communications. These results add laboratory confirmation to Piaget's notions concerning the development of cooperative communications between the same aged children. They are also in general agreement with results from other studies (1, 2, 3, 5), which presented different aged children with tasks requiring the ability to shift perspective and which showed a diminution of egocentric communications with age.

Taken as a whole, the results of these studies show that the child's level of cognitive development, as indexed by age or, in the Cowan study (1), by performance on Piagetian tasks, has predictable effects on his interpersonal behaviors which are mediated by language. With the assumption that these results represent a fairly normative estimate of the nature of the interaction between cognitive level and communication skill for the age groups studied, future research devoted to the following three interrelated questions seems most in order. (a) What are the antecedents of the ability to shift perspective and consequently the antecedents of cooperative communication? A first step toward answering this question might be to explore the effects of different child-rearing practices on the rate of attainment of this ability. Would, for example, the various child-rearing practices noted by Harvey, Hunt, and Schroder (6) have differential effects on the rate of attainment? (b) What if anything can be done to accelerate the attainment of the ability to shift mental perspective and thereby accelerate the age at which the child's communications become cooperative? A first step here might be to explore the possibility that the already existing preschool training programs, "Head Start" and nursery school programs, accelerate the attainment of this cognitive ability. (c) What can be done to improve the efficiency of the older child's cooperative communications? One study has already been devoted to this question. Using pairs of fifth-grade girls, Fry (4) was able to show that training in taking another's viewpoint did improve performance on subsequent tasks that required the ability to shift perspective. But this improvement only held up when the subsequent tasks were similar to the training tasks. The training tasks required succinct and nonredundant messages. When the subsequent task required detailed and extended messages, the trained and nontrained groups did not differ in performance. Though this study is disappointing in the sense that it failed to show that training leads to a more generalized improvement in communication skills, it still leaves unattended the possibility that other less situation-specific training procedures could produce a more generalized and flexible improvement in cooperative communications.

Since the study reported here was concerned with a construct (cognitive shifts of mental perspective) that is inferred from external verbal behavior, only one measure of the children's nonverbal behavior was taken (pictures matched). But other nonverbal behaviors observed by the experimenter suggest that if additional measures are employed the same experimental procedure can yield data that are relevant to other constructs which are not necessarily indicated through external verbal behavior. The following two observations led to this consideration. (*a*) On the first picture handed to the children during the practice matching procedure, many of them looked at the picture, then looked down at the nine pictures on the table and quickly matched the picture in their hand with the first one on the table that approximated it. They did not scan the entire set of pictures before making a choice. This sort of behavior was most prevalent with the 6 year olds. (*b*) During the testing procedure, many of the speakers appeared to be concerned with one picture at a time and not with the task as a whole. These speakers rarely scanned the set of pictures before choosing one to describe. They usually picked up the first picture that came into their field of vision. Once having picked up this picture, they addressed themselves solely to it. It seemed, for all practical purposes, that once they focused on this picture the other pictures no longer existed. Even when they were asked questions which referred to the other pictures, their focus remained on the picture in hand. Again, this sort of behavior was most prominent among the 6 year olds. Indeed, it seemed as if all the 6-year-old speakers oriented themselves toward the task in this way. Two constructs to which these observations are definitely relevant are (*a*) an impulsive as opposed to an analytic or reflective conceptual style (7) which is indicated by relatively quick responses to stimulus configurations, and (*b*) Piaget's construct of cognitive egocentrism which is indicated, among other ways, by preferential visual focusing on one or some aspects of a stimulus configuration to the exclusion of the other aspects. Thus, if measures of reaction time and eye movements are taken, the present experimental procedure should yield data relevant to constructs which are not necessarily inferred from external verbal behavior.

E. Summary

This paper was concerned with two forms of verbal communication, egocentric and cooperative, which, according to Piaget, are differentiated in terms of the absence and presence of a specific underlying cognitive operation, the ability to shift mental perspective in order to consider the hearer's point of view. Piaget hypothesizes that egocentric communication decreases and cooperative communication increases with age. The following study, which was designed to further the empirical exploration of these notions within a developmental context, was reported.

Sixteen pairs of 6, 8, and 11 year olds were tested on a verbal communication task where success was assumed to be a function of the ability to take each other's viewpoint. The members of a pair were separated by an opaque screen. Each had before him a set of nine pictures of boys expressing various affective states. The object was for the listener to select the picture being described by the speaker. Each pair was given three trials (a trial consisted of a run-through of all nine pictures). After each individual selection, E held up the pictures so that both children could see whether a match had occurred.

Comparisons of the percentages of matched pictures between 6 and 8, and 8 and 11 year olds resulted in z scores significant beyond the .01 level. Analysis of protocols revealed two major sources underlying the differences among the groups: decreases in egocentric communications and increases in verbal exchange as a function of age.

These results were interpreted to add laboratory confirmation to Piaget's notions concerning the development of cooperative communications between same aged children, and they were related to results from other studies in the same area. Suggestions for future research concerned with the development of the child's interpersonal verbal behaviors as well as suggestions for using the current experimental procedures to explore constructs which are not inferred from verbal behavior (impulsive conceptual style and cognitive egocentrism) were made.

References

1. Cowan, P. A. Cognitive egocentrism and social interaction. *Amer. Psychol.*, 1966, **21**(7), 623 (Abstract).
2. Feffer, M. H., & Gourevitch, V. Cognitive aspects of role-taking in children. *J. Personal.*, 1960, **28**, 383-396.
3. Flavell, J. H. Role-taking and communication skills in children. *Young Child.*, 1966, **21**(3), 164-177.
4. Fry, C. L. The effects of training in communication and role perception on the communicative abilities of children. Unpublished Doctoral dissertation, University of Rochester, Rochester, New York, 1961.

5. GLUCKSBURG, S., KRAUSS, R. M., & WEISBERG, R. Referential communication in nursery school children. *J. Exper. Child Psychol.*, 1966, **3**(4), 333-342.
6. HARVEY, O. J., HUNT, D. E., & SCHRODER, H. M. Conceptual Systems and Personality Organization. New York: Wiley & Sons, 1961.
7. KAGAN, J., ROSMAN, B. L., DAY, D., ALBERT, J., & PHELPS, W. Information processing in the child: Significance of analytic attitudes. *Psychol. Monog.*, 1964, **78**(1), Whole No. 578.
8. PIAGET, J. The Language and Thought of the Child. New York: Harcourt, Brace, 1926.
9. ————. Comments on Vygotsky's Critical Remarks. Cambridge, Mass.: M.I.T. Press, 1962.

Psychology Department
State University of New York at Albany
1400 Washington Avenue
Albany, New York 12203

EDITORIAL COMMENTS

In describing the development of role-taking and communication skills in children, Flavell (1968) identifies five major aspects of cooperative communication, as follows:

1. *Existence*—that there *is* such a thing as "perspective," that is, that what you perceive, think, or feel in any given situation need not coincide with what I perceive, think, or feel.
2. *Need*—that an analysis of the other's perspective is called for in this particular situation, that is, that such an analysis would be a useful means to achieving whatever one's goal is here.
3. *Prediction*—how actually to carry out this analysis, that is, possession of the abilities needed to discriminate with accuracy whatever the relevant role attributes are.
4. *Maintenance*—how to maintain in awareness the cognitions yielded by this analysis, assuming them to be in active competition with those which define one's own point of view, during the time in which they are to be applied to the goal behavior.
5. *Application*—how actually to apply these cognitions to the end at hand, for example, how to translate what one knows about the other's listener role attributes into an effective verbal message (page 208).

The student investigator may wish to attempt to classify the communications into these five categories.

Although tape-recorded sessions are preferable, the investigation can be conducted without a tape recorder by employing two investigators, one to give the instructions and the other to record the communications. If such a procedure is followed the two investigators should alternate roles.

The number of subjects can be reduced by using two samples instead of the three as in the Alvy study. This would require only 32 pairs of subjects— 16 pairs from the first grade and 16 pairs from the third or fourth grade. A further reduction in sample size can be achieved by using only male or female subjects—8 or 10 pairs for each group.

Clarification of Procedure

Alvy makes the following ambiguous statement about the procedure: "After the speaker described a picture and the listener made a choice from the pictures before him, they handed their respective pictures to *E*. *E* recorded whether a match had occurred and then showed both pictures to the *S*s, indicating verbally as well as visually whether a match had occurred. *E* told *S*s to continue playing the game." It isn't clear from this statement whether the *E* keeps the pictures or whether he returns them to the *S*s. In a personal communication Alvy explains that the *E* kept the pictures. This, however, increases considerably the possibility of a subsequent mismatch in the event of an earlier mismatch. It would appear that the best way to handle this is to return the picture to the listener but not to the speaker. This is to be done both in the case of a correct and an incorrect match. Such a modification in procedure may produce some differences in results, but the trends should be the same.

REFERENCE

J. H. Flavell, *The Development of Role-Taking and Communication Skills in Children.* New York: Wiley, 1968.

STUDIES IN SOCIAL DEVELOPMENT

CHILDREN'S CONCEPTS OF MALE AND FEMALE ROLES[1]

RUTH E. HARTLEY[2]

The City College of New York

The study reported here is an exploratory one which has as its principal focus women's social roles. This study was proposed in the first place because the nature and quality of women's adjustment to their status and function in the current social scene have been causing much concern to thoughtful observers. We proposed to study girls' perceptions of female roles because it seemed to us that these perceptions, with possibly differential impact at different developmental levels, might furnish some clues to the basic difficulties implicit in the adult role, and might suggest some techniques of guidance to ameliorate the difficulties of future generations of women. We had not proceeded very far in our planning, however, before it became quite clear that, since the demands of women's roles are complementary to the demands of men's roles, we needed to know something about girls' perceptions of male roles as well as of female roles. Similarly, since our female subjects would most likely be filling their roles vis-a-vis male partners, it seemed wise to obtain a sampling also of boys' perceptions of both male and female roles. Findings obtained from male subjects are regarded mainly as supplementary, however, a kind of checking device against which to test our interpretations of data obtained from female subjects. The techniques dealing with female roles are more elaborate and extensive than those dealing with male roles, and we have many more female subjects than male subjects. The insights we have incidentally obtained into male functioning, even under these limitations, are so provocative, however, that they suggest the desirability of a study that will permit us to focus on the male of the species in as concentrated a fashion as we have been focusing on the female(1).

[1] An address delivered at the Biennial Meeting of the New York-New Jersey Regional Committee of the American Association of Psychiatric Clinics for Children, June 5, 1959. The investigation referred to here was supported by a research grant, M 959 (C, C-1, C-2, C-3) from the National Institute of Mental Health, Public Health Service.

[2] The author wishes to indicate her warm appreciation of the extensive and skilled participation of Dr. Frank Hardesty, Research Associate on the project, in collecting much of the data and handling many of the analyses reported here. She also wishes to acknowledge the help of Mr. David Gorfein, research assistant, with the analyses of the "Mars story" data.

Turning to the *design* of this study, I must again emphasize its exploratory nature. Because so little is really known about the processes by which social roles are internalized, it seemed wise to give this investigation something of a pilot quality, striving for a rich variety of data, obtained from relatively few subjects, which could form the basis for more precise and testable hypotheses. We expect our finding to be suggestive rather than conclusive, and our most important results to take the form of hypotheses which can subsequently be put to definitive test. Of course, we had some implicit hypotheses to begin with; these concerned among other items, relationships between parental attitudes and children's perceptions, between mother's attitudes and girl's attitudes, between the quality of every day experiences and both perceptions and attitudes, between the individual's capabilities and his attitudes toward sex-role activities, between the age of the child and the effect of certain experiences. Techniques were designed to elicit materials that would help us identify which of these hypotheses seemed worth working out more explicitly and pursuing further.

To keep the project within manageable limits, it was decided to confine this inquiry to the pre-pubertal years. The ages five, eight and 11 years were chosen for several reasons: five was judged the earliest age at which we could expect responses that could be compared to those of the older children. Eleven was as close as we dared get to puberty and still hope to steer free of the complex pubertal problems. Eight seemed a good point in between, when the child might be expected to be well advanced in weaning from the family, well integrated in peer groups, yet not completely independent of parents.

The variables which influenced our choice of subjects were implicit in our hypotheses and consisted of age, socio-economic class, work status of the mother and sex. Our original design called for equal numbers of five-, eight-, and eleven-year-old girls, with each age group divided into upper-middle and lower-middle class subjects, and each class group containing equal numbers of children with working and with non-working mothers. We planned to have similarly balanced groups of boys, but the male sample was to be only about half as large as the female.

To avoid having to deal with too many unpredictable variables, we decided not to include recent immigrants or members of minority groups having sex-role patterns differing from those common to the majority group culture. Only subjects born in the U.S., coming from two-parent homes, and without outstanding emotional difficulties were to be used.

Unfortunately, the practical exigencies of finding cooperative centers and our own time limits interfered somewhat with our carrying out our original sample design. We had to content ourselves with fewer and less well balanced groups of five-year olds among the girls and of all ages among the boys than we had originally planned. This means that some comparisons we had hoped to be able to make will not be possible, but by concentrating our smaller sample of the youngest subjects into one class-grouping, the upper-middle class, we were able to rescue a usable segment of material which can at least tell us some things about age and sex-role development at that socio-economic level.

At present we have data from 157 subjects, 47 boys and 110 girls. Age-wise, they are divided into 23 five-year-olds, 63 eight-year-olds, and 71 eleven-year-olds. The whole sample is approximately equally divided between those coming from families where mothers are employed and from families where the mothers are not employed. We used a variety of techniques, including play, pictorial and purely verbal approaches; some were projective types, others simply factual and repertorial. The complete battery took from eight to twelve sessions to administer, exclusive of fairly lengthy interviews with the mothers and fathers of the female subjects. The findings I will report here are derived for the most part from a small segment of our battery of techniques, consisting of one pictorial projective-type and one indirect verbal device, each designed to give us answers to different questions.

One question derived from the insistence in recent years by a wide variety of "experts" is that current changes in sex-role mores are confusing the children and that this confusion is interfering with their own sex identification. The question we put to the data was simple. We wanted to find out how the world actually does appear to the children growing up in it, in relation to male and female functioning. One way we tried for an answer was to say to our subjects:

1. Suppose you met a person from Mars (the moon) and he knew nothing about the way we live here, and he asked you to tell him about girls (your age) in this world—what would you tell him girls need to know or be able to do?
2. What would you tell him boys need to know or be able to do?
3. What would you tell him women (ladies) need to know or be able to do?
4. What would you tell him men need to know or be able to do?

When we had analyzed the responses in the simplest possible way, by counting the number of times an item was mentioned and totalling the number of item-mentions in each of the several categories into which the answers seemed to fall, this is what we found. Of a total of 640 item-mentions for women, 64.5% were in the traditional domestic activities having to do with household care and management, child care, and relations with husbands. Items relating to the work-role made up only six per cent of the total number of item-mentions for women and other items were distributed among a variety of categories, such as general traits, skills, general capability, recreation, self maintenance and extra-familial relationships. Responses from boys and girls were very similar in distribution. From a child's-eye view, the traditional picture of women's roles does not seem to have changed much, if at all, and no confusion is perceptible.

With reference to men, approximately 32% of the item-mentions referred to domestic activities also; of these, about 26% were traditionally masculine activities while six per cent fell in the area we tend to think of as "woman's work"—cooking, cleaning, etc. Activities related to work-roles came next; they accounted for approximately 27% of the total. Compared with women, men had a slight edge in the proportion of items falling into such areas as extra-familial relationships, recreational activities, self-maintenance, mobility, generalized traits, education and acquired skills. It is possible that the relatively high proportion of domestic activities for both men and women reflects the limitations of the child's experiences— these are the activities of adults of both sexes with which he is most familiar and which he can recount in greatest detail. Activities related to work-roles take place outside his ken and are more often dismissed with a non-specific phrase like "go to work". Still, the comparative concentration of women's role activities within the home and family is striking, particularly since half our subjects came from "working mother" families. There is no area in male activities which approaches it.

Another way to check on the extent to which certain aspects of sex-roles are perceptible to children is to ask how many subjects out of the total sample mention such aspects at all. We did this in relation to work-roles for women and non-traditional domestic activities for men, since these seemed logically the categories most likely to reflect changes from traditional sex-role pictures. We found that, although only six per cent of all feminine item-mentions had related to work-roles, 29% of the boys and 24% of the girls had contributed one or more items in this category. In relation to men's non-traditional domestic roles, only 23% of the girls had contributed items, but about 37% of the boys had.

When we compared sub-groupings within our sample on the basis of our four major variables, this is what we found. In relation to the assigning of work-role activities to women, only one variable, the work-status of the mother, seemed to have a statistically significant effect, and that effect was perceptible only among the boys. Significantly more sons of working mothers than sons of non-working mothers ($p < .05$) assigned work-role activities to women. Among girls, the fact of having a working mother apparently had less impact. In terms of percentages, approximately 28% of the daughters of working mothers mentioned work-role activities for women, while 21% of the daughters of non-working mothers did this. Among the boys, the comparable figures were 43% for the sons of working mothers and 15% for sons of non-working mothers.

It was among the boys, also, that we found a significant variable in relation to non-traditional domestic activities assigned to men. Here, however, it was the *class* variable that made the difference. Boys from lower middle class and working class homes mentioned such activities for men significantly more frequently than boys from upper middle class homes (p<.01). Compared with girls from the same class category, the boys still come out ahead (p<.05). Moreover, this tendency had no perceptible connection with the work-status of their mothers. In fact, careful examination of the individual protocols revealed that the greatest contribution to this category was made by boys coming from homes where the mother had no outside employment.

Now let us turn from the general picture to a specific question. Because much of current concern about women's role centers around the work role, we wanted to find out how children perceived this role, both in relation to the woman involved and in relation to the child or children from whom she must be separated to fulfill the role. In order to assess our findings concerning women's work-roles, however, we believe we also needed to know how the male counterpart of the working mother was perceived. To obtain these materials, we used two pictures, one showing a woman with a briefcase, walking away from the partly opened door of a house through which a small child watched, and one of a man also apparently leaving a watching child. These pictures were presented one at a time, interspersed among other pictures to which the subjects also reacted; they were separated from each other in the order of presentation by several other pictures.

The interviewer introduced the picture containing the woman with the following words, "This little girl is at home and her mother is going to work—how does the little girl feel about that?" The child's first response was followed by, "What makes you think so?" and by the following series of questions, asked in whatever order was most appropriate to the direction the subject's replies took:

> "Does her mother know how she feels?
> "What is the little girl going to do now?
> "Who will take care of her?"
> "How old do you think the little girl is?
> "How would she feel if she were older?
> "How would she feel if she were in school when her mother went to work?"
> "How does the mother feel about going to work?
> "What makes you think so?"

If the subject stated that the mother was "unhappy" about going to work, the examiner inquired:

> "Why does she go to work if she doesn't like to?
> "What would she rather do?"

If the response to the last question referred primarily to monetary need, the examiner asked:

> "What do you think would happen if she didn't work?
> "Is that the *only* reason that mothers work—to get money?"

"Do they ever enjoy their work?
"Do you know any mothers who go to work?
"How is it in most families?"

The following was asked if the subject indicated that the *child* in the picture felt "badly" about being separated from the mother by the latter's going to work.

"Did *you* ever feel like this little girl does?
"Tell me about it."

The picture of the man was presented with a similar series of remarks and questions, except that at the end the following questions were added:

"In general why do *most* people work?
"If they had enough money without working what would they do?"

Subjects' responses were coded in terms of the global affect they communicated, and we have currently been able to analyze them in relation to three components in the situation: the feeling of each adult about the total situation, the feeling of each adult about his or her work *per se* and the child's feeling. We shall report here on the first two components only.

In relation to the first question, we tried to assess the responses according to what they showed about the respective adult's feelings about the total situation of going-to-work-and-leaving-the-child. We found the most reliable coding scheme was a simple dichotomy which divided the data into answers indicating some degree of discomfort, conflict or unhappiness on the part of the adult, and answers indicating no such feelings. Below are some verbatim examples, showing the range of affect we encountered. They all refer to the woman in the picture, and are responses to the question, "How does she feel about going to work?"

Strongly negative:

"She feels miserable, because she's leaving the little girl behind. . . . If she didn't work, she'd take care of her little girl. . . . She doesn't like working, at least while the girl is so young." (F: 11 yrs.)

Moderately negative:

". . . the mother probably doesn't want to go to work, but the family needs the money. She'd rather stay home and take care of the child, I think, but that's not possible. She feels bad about it all. . . . (Why do you think so?) . . . he's very young and she wants him to love her when he gets older and not say things about her not taking care of him when he was younger. She thinks if he didn't love her, he might start doing bad and become a juvenile delinquent." (M: 11 yrs.)

On the positive side:

"She feels O.K. about it. It's a regular thing. . . . It helps support the family." (F: 11 yrs.)

"She looks like she likes it. She likes it, well, pretty much. . . . They work because they haven't anything to do hardly. . . . She looks like the type who would work, not the type that likes to stay home." (F: 11 yrs.)

". . . she likes going to work, so she won't have to keep yelling at her girl so much. When she's at work she's peaceful and quiet. . . ." (F: 11 yrs.)

Out of 143 subjects who gave us scoreable responses, approximately 64% perceived the woman as suffering some degree of discomfort at leaving a young child to go to work. Only 36% thought she might feel good about it—or, at any rate, have no pangs. These percentages were virtually duplicated in almost all sub-group comparisons. Sex, social class, mother's work-status—none of these made much difference. Only the age variable seemed to have any effect on the responses—there was a steadily rising proportion of discomfort perception from age five through age eleven—from 53% at five, to 60% at eight, to 73% at eleven. Perhaps the reason for this lies in the kinds of work commitment mothers of eleven-year-olds take on, in comparison with mothers of younger children, as well as in the lesser ego-centricity of the older child, and his greater ability to put himself in another's place. Whatever the basis for it may be, the finding itself is provocative. It may explain why significantly fewer eleven than eight-year-old girls said they expected to work after they have a family.

When we turned to the responses concerning the father-going-to-work-and-leaving-a-child, we received something of a surprise, for even *more* of our subjects (69%) thought the *father* felt unhappy or uncomfortable about the situation, with the boys slightly outranking the girls in this judgment (72% to 68%). Here, also, we found an age trend, even more striking in some ways than the other. While approximately 53% of the five-year-olds (and 58% of the eight-year-olds) saw something negative in the situation for the father, 83% of the eleven-year-olds did so. Slightly more children of working mothers than of non-working mothers (73% to 65%) made this kind of judgment.

When we scored the responses for attitude toward work, *per se*, however, the distribution of affect was strikingly different. Considering only the mothers attitude toward her *work per se*, without regard to sources of conflict other than work, we found approximately 54% of the subjects (N = 108)[3] making a positive or neutral judgment and only 45% expressing a negative one. Concerning the father's attitude toward his work, about 61% (N = 84) thought he liked it or didn't mind it, while only 39% thought he felt negative toward it.

Differences between boys and girls were more perceptible in this area. While they did not differ much in their judgments of the woman's feelings, a considerably larger proportion of boys than girls thought the man might

---

[3]N refers here to the number of responses available in which attitude toward work could be clearly differentiated from attitude toward the total complex of leaving-child-to-go-to-work.

have negative feelings about his work (54% boys to 33% girls). Age trends were similar in direction to those reported above, but were not quite so extreme. While only 30% of the eight-year-olds thought the woman might not like her work, 61% of the elevens made this judgment. In relation to the man, corresponding figures were 29% for the eight-year-olds and 44% for the elevens. (We are eliminating the five-year-olds in this comparison because we have so few scorable responses for this category from them that we do not believe any comparison would be meaningful.) There was a slight tendency for more upper-middle-class children than lower-middle-class children to judge work to be pleasant or at least neutral in its impact for both women and men—58% of upper-middle-class subjects to 50% of the others for the women, and 65% of the higher socio-economic group to 56% of the lower for the men.

Interestingly, relatively fewer children of working mothers than of non-working mothers thought work had unpleasant connotations for the woman (37% to 54%). This trend was reversed in judgments about work and the man—here fewer children of *non-working* than of working mothers thought the man might *not* like going to work—34% of the first group to 45% of the second. Comparing these figures in another way, we find that while of the children of working mothers, 37% think mothers might not like to go to work and 45% think fathers might feel this way, of the children of non-working mothers 54% think going to work is unpleasant for mothers while only 34% think this might be so for fathers. Apparently, having a working mother has a considerable effect on the way in which one perceives both work and people.

This qualitative difference in the perception of the work role seems to be reflected in our subjects' future plans. When asked what they expected to do or be when they grow up, significantly more (p<.05) daughters of non-working mothers gave "housewife" as their primary choice and more daughters of working mothers mentioned non-traditional professional areas (such as doctor, lawyer, creative worker) as their vocational choices (p<.20). In relation to work after marriage and the coming of children, also, more daughters of working mothers said they thought they would continue working (p<.05).

When the responses of all the girls were compared with those of all the boys, the proportion of girls who indicated they planned to work was significantly higher than the proportion of boys who indicated they might consent to their wives' working (p<.01). This finding is in line with those reported by other investigators, who have mostly worked with older male subjects (2), and suggests that the attitudes of the male of the species will continue to act as a brake in relation to speed of sex-role changes.

In conclusion, I should like to emphasize a few points that seem to me to be important. In response to those who are overly concerned about the effect of apparent recent sex-role changes, I would like to point out that from the child's point of view, there are no "changes"; he sees only the picture as it appears in his time, and this picture, as it is reflected in our data, shows remarkably little change from traditional values. If the forms of sex-role activities have changed somewhat, from the child's point of view their *functions* have not. Our subjects clearly tell us that the basic home-making duties are still the woman's; the money-getting role is still primarily the man's. Whenever women are perceived to have assumed the work-role, they are generally perceived to do so as "helping" persons within the family group—to help out when the family needs more money than the father earns, or when the father cannot earn. Similarly, fathers occupied with domestic activities are seen as "*helping*" the mother in her myriad home-centered responsibilities, not *supplanting* her. Finally, we find no hint of female-male competitiveness in the picture of sex-role functioning as the children reflect it. Whatever changes have occurred, seem to be in the direction of greater flexibility and egality of activities in the service of maintaining established functions. On the whole, they suggest an increasingly realistic adjustment to the demands of modern living, without the enforced trauma of radical innovation.

REFERENCES

1. Hartley, Ruth E. Sex-role pressures and the socialization of the male child. *Psychological Reports*, 1959, 5, 457-468.
2. Payne, R. Adolescents' attitudes toward the working wife. *Marriage and Family Living*, 1956, 18, 345-348.

EDITORIAL COMMENTS

One of the most obvious bases for classification of human beings is that of sex. In most cultures, differentiation on the basis of sex is not considered merely biological in origin, but different skills, social behaviors and attitudes, and relationships are associated with being male or female. One aspect of the socialization of children concerns the development of such different behaviors—that is, the child's learning of appropriate sex-role behaviors. This has been studied extensively, and many theorists consider this aspect of development to be of major importance with respect to the development of personality and moral behavior.

Hartley's investigation looks at a facet of the area of development slightly different from that on which most research has focused. Hartley studied the child's perception of the adult sex role, and the influence on this perception of apparent changes in the traditional definitions of such roles that result from increasing numbers of women (mothers) being employed outside of the home.

Hartley concluded that her findings indicate that the child's perceptions of sex roles seem not to differ from the traditional values and definitions of such roles. However, this conclusion was based only on the agreement of the children's answers with her assumptions concerning the traditional definitions, and not on any formal comparison with similar answers obtained at a different time. Comparison of her findings with those obtained more than a decade later would afford an interesting opportunity to examine more precisely the effects of changes over time in acceptable sex-role behavior on children's perceptions.

Modifications of Sample and Procedure

In the original investigation more girls than boys were involved, as Hartley's concern was primarily with girls' perception of the female role. For purposes of replication, equal numbers of each sex may make the results easier to interpret.

Hartley classified her subjects in terms of their membership in different socioeconomic classes and according to the presence of working or nonworking mothers. Information as to whether or not a child's mother is employed may be relatively easy to ascertain. However, Hartley does not specify the criteria used for the socioeconomic classification of her subjects, so that this aspect of her study cannot be replicated; also, this information may be more difficult for students to obtain. If subjects are drawn from markedly different neighborhoods, or if students obtain subjects from two settings that differ in some particular way that seems relevant to the purpose of the study, comparison of subgroups could be made here. However, use of subgroups differing only with respect to age and sex would still make this an interesting study to carry out.

In replicating this study, students may wish to include both aspects, that is, traditional sex role and attitudes toward work, or they may wish to replicate only one part of the study and employ a larger number of subjects than if both parts were utilized.

Hartley classified the children's answers to questions as to whether they reflected traditional sex-role activities, work roles, or other behaviors. Specification of the behavior included in these categories is not very complete or precise. If two students work together on this project, it would be interesting to determine the extent of agreement of two judges concerning the assignment of the children's responses to these categories. The same problem exists concerning the classification of the children's answers with regard to their perception of the parents' attitudes toward going to work; a similar procedure might be carried out in replicating this aspect of the study. (See editorial comments for the Graham *et al.* study and the Sigel study for assuring judges' reliability.)

Treatment of Data

Understanding of Hartley's results, as well as comparison of her findings with those of a replication, may be facilitated if these results are summarized in tabular form. It should also be noted that while the article indicates that a statistical analysis of the results was carried out (statistical significance of results is reported), there is no indication as to what statistical procedures were employed.

The student should also be aware that when results are reported in percentages, and when there are few subjects in each subgroup, the proportion of results contributed by one subject becomes rather large—with only three subjects per group, each subject provides 33 percent of the results for that category.

THE DEVELOPMENT OF CONSCIENCE:
A COMPARISON OF AMERICAN CHILDREN OF
DIFFERENT MENTAL AND SOCIOECONOMIC LEVELS

Leonore Boehm,[*] *Brooklyn College*

This is the first of four reports on an investigation of moral judgment and conscience development, and subcultural differences due to religion, socioeconomic class, and mental level. The writer agrees with Piaget (10) that the cognitive ability to distinguish between right and wrong is one of the ingredients in conscience development, and she was interested in investigating at what age different groups of American children learn to distinguish between intention and result of an action. Another closely related question arose from Piaget's belief, which the author questioned, that the child cannot attain "morality" until he becomes independent of adults and achieves peer reciprocity.

The subcultural comparisons were made by studying boys and girls of two intelligence levels in upper middle class and working class attending public[1] and parochial schools. The parochial schools were Jewish and Catholic (2).

After having interviewed a number of children, the author formulated the hypotheses that, in answer to questions concerning intention versus result: (a) academically gifted children might respond with earlier maturity than children of average intelligence and (b) upper middle-class children might respond with earlier maturity than children of working-class parents; but that, in answer to questions regarding independence from adult versus peer reciprocity, (a) gifted children might be less mature than children of average intelligence and (b) upper middle-class children might be less mature than working-class children. A further hypothesis was that there would be individual and subcultural differences in the age of mature response, depending upon the area of conscience development under investigation and specific aspects of that area.

Procedure

Table 1 shows the distribution of children interviewed in the study according to above-average intelligence (IQ over 110) and average intelli-

[*] Department of Education, Brooklyn College, Brooklyn 10, New York.

[1] A study of children of average intelligence attending public schools was conducted jointly with Martin Nass. These investigations have been supported by a PHS research grant M-2528 from the National Institute of Mental Health, Public Health Service.

Child Develpm., 1962, 33, 575-590. © Society for Research in Child Development, Inc., 1962.

gence (IQ 90 to 110), socioeconomic class, and the school attended.[2] These children ranged from 6 to 9 years of age. It was decided to set an upper limit of 9 years, because analysis of data in the previous study (3), which had included children from 6 to 11 years, indicated little change in response after the age of 9.

TABLE 1

POPULATION: CHILDREN BY SCHOOL AND GROUP

| | | | SCHOOL | | |
| | | | CATHOLIC PAROCHIAL | | |
Group	TOTAL	PUBLIC	Natick	Brooklyn	JEWISH PAROCH'L
Total	237	112	44	66	15
Gifted					
Upper class	80	22	20	23	15
Working class	43	19	8	16	..
Average					
Upper class	56	34	8	14	..
Working class	58	37	8	13	..

The children comprised all students available in their grades who fell into the desired categories, except in the Jewish parochial school where the principal selected the small number of children we were allowed to interview.

Warner's norms were used as a basis for assigning social class position of the subjects studied.

Using Piaget's "clinical method," each child was seen individually and told four stories. Two stories were by Piaget, the Cup story with slight cultural adaptation and the Lost story. The other two stories (1), Fight and Scout, had been constructed and tested in collaboration with Alina Szeminska. Interviews were recorded on tape. The Cup and Lost stories are concerned with the evaluation of an act as to intent or result, while Fight and Scout are concerned with peer reciprocity versus dependence on adult authority.

The stories were used as semiprojective tests. It was hoped that the children tested would identify with the children in the story and would respond on an affective, as well as on a purely intellectual level.

The stories are presented below with questions illustrating the type of question used in the interviews. All but the Lost story were interrupted by

---

[2] The investigator realizes that the samples when grouped by age, intelligence and class, as well as by type of school attended, are small; however, age development can be observed when all children of a given age are grouped together.

questions before the stories were completed. In the clinical method the investigator formulates each question on the basis of the response to the preceding question and a uniform questionnaire cannot be used. In the course of probing, the investigator asked a large number of questions, making sure to pick up the child's exact terminology in order to preserve the child's emotional reaction.

CUP STORY (after Piaget):

A little boy named John (or a girl named Mary, depending on the sex of the subject) is called to dinner by his mother. Between the room where John is and the kitchen (or dining room) there is a swinging door. Behind the door is a chair with fifteen cups on a tray. John has no way of knowing that the chair with the cups is there. When he opens the door, the door swings into the chair, the chair and the tray tumble and all the cups break.

How do you think his mother felt about this?
Was she angry at John?

A boy named Henry (or a girl named Margaret) is told by his mother not to take any cookies from the jar, since the mother needed the cookies for guests. The mother leaves the house and Henry wants to snitch one cookie. Since the mother has placed the jar out of his reach, Henry has to climb up on a chair in order to reach the jar and he knocks over a cup on a lower shelf while doing so.

How will Henry's mother feel when she comes home?
Which mother is more angry, John's or Henry's?
What do you think about these two boys?
Are they both naughty? Is one naughty?
If you were the father (or mother) would you punish both?
Would you punish one more than the other? Which one?

LOST STORY (after Piaget):

A boy named Joe (or a girl named Alice) has just moved into the neighborhood and does not know the names of the streets very well. One day while he is playing, a man stops him and asks him where ———— Street (street near child's school) is. Joe is not sure of the direction, but answers: "I think it's over there." But it was not there. The man walks and walks and walks and cannot find the house he is looking for.

A boy named Mike (or a girl named Louise) knows the neighborhood very well. One day a man asks him where ———— Street is. Mike knows, but he wants to play a trick on the man and says, "It's there," and shows him the wrong way, but this man is smart and finds his way.

What do you think of the two boys?
Why?
Were both these boys equally naughty?

FIGHT STORY (Boehm and Szeminska):

Two boys, Louis and George, very good friends, want to find out whether one of them is stronger than the other. So they decide to have a match, a fun fight, to see who is stronger. The next morning they meet early in the school yard for their fight. While they are fighting, by accident Louis hits George on the nose which begins to bleed badly.

How do you think George felt about Louis?
How did Louis feel?

Because Louis felt sorry (or whichever term the child used) he wanted to do something about it, and wondered what to do. He could ask his teacher. Louis thought the teacher might tell him to write "I should not fight," 100 times. Or he could ask some of his friends. One of them might say, "Why don't you bring George your favorite toy to play with?" Another one might say, "Buy him a gift." A third might say, "Just go to George and tell him you're sorry."

What do you think Louis did?
Why?

Louis went to George to tell him he was sorry (using the child's term) and he also brought him his toy. But George said, "You don't need to give me anything. You didn't mean to hurt me. It was an accident. I could have hurt you just as easily."

Do you think Louis left the toy or took it home?
Why?
When do you think George forgave him, when Louis said he was sorry, or when he gave him the toy?
Would the toy make George be a better friend again?
What do you think made Louis feel better, writing 100 times "I should not fight," giving his toy to George, or hearing George say everything was all right?

SCOUT STORY (Boehm and Szeminska):

A group of children X years old (the subject's age) want to give a surprise birthday party for their scout leader. One boy, Charles, is to decorate the room. He has never done this before and wonders whom he should ask for advice. He could ask his home room teacher. This teacher does not teach arts and crafts because he is not good in it, although he is very good in English, social studies, mathematics, etc. Or Charles could ask a boy in his classroom who takes lessons in arts and crafts at the museum once a week and is excellent. He is so talented that he has won a prize at the museum.

Whom do you think he asked?
If he asked both and they gave him different ideas, whose advice would he follow?
If he thought both ideas were equally good, whose would he use?
A friend told him he liked the classmate's plan much better than the teacher's. Would Charles still rather use the teacher's?
If he follows the friend's advice and uses the boy's plan, will the teacher be hurt or angry?[3]

Treatment of Data

Each child's protocol was scored independently, from transcriptions of the tape, by three judges, one of whom was the investigator. The other two judges were graduate education students, both teachers.[4] Responses to each

---

[3] These stories are in a slightly altered form than when first used.

[4] Mrs. Doris Danto and Mrs. Esther May, former graduate students, who had done similar research.

story by each child were classified according to Piaget's three levels of morality (10):

> 1. "Morality of constraint." This is defined to mean automatic obedience to rules without reasoning or judgment, with adults viewed as omnipotent. Punishment is seen as a necessary retribution of justice and given in proportion to size or result of the misdeed, independent of motive. Intentions are not taken into consideration.
> 2. An intermediary stage in which the child internalizes rules without evaluating them, or alternates in his responses to the situation.
> 3. "Morality of cooperation." This is defined to mean that the child evaluates intentions rather than deeds or outcomes alone. Moral behavior is engaged in for its own sake, not out of fear of punishment. Cooperation and mutual respect among peers have taken the place of former unilateral respect for adults.

Because of the relatively small numbers of responses, it was not expedient to examine responses "1" and "2" separately in the statistical analyses.

RESULTS

Our findings were analyzed by two different statistical methods: (a) tests of interactions (Table 2) and (b) significance tests on various proportions (Table 3). In the tests of interactions (11) the responses (omitting the small Jewish group) were classified according to three independent variables (mental level, socioeconomic level, and stories) and their combinations.

TABLE 2

TESTS OF INTERACTIONS

Classifications	df	χ^2
Mental level	1	15.03*
Socioeconomic class	1	2.11
Mental level by socioeconomic class	1	11.49*
Stories	3	30.20*
Stories by mental level	3	1.40
Stories by socioeconomic class	3	8.11*
Stories by mental level by socioeconomic class	3	.56

* $p \leq .05$.

Both types of analysis show that mental level is significant and is modified by class membership. When in the tests of interactions the results of all four stories are combined, socioeconomic class differences are masked, be-

TABLE 3

DIFFERENCES IN PROPORTIONS OF "3" RESPONSES FOR COMPARABLE CATEGORIES

SECTION 1. GIFTED (A) vs. AVERAGE (B)

Group	CUP STORY Number of Responses	"3" Responses No.	%	Difference between Percentages	LOST STORY Number of Responses	"3" Responses No.	%	Difference between Percentages	FIGHT STORY Number of Responses	"3" Responses No.	%	Difference between Percentages	SCOUT STORY Number of Responses	"3" Responses No.	%	Difference between Percentages
A, Age 6	28	12	42.8	+20.6	28	19	67.9	+19.8	21	9	42.9	+5.4	28	13	46.4	— 1.7
B, Age 6	27	6	22.2		27	13	48.1		24	9	37.5		27	13	48.1	
A, Age 7	35	17	48.6	+16.3	34	28	82.4	+20.3*	26	16	61.5	+22.4	35	29	82.9	+36.0**
B, Age 7	31	10	32.3		29	18	62.1		23	9	39.1		32	15	46.9	
A, Age 8	30	15	50.0	+ 5.2	31	26	83.9	+11.5	25	20	80.0	+34.2**	31	20	65.7	— 3.3
B, Age 8	29	13	44.8		29	21	72.4		24	11	45.8		29	20	69.0	
A, Age 9	29	26	89.7	+ 9.6	28	27	96.4	+11.8	21	15	71.4	+ 8.9	29	20	69.0	— 4.1
B, Age 9	26	21	80.1		26	22	84.6		24	15	62.5		26	19	73.1	
A, Ages 6–9	122	70	57.4	+13.2**	121	100	82.6	+15.9**	93	60	64.5	+18.2**	123	82	66.7	+ 7.9
B, Ages 6–9	113	50	44.2		111	74	66.7		95	44	46.3		114	67	58.8	

* $p \leq .10$.
** $p \leq .05$.

TABLE 3 (*continued*)

DIFFERENCES IN PROPORTIONS OF "3" RESPONSES FOR COMPARABLE CATEGORIES

SECTION 2. GIFTED, UPPER CLASS (A) vs. AVERAGE, UPPER CLASS (B)

Group	CUP STORY Number of Responses	"3" Responses No.	%	Difference between Percentages	LOST STORY Number of Responses	"3" Responses No.	%	Difference between Percentages	FIGHT STORY Number of Responses	"3" Responses No.	%	Difference between Percentages	SCOUT STORY Number of Responses	"3" Responses No.	%	Difference between Percentages
A, Age 6	17	9	52.9	+14.4	17	11	64.7	− 4.5	12	4	33.3	+ 2.5	17	10	58.8	+20.3
B, Age 6	13	5	38.5		13	9	69.2		13	4	30.8		13	5	38.5	
A, Age 7	23	12	52.2	+27.2*	22	21	95.5	+38.4**	16	11	68.8	+35.5*	23	19	82.6	+35.5**
B, Age 7	16	4	25.0		14	8	57.1		12	4	33.3		17	8	47.1	
A, Age 8	20	11	55.0	+12.1	21	21	100.0	+28.6**	17	14	82.4	+55.1**	21	13	61.9	− 16.7
B, Age 8	14	6	42.9		14	10	71.4		11	3	27.3		14	11	78.6	
A, Age 9	19	18	94.7	+ 3.0	18	17	94.4	+ 2.7	14	9	64.3	+ 0.7	19	11	57.9	− 0.4
B, Age 9	12	11	91.7		12	11	91.7		11	7	63.6		12	7	58.3	
A, Ages 6–9	79	50	63.3	+16.0*	78	70	88.6	+16.9**	59	38	64.4	+26.1**	80	53	66.2	+10.8
B, Ages 6–9	55	26	47.3		53	38	71.7		47	18	38.3		56	31	55.4	

* $p \leq .10$.
** $p \leq .05$.

TABLE 3 (continued)

DIFFERENCES IN PROPORTIONS OF "3" RESPONSES FOR COMPARABLE CATEGORIES

SECTION 3. GIFTED, WORKING CLASS (A) vs. AVERAGE, WORKING CLASS (B)

Group	CUP STORY				LOST STORY				FIGHT STORY				SCOUT STORY			
	Number of Responses	"3" Responses No.	%	Difference between Percentages	Number of Responses	"3" Responses No.	%	Difference between Percentages	Number of Responses	"3" Responses No.	%	Difference between Percentages	Number of Responses	"3" Responses No.	%	Difference between Percentages
A, Age 6	11	3	27.3	+20.2	11	8	72.7	+44.1**	9	5	55.6	+10.1	11	3	27.3	−29.8
B, Age 6	14	1	7.1		14	4	28.6		11	5	45.5		14	8	57.1	
A, Age 7	12	5	41.7	+1.7	12	7	58.3	−8.4	10	5	50.0	+4.5	12	10	83.3	+36.6*
B, Age 7	15	6	40.0		15	10	66.7		11	5	45.5		15	7	46.7	
A, Age 8	10	4	40.0	−6.7	10	5	50.0	−23.3	8	6	75.0	+13.5	10	7	70.0	+10.0
B, Age 8	15	7	46.7		15	11	73.3		13	8	61.5		15	9	60.0	
A, Age 9	10	8	80.0	+8.6	10	10	100.0	+21.4	7	6	85.7	+24.2	10	9	90.0	+4.3
B, Age 9	14	10	71.4		14	11	78.6		13	8	61.5		14	12	85.7	
A, Ages 6–9	43	20	46.5	+5.1	43	30	69.8	+7.7	34	22	64.7	+10.5	43	29	67.4	+5.3
B, Ages 6–9	58	24	41.4		58	36	62.1		48	26	54.2		58	36	62.1	

* $p \leq .10$.
** $p \leq .05$.

TABLE 3 (*continued*)

DIFFERENCES IN PROPORTIONS OF "3" RESPONSES FOR COMPARABLE CATEGORIES

SECTION 4. GIFTED, UPPER CLASS (A) vs. GIFTED, WORKING CLASS (B)

Group	CUP STORY			LOST STORY			FIGHT STORY			SCOUT STORY		
	Number of Responses	"3" Responses No. %	Difference between Percentages	Number of Responses	"3" Responses No. %	Difference between Percentages	Number of Responses	"3" Responses No. %	Difference between Percentages	Number of Responses	"3" Responses No. %	Difference between Percentages
A, Age 6	17	9 52.9	+25.6	17	11 64.7	− 8.0	12	4 33.3	−22.3	17	10 58.8	+31.5*
B, Age 6	11	3 27.3		11	8 72.7		9	5 55.6		11	3 27.3	
A, Age 7	23	12 52.2	+10.5	22	21 95.5	+37.2**	16	11 68.8	+18.8	23	19 82.6	− 0.7
B, Age 7	12	5 41.7		12	7 58.3		10	5 50.0		12	10 83.3	
A, Age 8	20	11 55.0	+15.0	21	21 100.0	+50.0**	17	14 82.4	+ 7.4	21	13 61.9	− 8.1
B, Age 8	10	4 40.0		10	5 50.0		8	6 75.0		10	7 70.0	
A, Age 9	19	18 94.7	+14.7	18	17 94.4	− 5.6	14	9 64.3	−21.4	19	11 57.9	−32.1*
B, Age 9	10	8 80.0		10	10 100.0		7	6 85.7		10	9 90.0	
A, Ages 6-9	79	50 63.3	+16.8*	78	70 88.6	+18.8**	59	38 64.4	− 0.3	80	53 66.2	− 1.2
B, Ages 6-9	43	20 46.5		43	30 69.8		34	22 64.7		43	29 67.4	

* $p \leq .10$.
** $p \leq .05$.

TABLE 3 (*continued*)

DIFFERENCES IN PROPORTIONS OF "3" RESPONSES FOR COMPARABLE CATEGORIES

SECTION 5. AVERAGE, UPPER CLASS (A) vs. AVERAGE, WORKING CLASS (B)

Group	CUP STORY Number of Responses	"3" Responses No.	%	Difference between Percentages	LOST STORY Number of Responses	"3" Responses No.	%	Difference between Percentages	FIGHT STORY Number of Responses	"3" Responses No.	%	Difference between Percentages	SCOUT STORY Number of Responses	"3" Responses No.	%	Difference between Percentages
A, Age 6	13	5	38.5	+31.4**	13	9	69.2	+40.6**	13	4	30.8	−14.7	13	5	38.5	−18.6
B, Age 6	14	1	7.1		14	4	28.6		11	5	45.5		14	8	57.1	
A, Age 7	16	4	25.0	−15.0	14	8	57.1	− 9.6	12	4	33.3	−12.2	17	8	47.1	+ 0.4
B, Age 7	15	6	40.0		15	10	66.7		11	5	45.5		15	7	46.7	
A, Age 8	14	6	42.9	− 3.8	14	10	71.4	− 1.9	11	3	27.3	−34.2**	14	11	78.6	+18.6
B, Age 8	15	7	46.7		15	11	73.3		13	8	61.5		15	9	60.0	
A, Age 9	12	11	91.7	+20.3	12	11	91.7	+13.1	11	7	63.6	+ 2.1	12	7	58.3	−27.4
B, Age 9	14	10	71.4		14	11	78.6		13	8	61.5		14	12	85.7	
A, Ages 6-9	55	26	47.3	+ 5.9	53	38	71.7	+ 9.6	47	18	38.3	−15.9	56	31	55.4	− 6.7
B, Ages 6-9	58	24	41.4		58	36	62.1		48	26	54.2		58	36	62.1	

* *p* ≤ .10.
** *p* ≤ .05.

cause the pairs of stories operate in different directions concerning class level. When considered individually, however, the stories are sensitive to socioeconomic class membership. Although the four stories vary in difficulty, their relative difficulty does not vary for the different IQ groups.

In each pair of stories one story received fewer "3" responses than the other. Cup and Fight presented much greater difficulties to the respondents, whose scores on both stories were lower than expected on a chance basis. Cup scored lowest, while Scout and Lost exceeded the expected number of "3" responses, Lost more than Scout.

The percentage of "3" responses to the Cup and Lost stories (concerned with intention and result of action) and to the Fight and Scout stories (concerned with adult authority and peer reciprocity) are not significantly different: 62 per cent in the case of the former, and 59 per cent in the case of the latter.

Responses to the stories were compared according to age groups (*see* Table 3). Gifted children gave "3" responses at an earlier age and at each age level received more "3" scores than children of average intelligence, except for the Scout story, when the socioeconomic classes were combined (*see* section 1, Table 3).

These differences between gifted children and those of average intelligence were accounted for mainly by the upper middle-class group, as shown in section 2, Table 3. While the gifted upper middle-class children gave significantly more "3" responses (except for the Scout story) than subjects of average intelligence in the upper middle class, gifted working-class children (in all but the Scout story) showed only a slightly higher (and nonsignificant) proportion of "3" responses than their counterparts of average intelligence (*see* section 3, Table 3).

Responses to the separate stories were compared by socioeconomic class (*see* sections 4 and 5, Table 3). In the Cup and the Lost stories, in which children evaluated a deed as to either intention or result, the upper middle class, of both levels of intelligence, gave more "3" answers at an earlier age. In the Cup story there was a larger difference favoring the upper middle class among gifted children than among those of average intelligence. Among the latter at ages 7 and 8, there were small but nonsignificant differences in favor of the working-class group.

The Lost story also showed higher scores for upper middle class with all ages combined, although at ages 6 and 9 gifted working-class children scored more "3's" than gifted upper middle-class children. At ages 7 and 8, working-class children of average intelligence scored more "3's" than upper middle-class children of average intelligence. These differences in favor of working-class children were less marked than the ones in favor of upper middle-class children.

For the Fight and the Scout stories which are concerned with peer reciprocity versus dependence on authority, the working-class child at both intelligence levels scored higher than the upper middle-class child. In the Fight story, with a few exceptions, the working-class children tended to give more "3" responses than middle-class children of comparable age and intelligence. In the Scout story the scores are slightly, though insignificantly, in favor of working-class children at both intelligence levels when ages are combined.

The age at which a majority of the children tested gave level "3" responses varied with the specific situation and the child's socioeconomic class and level of intelligence. The response to the Cup story by gifted children showed that a majority in the upper middle class gave "3" level responses at age 6, while the majority of the working class did so at age 9. Among children of average intelligence, there was no class difference, the majority scoring "3" only at 9 years.

Level "3" responses were given to the Lost story at age 6 by a majority of the gifted and average upper middle-class children and the gifted working-class children. The majority of working-class children of average intelligence were 7 years old before they gave a "3" level response.

In the Fight story, the gifted group in the upper middle class scored "3" at age 7, and the gifted in the working class at age 6 (although there is an exception at age 7). In the group of average intelligence, the upper middle class scored "3" at age 9 and the working class at age 8.

In the Scout story a majority of "3" answers were given at age 6 by gifted upper middle class, at age 7 by gifted working class, and at age 8 by upper middle class of average intelligence. With the responses available, it was not possible to determine a "3" level response for the working-class child of average intelligence since, although the majority scored "3" at ages 6 and 8, at age 7 only 47 per cent scored "3."

Gifted children scored "3" responses at least a year earlier than those of average intelligence, except for the Scout story.

The majority of gifted children in both socioeconomic groups scored "3" at age 9 for the Cup story, at age 7 for the Fight and Scout stories, and at age 6 for the Lost story.

The majority of children of average intelligence in both socioeconomic groups scored "3" at age 9 in the Fight and Cup stories, at age 8 in the Scout story, and at age 7 in the Lost story.

The findings regarding class and intelligence show that, in stories concerned with motivation versus outcome, gifted upper middle-class children had the greatest relative number of "3" scores. They were followed by upper middle-class children of average intelligence. Gifted working-class children received somewhat fewer "3" scores than upper middle-class children of average intelligence. Working-class children of average intelligence had the lowest number of "3" scores.

In stories concerned with the child's independence from adult authority, the picture is somewhat reversed. Gifted working-class children had significantly more "3" scores, followed by gifted middle-class children. Working-class children of average intelligence had more "3" scores than upper middle-class children of average intelligence, the difference approaching significance.

Discussion

These results generally confirm the hypothesis of a difference between gifted children and those of average intelligence with regard to maturity of moral judgment (as defined by Piaget).

A review of the literature on this subject discloses that other investigations did not find this distinction. The findings of these studies, which are also built on Piaget's method and concepts, are at variance with the present findings because of such factors as the smaller number of subjects at each age, differences in range of age groups, differences in range of IQs in the gifted and average categories, and in the specific aspect within the area of moral development being investigated.

Kohlberg (7) investigated Piaget's concept of morality as related to peer reciprocity among boys from the fourth, seventh, and tenth grades. These subjects consisted of six disturbed isolates and six integrates, half each from the upper and lower socioeconomic classes in each age group. Kohlberg found no significant difference in responses between the higher and lower intelligence levels, although he did find differences "in level of sophistication" in the replies. His results are similar to those of the present study at the fourth grade level where little difference in response was found between children at the two intelligence levels.

Durkin (4, 5, 6) used Piaget's clinical method in interviewing boys and girls in grades 2, 5, 8, and 11 on the development of concepts of justice. In her first study (4) of fifth grade children, Durkin felt there was a possible difference in level of responses due to intelligence level; children of higher intelligence were less inclined to seek help from an authority figure than those of lesser intelligence. Older and younger subjects, regardless of intelligence level, however, preferred to report an incident to a person in authority rather than settling it among themselves.

In a later paper Durkin (6) concluded that this difference among fifth grade subjects was due to chance and that there was no difference in response between intelligence levels. Several factors may account for the fact that her findings differ from those of the present study. The subjects from a small midwestern, mostly farming, community, though considered by Durkin to be middle class, were a mixed group economically and from a lower middle-class group than those in the present study. The IQ scores of her subjects also differed, ranging from 92 to 114 in the second grade, from 69 to 122 in the fifth grade, and from 77 to 148 in the eighth. Subjects of above-average intelligence in the present study had IQs higher than those in Durkin's above-average group.

A few of the gifted children in the present study, like those in Durkin's, chose adult help over peer help, but they obviously were trying to please the investigator with their replies. They "changed" their opinions at the slightest suggestion from the interviewer. Bright children are more likely to try to please teachers, since they have more foresight and are aware of possibilities for ingratiating themselves with persons in authority. Often they identified with the interviewer who represented a teacher to them and gave the answer they thought was expected.

MacRae (8, 9) investigated Piaget's concept of morality, using Piaget's stories in interviews with younger children and in questionnaires filled out by older children. His subjects from grades 5 to 8 consisted of a small group of boys of higher IQs (over 105) who were compared with those of average intelligence, each group being composed of higher and lower socioeconomic classes.

MacRae found more adult dependency among the gifted children in the fifth grade. MacRae's fifth-graders of above-average intelligence believed more in immanent justice or punishment and thus judged more absolutely and rigidly than those of average intelligence in the same grade. His gifted and upper-socioeconomic-class boys allowed no exception in breaking of norms, even in circumstances where a violation of a norm would appear more moral than keeping it.

In this respect, his older subjects responded alike without regard to intelligence levels, but at all ages children of above-average intelligence and those of upper socioeconomic class responded more maturely to questions concerning intention and result and took into account foreseeable consequences of actions. They responded more maturely with regard to strict punishment and in showing they knew when they were capable or not to judge.

MacRae decided that children of above-average intelligence and upper socioeconomic class respond more maturely to "cognitive" aspects of moral development. Cognitive responses, according to MacRae, are based on knowledge of adult expectations and are due to cultural indoctrination and learning of norms. He believes that the bright child and the child of upper socioeconomic class internalizes parental rules more strongly and remains dependent upon parents longer than those of average intelligence and the lower class. Because of this, they cannot be flexible about rules and will not accept any change in rules. The present findings do not bear out MacRae's findings of longer or stronger dependence on adults by gifted children than by children of average intelligence. Gifted children at almost all ages—there are exceptions in the Scout story—responded with less adult dependency than those of average intelligence.

Differences in responses between gifted upper middle-class and gifted working-class subjects are less surprising than would first appear. Piaget pointed out that children's actions are "moral" far earlier than their theoretical verbal judgments. On this point MacRae's (8) findings and conceptions of moral evaluations and adult independence in the working-class group may well be correct. These children, regardless of intelligence level, are certainly less accustomed to formalized thinking. The less verbally inclined, though gifted, working-class child could be as "moral" in his actions as gifted upper middle-class children, but might appear less mature because of an inadequate way of expressing himself in judging actions. However, in his responses it was not only the quality and length of expression which differed, but the level of moral judgment.

In calling for a distinction between intention and consequence, the Cup and Lost stories could have involved a higher thought process than the other stories, a more complex "operation" (Piaget) and a more conceptually abstract thought. Both the Cup and Lost stories, in contrast to the other two, contain a pair of plots similar in some respects and different in others. However, more younger children from both levels of intelligence distinguished between intention and result in the Lost than in the Cup story, although both stories are concerned with the same problem.

In the Cup story, working-class children often judged "maturely" (according to Piaget's definition) after hearing the first plot but changed to an "immature" response when hearing the second plot and being asked to compare them. While at first they were able to judge the action without regard to result, in the second part of the story they evaluated outcome, impressed by the comparison of 15 versus one broken cup. Perhaps they would have remained more objective if the number of broken cups had varied less. As it was, emotions might have interfered with logical thought. Personal experience with scoldings and punishment for dishes broken accidentally might be remembered. A belief in "immanent justice" returned and with it the expectance of dire results as a consequence of behavior causing harm.

Contrary to Piaget, our data do not show that "maturity of moral judgment" increases as the child becomes independent of adults and achieves peer reciprocity. In the present study there seemed to be no connection between "mature" responses concerning right and wrong and responses indicating adult independence. Rather, working-class children who gave early "3" level responses to the stories concerning adult independence scored more lower level responses at the same age when distinguishing right from wrong in considering intention and result of actions. Upper middle-class subjects, who were more discerning at an earlier age than working-class children with regard to intention and consequence, scored more lower level responses at the same age regarding issues of adult independence and peer reciprocity.

SUMMARY AND CONCLUSIONS

In a study of some aspects of conscience development in public schools, two Catholic parochial schools, and one Jewish parochial school, academically gifted children were compared with children of average intelligence, and upper middle-class children with children of the working class. The following findings emerged:

1. Academically gifted children mature earlier in their moral judgments concerning distinctions between intention and outcome of an action than children of average intelligence.

2. Upper middle-class children develop earlier in this aspect than working-class children.

3. There is a greater difference between responses of academically gifted children and children of average intelligence of the upper middle-class than between gifted children and those of average intelligence in the working class.

4. Working-class children at both intelligence levels show earlier peer reciprocity and adult independence than upper middle-class children.

REFERENCES

1. BOEHM, L. The development of independence: a comparative study. *Child Develpm.*, 1957, 28, 85-92.
2. BOEHM, L. The development of conscience: a comparison of upper-middle-class, academically gifted, children attending Catholic and Jewish parochial schools. *J soc. Psychol.*, in press.
3. BOEHM, L., & NASS, M. Social class differences in conscience development. *Child Develpm.*, 1962, 33, 565-574.
4. DURKIN, D. Children's concepts of justice. *Child Develpm.*, 1959, 30, 59-67.
5. DURKIN, D. Children's acceptance of reciprocity as a justice-principle. *Child Develpm.*, 1959, 30, 289-296.
6. DURKIN, D. Children's concept of justice. *J. educ. Res.*, 1959, 52, 252-257.
7. KOHLBERG, L. Moral judgment in the years ten to sixteen. Unpublished doctoral dissertation, Univer. of Chicago, 1958.
8. MACRAE, D. The development of moral judgment in children. Unpublished doctoral dissertation, Harvard Univer., 1950.
9. MACRAE, D. A test of Piaget's theories of moral development. *J. abnorm. soc. Psychol.*, 1954, 49, 14-18.
10. PIAGET, J. *Le jugement moral chez l'enfant.* Alcan, 1932.
11. SUTCLIFFE, J. P. A general method of analysis of frequency data for multiple classification designs. *Psychol. Bull.*, 1957, 54, 134-139.

EDITORIAL COMMENTS

Boehm's study compares moral judgments made by children of different socioeconomic backgrounds (upper-middle and working class) and of different degrees of academic performance (average and academically gifted) and the interaction of these variables.

Modifications of Sample and Procedure

Several possible modifications, particularly in sample selection, are possible in replicating this study. The student may elect to make only a limited number of comparisons rather than use all of the subgroups in the original study.

Boehm's subjects were selected from four different age groups. Students may use only two age groups in order to obtain a larger number of subjects in each of the subgroups in the study. Investigation of responses to the four stories for several age groups in itself would be an interesting project. In some schools it may not be possible to identify academically gifted students, or such information about children may not be available to the student investigators, so that these classifications of subjects may not be possible. Boehm has also classified children into social class groups, and the information necessary to do this may also not be available to student investigators. However, data could be gathered from two groups of children attending schools in different neighborhoods, in urban or surburban school districts, and so on, and the results from such groups compared.

Boehm utilized a "clinical method," similar to that used by Piaget, in interviewing her subjects about their reactions to the stories. It may not be possible to tape-record the subjects' responses as she did, but the investigator should try to record the exact words used by the subjects as well as the questions asked by the examiners. Two students working together provide two judges for scoring the responses, and the report should include a statement of the degree of agreement in their judgments. If a single student works on this project, it may be necessary to cooperate in being a judge for another project, thus gaining experience with two different studies.

Analysis of Results

The results of this study were analyzed using the chi-square test for independence. This test is referred to by Boehm in discussing the tests of interactions and the test for differences in proportions. (See appendix.)

PREPARING THE REPORT

A primary purpose in carrying out a research project in psychology is to add to accumulated knowledge with respect to greater or improved understanding of behavior. After a question has been posed, in answerable form, and data concerning it have been collected and analyzed, the investigator communicates his efforts to answer this question, sharing his findings and his interpretation of them with an audience of others who are interested in his area of research.

For readers of this collection of studies, the reports of their research will probably be written primarily to satisfy a course requirement and for an audience composed primarily of their course instructor. However, the greater the degree to which the student becomes actively involved both in carrying out the research and in writing up the report, the greater should be the gains from doing it, both in knowledge and in satisfaction.

Sarbin and Coe (1969) suggest that a student reaps many benefits from carrying out and reporting on a research project: (1) answers to interesting questions are discovered, and the problems and difficulties in trying to do this are experienced directly; (2) the student gains a degree of expertise about an area of research, and he may organize his information and hypotheses about this area in a new way; (3) firsthand information about the scientific methods used for solving problems in the topic area is gained; (4) the student gains increased competence in performing scholarly work; and (5) the familiarity and experience gained with the conventions and formats of scientific writing are also of value to the student.

Articles describing research generally follow a fairly standard pattern. A suggested outline for writing such a report on the research that the student has done is presented below:

Purpose: This introductory section should contain a statement of the problem that was investigated, an explanation as to why this problem was of interest, and a statement of expectations (hypotheses) concerning the findings.

Procedure: This section of the report should describe in detail the procedures that were used in carrying out the project, including the materials or apparatus used, the setting in which the study was performed, the selection and characteristics of the subjects, the exact instructions given to the subjects, and the recording, scoring, or judging of the subjects' responses. The procedures should be described in sufficient detail that someone else could replicate the study and expect to obtain the same or similar results.

Results: This section of the report should present the findings. The data should be clearly presented in tables, graphs, and so forth that are clearly labeled, and the procedures by which the data were analyzed should be specified. (The background of students who will be replicating the studies in this collection will probably vary widely with respect to their sophistication in use of statistical procedures. Therefore, we have suggested that simple statistics be used to summarize the data. The results for many of the studies in this collection can be handled by use of the chi-square test. This statistical test is appropriate when the data can be classified into separate categories, and the hypothesis to be tested is to determine whether two variables are independent of each other. For assistance in the use of this procedure, the student is referred to the appendix. Students with more extensive background in statistics may use more complex procedures if they so desire.)

Discussion: This section of the report presents the author's attempt to explain the meaning of the obtained results. It should include:

1. a decision as to whether the data tend to confirm or disconfirm the expectations stated in the Purpose section of the report;
2. a comparison of the findings of the student's replication study with the findings presented in the original study and an attempt to account for differences that occurred;
3. an effort to interpret the results in terms of what the student has learned about the behavior being studied and related developmental processes.

Conclusion: This section should contain a statement about the general findings of the project, suggestions as to how such a study might be improved or modified at another time, and suggestions as to what further research might be done, and what other variables might be investigated.

References: All the articles referred to in the project should be listed alphabetically in this section of the report. Students may use the reference sections of their textbooks as a model. The first mention of a study in the body of the report should be followed by the name of the author and the year of publication in parentheses. For example: "in a study by Sigel (1952)," or ". . . which agrees with previous findings (Jones, 1963; Smith, 1967)." If all that is known about a citation is derived from some other source, this should be indicated by the following form: "Hunt, as cited in Jones (1968)."

REFERENCE
T. R. Sarbin and W. C. Coe, *The Student Psychologist's Handbook: A Guide to Sources.* Cambridge, Mass.: Schenkman Publishing Company, 1969.

APPENDIX

The Chi-Square Test for Independence

The analysis of the results obtained in replicating many of the studies in this collection can be carried out satisfactorily by using a simpler procedure than is involved in some of the original studies. In many cases, we are interested in the number of observations that can be assigned to specified categories, and when this is the case it is possible to utilize the χ^2 test, a relatively simple procedure.

The χ^2 test of independence is appropriate whenever the data can be classified into categories. This test of independence is utilized to evaluate the hypothesis that two (or more) variables are independent of each other; for example, that the distribution of the types of responses given by children in solving a problem is not related to, or is independent of membership in a particular age group, sex group, and so on. If this hypothesis (commonly called the null hypothesis) is rejected, it can be concluded with a specified degree of probability that there is some association between the two variables, or that differences in types of response are associated with difference in age or sex group membership.

In order to carry out this type of analysis of data, the χ^2 statistic is calculated and then this is interpreted in terms of probability from a table of the χ^2 distribution. The size of the χ^2 statistic is used to determine whether the distribution of the frequency of the responses in each category is that which would be expected if assignment to a particular category was a result of chance sampling fluctuations. That is, we examine whether the differences between the observed frequencies (o) in any number of categories and the theoretical or expected frequencies (e) that would follow from the hypothesis are relatively small and could be accounted for by chance variations in sampling, or whether these differences are relatively large and represent a probable relationship between the variables under investigation. That is, are the differences more than would be expected on the basis of chance variation?

249

In using the χ^2 procedure as a test of independence, the expected value, or theoretical frequency of observations in any category, would be the number of responses we would expect to find in that category by assuming the same distribution in type of response for each subgroup of subjects.

Let us illustrate the procedure with an example. Suppose that in replicating the study by Graham *et al.* the drawings for each subject are classified as primitive (*P*) or nonprimitive (*NP*) for some particular characteristic (open–closed, for example). Let us also suppose that we have fifteen drawings produced by the children in each of three age groups—three-year-olds, four-year-olds, and five-year-olds. Then, if there is no relationship between type of drawing (*P* or *NP*) and age of subject, and if these two characteristics (age and quality of drawing) are independent, we would expect an equal number (or an equal proportion if the groups have produced different numbers of drawings) of *P* drawings from each age group, and the same distribution of *NP* drawings in each age group.

Now, let us suppose that we obtain a total of 15 *P* and 30 *NP* drawings from all our subjects across the three age groups. Then the theoretical frequencies in the cells of a table of results would be as follows:

Table A

Theoretical Frequencies for Calculation of χ^2 for a 2 × 3 Table in a Test of Independence (Testing Hypothesis That Quality of Drawing Reproduction Is Independent of Age)

Drawing Characteristic	3-year-olds	4-year-olds	5-year-olds	Total
P	5	5	5	15
NP	10	10	10	30
Total	15	15	15	45

The entries in the above table constitute the theoretical frequencies, or the number of observations we would expect to find in each cell of the table if there were no relationship between age of child and type of drawing. The numbers in this example have been chosen for convenience of illustration. It is not necessary that the numbers of subjects in the subgroups be equal as they are in this illustration. The same procedure would be followed if there were unequal numbers of drawings produced by the different age groups. For any table, the theoretical frequency (*e*) for any cell can be calculated by dividing the product of the two marginal totals, that is, multiplying the total for the rows by the total for the columns, for that cell by the grand total of observations. For the top left cell in the table (3-year olds producing *P* drawings)

$$P = \frac{(15)(15)}{45} = 5$$

Now, suppose the results obtained or the observed frequencies in the replication study are as follows:

Table B

Observed Frequencies for Calculation of χ^2 for a 2 $\times$ 3 Table in a Test of Independence (Testing Hypothesis That Quality of Drawing Reproduction Is Independent of Age)

Drawing Characteristic	3-year-olds	4-year-olds	5-year-olds	Total
P	10	5	0	15
NP	5	10	15	30
Total	15	15	15	45

Once we have determined the theoretical and observed frequencies, χ^2 can be calculated by using the formula:

$$\chi^2 = \sum \frac{(o - e)^2}{e}$$

where o represents the observed frequency and e represents the theoretical frequency, and the values of $\frac{(o - e)^2}{e}$ are calculated for each cell in the table and then summed. In the above example then.

$$\chi^2 = \frac{(10 - 5)^2}{5} + \frac{(5 - 5)^2}{5} + \frac{(0 - 5)^2}{5} + \frac{(5 - 10)^2}{10}$$

$$+ \frac{(10 - 10)^2}{10} + \frac{(15 - 10)^2}{10} = 5 + 0 + 5 + 2.5 + 0 + 2.5 = 15$$

For the interpretation of the value of χ^2 obtained, the student must consult a table of χ^2, which can be found in most texts of statistics, and determine the probability of obtaining such a value in terms of the number of degrees of freedom (column labeled *d.f.* in the χ^2 table). In general, the number of degrees of freedom refers to the number of cells in the table for calculating χ^2 for which the theoretical frequency can be filled in arbitrarily under the condition that the marginal totals of the table are fixed. This number (*d.f.*) can be calculated by using the simple formula

$$d.f. = (r - 1)(c - 1)$$

where r equals the number of rows in the table, and c equals the number of columns. In the example

$$d.f. = (2 - 1)(3 - 1) = 2$$

Now, by consulting a table of χ^2 we find that our value of χ^2, 15, for 2 degrees of freedom, has a *P* value of less than .01. This means that a value of χ^2 as large or larger than we have obtained would occur by chance fewer than 1 time out of every 100 random similar samples if there were no association between age and quality of drawing.

In psychological research, we generally say that a result is statistically significant when the probability that it is a result of chance sampling fluctuation is equal to or less than .05, or would occur by chance with less frequency than 5 in 100 times.

For the χ^2 test to be valid, the theoretical or expected frequencies in each of the cells should not be too small. A frequently used rule-of-thumb suggests that none should be less than 5. However, if fewer than 20 percent are less than 5, and if none are extremely small (less than 2), the probability statements associated with the test will be reasonably accurate. When this is not the case, the student should consult a more detailed presentation concerning χ^2, or contact someone with reasonable statistical sophistication for advice.

It should be noted that the analysis described above could be carried out for each of the primitivation characteristics that Graham *et al.* discuss. It could also be done for each of the figures reproduced by the children. A further analysis could also be carried out to determine whether there is any relationship between use of one characteristic of type of drawing and another—that is, do those children whose reproductions are more closed than the original drawing also produce drawings which are simplified rather than made more complex. This could be done for the total sample of subjects, or separately for each group if desired.

The discussion presented here has dealt only with the χ^2 procedure for analyzing the results of a study. This is not necessarily the best procedure in every instance, and it certainly is not the only one available. Indeed, in reading the studies in this collection the student will become aware of other possible methods of data analysis. Graham *et al.*, in the study used above for purposes of illustration, utilize an analysis of variance in their investigation. The presentation of statistical procedures here has been restricted to the χ^2 procedure because it is one of the simplest procedures, an important consideration for students with relatively little sophistication in statistical analysis, and because in many of the studies the responses made by different groups of subjects are categorized, thus providing data that is particularly suited to analysis by this procedure. Students who wish to use other methods of data analysis should consult more extensive presentations for assistance with other procedures.